THE STUDENT'S INTRODUCTION TO
THE SYNOPTIC GOSPELS

LONGMANS, GREEN AND CO. LTD.
39 PATERNOSTER ROW, LONDON, E.C. 4
6 OLD COURT HOUSE STREET, CALCUTTA
53 NICOL ROAD, BOMBAY
36A MOUNT ROAD, MADRAS

LONGMANS, GREEN AND CO.
114 FIFTH AVENUE, NEW YORK
221 EAST 20TH STREET, CHICAGO
88 TREMONT STREET, BOSTON

LONGMANS, GREEN AND CO.
480 UNIVERSITY AVENUE, TORONTO

THE
STUDENT'S INTRODUCTION
TO
THE SYNOPTIC GOSPELS

BY

E. BASIL REDLICH, B.D.

CANON THEOLOGIAN OF LEICESTER

AUTHOR OF "S. PAUL AND HIS COMPANIONS"; "INTRODUCTION
TO OLD TESTAMENT STUDY"; "OLD TESTAMENT STORIES AND
HOW TO TEACH THEM"; "THE CHURCH CATECHISM: ITS
HISTORY AND MEANING"; "HISTORY OF TEIGH," ETC.

LONGMANS, GREEN AND CO.
LONDON • NEW YORK • TORONTO

First published . . . . *January 1936*

Printed in Great Britain

Dedicated

TO

VIOLET AND MONICA

PREFACE

THIS book is an attempt to bring before teachers and students the new knowledge of the study of the Gospels that has been made available through the methods of documentary and textual criticism. The critical study of the Gospels was inevitable after similar methods had been applied successfully to the study of the Old Testament. There was a time when the modern approach to the Old Testament caused disquiet and alarm, for it was then held that it was impious to doubt its being verbally inspired. Yet the vast majority of instructed Christian people has accepted thankfully the new light that has been thrown on the Old Testament by new methods of study. No fear was felt for the New Testament, especially for the Gospels; it was possible to harmonise the Gospels and thereby to write a biography of the life of our Lord as it was possible to write a coherent life of S. Paul from the Acts and the Epistles.

In recent times, however, it has been recognised that a harmony of the Gospels is not so simple a matter; that there are contradictions in them which cannot be explained away, that not only Matthew, Luke and John, but also Mark were all written with special aims, that the Gospels cannot be understood without reference to the circumstances of the great centres of Christianity, that behind the Gospels are certain documents to which Luke referred in his preface, just as behind the Pentateuch lay sources known as J, E, D and P. But there is this difference

between the Pentateuch and the Gospels; the interval of
time between the basic Gospel records and the ministry
of Jesus is only a generation, as compared to the centuries
between Moses and the earliest Old Testament document,
and therefore the evidence for the main events of the
ministry of Jesus and for His teaching is of a reliable and
trustworthy character.

This book is based on the researches and studies of
English scholars. It is impossible to limit my indebtedness
to them; every chapter will show traces of their influence,
even to their very words, and if in the book I have
mentioned only a few of them by name, it is solely from a
desire not to hamper the student by innumerable footnotes
referring them to standard works by well-known and
distinguished scholars such as Allen, Burkitt, Charles,
Easton, Goudge, Hawkins, Foakes-Jackson, Kenyon, Kir-
sopp Lake, Manson, Milligan, Rawlinson, Raven, Sanday,
Stanton, Streeter, Taylor and Walker.

My great desire is to help those who were helped by
my "Introduction to Old Testament Study". In that
book I pleaded that those who taught the Old Testament
should safeguard the character of God; in this book I
plead that they would see Jesus set forth before us by
various writers, each in his own way, not only as the
Messiah expected by the Jews, but as the Saviour of all
men, and as One who was as fully man as He was and is
truly God.

The chapters on the text of the Gospels may seem
exacting, but they are as necessary to the study of the
Gospels as five-finger exercises and scales are to the
musician.

E. BASIL REDLICH.

CONTENTS

INTRODUCTION

CANON REDLICH'S book, which I count it an honour to introduce, has the unusual merit of serving, and serving successfully, three distinct ends.

In the first place it fulfils its title by introducing the reader—that is, any interested but not necessarily expert person—to the intelligent study of the Gospels. It has long been plain that the habit of Bible-reading has largely disappeared. Experience suggests that traditional methods are not succeeding in restoring it. But those who have discovered the fascination of a more scientific type of study are encouraged to claim that no ordinary person, if he once begins such study, will fail to enjoy it and profit by it. Hitherto our claim has been mainly based upon the evidence of the Student Christian Movement and of classes and circles; and the chief difficulty has been that suitable books were few. Either they were too technical or they were too vague and slight. This book can be studied " without previous knowledge," and is sufficiently concrete and detailed not to require supplementing.

In the second place it is a text-book, setting out the principles and the results of critical research and bringing into convenient form much material otherwise only to be found in a variety of larger and more difficult volumes. It ought to be of very real value to teachers, to the senior forms in schools, and to those beginning the serious study of theology.

Finally, it is not merely a compendium. Its author has not been content only to survey and reproduce the findings of others; he has worked over the whole matter of his book for himself. Thus he handles his subject with freshness and a sense of adventure; and in many places puts forward suggestions of his own which are new and stimulating. It will thus appeal to the scholar who, whether he agrees or disagrees with Canon Redlich's conclusions, will find them deserving of serious consideration.

CHARLES E. RAVEN.

CHAPTER I

THE TEXTS OF THE GOSPELS

THERE are two versions of the New Testament in English, the Authorised Version of 1611 and the Revised Version of 1881. Two facts here need explanation. Why was a new version necessary ? How was an English version obtained ?

These questions involve the story of the texts of the New Testament, and in particular for our purpose the story of the texts of the Gospels. Let us begin with the word " version" ; it means a translation from another language ; thus the English versions are translations, and these translations were made from written Greek texts. But Greek was not the only, nor was it the chief language spoken by the people of Palestine in our Lord's day ; nearly all spoke Aramaic (this is not the same as Hebrew). Thus a Gospel in Greek would be in the main a translation of the spoken Aramaic ; Aramaic words are to be found in Mark's Gospel. Our English versions of the Gospels are therefore translations from Greek texts, which in turn are mainly translations from the Aramaic. Now the two English versions of the Gospels were produced by two bodies of scholars who had before them not the same but two different Greek texts, and these Greek texts did not always agree, because they were based on different manuscripts, which often varied in their accounts of incidents and sayings.

This is, in short, the chief explanation of the remarkable fact that there are about 4000 differences in the Gospels

alone between the Authorised Version and the Revised Version.

How then did different texts and manuscripts of the Gospel arise ?

The First Manuscripts.

The Gospels were written to meet a need, and they were written by men who lived in the first century A.D. These authors are known to us as S. Matthew, S. Mark, S. Luke and S. John ; but as the Gospels were written anonymously the attribution of the Gospels to their authorship has to be proved. None of these autograph Gospels contained a superscription of the kind we find in our versions ; in other words, the original copies did not begin with a heading such as " The Gospel according to S. Matthew," and so on. These original autographs do not exist; they have disappeared, and there is hardly any hope of their being discovered. One of the causes, if not the sole cause, of their non-existence to-day is that the material on which they were written was not durable. The Gospels were written on rolls made up of sheets manufactured from the papyrus reed which grew in Egypt on the banks of the Nile.

A sheet of papyrus was prepared by cutting the reeds into long strips, which were first placed vertically alongside each other ; over these were placed other strips in a horizontal position. They were then pressed down, treated with gum, and dried in the sun ; and finally the sheet was rubbed over with a round object to give it a smooth surface. The size of a sheet of this kind of paper was 9 to 11 inches long, and 5 to $5\frac{1}{2}$ inches wide ; rolls could be formed of any desired length by joining the sheets together. The price of a sheet varied according to quality ; a good sheet would cost about one shilling of our money, and one of inferior quality about 4d. The ink was a mixture of soot, gum and

water ; the pen was cut into shape from the reed. The early Christians preferred to use papyrus for religious scripts, whilst others preferred parchment made out of skins : the rolls of Old Testament books used in the synagogues were of parchment. References to these objects are to be found in the New Testament :

> " Having many things to write unto you, I would not write them with paper and ink."—2 John 12.
> " I am unwilling to write to thee with ink and pen."
> —3 John 13.
> " And the heaven was removed as a scroll when it is rolled up."—Rev. 6[14].
> " The books, especially the parchments."
> —2 Timothy 4[13].

(The paper in the first quotation is papyrus. The books in the last quotation are papyrus sheets, and the parchments are portions of the Old Testament on skins.)

The Greek word for a papyrus roll was *Biblos* or its diminutive *Biblion ;* hence our word Bible. The papyrus roll thus soon had a sacred connotation.

The length of a roll of any of the Gospels or Epistles naturally varied. Whilst 2 Thessalonians would be 15 inches long, Mark would be 19 feet, Matthew 30 feet, and Luke 31 feet. If the roll had to be read, it was wound up at one end and unwound at the other end at the same time, both hands being used in the process. The original autographs had no numbered chapters or verses, no spaces between the words, no inverted commas to denote quotations, no interrogation marks, and no punctuation marks. Hence, owing to the inconvenience in handling them and in referring to them, there would be great difficulty in comparing the Gospels one with the other ; reliance had often to be placed on memory.

Jesus did not write a book, though according to a tradition (John 8[6]) He could write ; there is no record that He gave any directions for the writing of a Gospel. He was learned, and could speak to Rabbis as a Rabbi, and He was often addressed thus. To the people He would speak Aramaic ; but He could read the Scriptures, which were written in Hebrew, at the age of twelve, and, later in life, was invited both to read and expound the Scriptures in the synagogue at Nazareth. He probably knew Greek, for He conversed with Pilate and toured the Decapolis. No written records of His life and teaching were, as far as we know, made during His ministry ; and for a short period after His death, whilst the Apostles were alive and there were eye-witnesses of His ministry, Passion and Resurrection, there was no need of written documents to tell the story of Jesus. Besides, the idea of writing a record would not suggest itself when the Parousia or the Appearance of the glorified Messiah with power was soon expected. But as this Appearance was delayed, and the Gospel was spreading in Gentile lands, new conditions and new problems arose. The admission of Gentiles into the Church, a desire to know the origins of Christian observances, attacks on the Christians and on their creed, the instruction of converts, and the preparation of missionaries for spreading the Gospel necessitated a knowledge, not so much of the earthly life of their Founder, but very specially of His views on the problems which faced the Churches. Oral information could not wholly supply answers to these problems, for such information might not be authentic or available. The circumstances of Christian history demand more than what can be supplied by oral tradition ; a Christian society cannot grow on cycles of tradition only, however valuable they are ; there must be a code of regulations of some kind, and this code must be authoritative, that is, must possess the imprimatur of an Apostle or of a great Church such as

Rome or Antioch. Historical probability therefore suggests that the earliest written documents would consist not of narratives, except the story of the Passion revealing Jesus as Saviour, but of discourses and sayings of our Lord, and in particular of such utterances as bore on the needs and circumstances of the Churches in the great centres of Christianity.

In time, when the number of original eye-witnesses began to diminish through death and martyrdom, the preservation of details of our Lord's life, over and above the Passion narratives, became urgent; collections of stories were formed to make narratives of our Lord's career. Gradually the sayings and narratives were united to give a single document such as a Gospel. Our four Gospels were not the only Gospels written; there were others, most of them of later date than our Gospels, which for a time were held in esteem, even though they contained imaginative and fanciful details. But these latter were rejected when the Canon was formed; they are known as the Apocryphal Gospels. The first of the four canonical Gospels that was written was Mark, and after Mark came Matthew and Luke, which were based on Mark and matter obtained from other sources.

According to this summary, our Four Gospels were preceded by earlier documents, namely collections of sayings and short narratives; these earlier written sources, as we shall see, can be traced in our Gospels.

The Transmission of the Gospel Texts.

One single autograph of the Gospels would not supply the needs of more than one Church. Books were not printed or produced mechanically, and therefore in identical words, in these early days. If Churches other than those for whom the original Gospels were produced needed copies, these

copies could be made only by hand. The early Christian copyists of the first and second and third centuries were not probably all professional scribes, but often men with no special qualification for the work ; they were untrained and possessed no critical ability ; but whether professional or amateur, they would make mistakes in copying, as we do. As time went on and Christianity spread, copies of the Gospels for new centres and for private use would be made from earlier copies. New scribes would at every stage add their contributions of mistakes to copies already faulty, with the result that variations from the original autographs would be multiplied at every stage of transcription.

Not only bad and unskilful copying, but free editing, deliberate alterations and omissions from the text, the error known as *homoioteleuton* when the eye skips over passages and continues at the same or a similar word lower down in the text (there are 48 examples of this in the Gospels in the Codex Sinaiticus), the guessing of an illegible word or phrase—all contributed their quota. But it must be emphasised that however many these variations of the text may be, the main facts of our Lord's ministry and of His teaching and doctrine remain unimpaired.

These were not the only contributory causes which affected the text of the original autographs ; for until the Emperor Constantine tolerated Christianity in A.D. 313, the Christians lived in constant fear of persecution and martyrdom. One of the acts of persecution of Diocletian was the destruction of copies of the Scriptures. In these dark days were created the problems which to-day await solution. Not only the original manuscripts of the Gospels, but nearly every one of the copies of them made during two centuries of persecution have been, we fear, irretrievably lost. One special calamity had befallen Mark's Gospel ; it was either not concluded by the author owing to some cause, such as persecution, or, if completed, it was damaged. A papyrus

roll is a delicate roll to handle, for it could easily suffer damage, especially at its ends ; whatever the cause, the final end of Mark was lost so early in its history that it would seem that Matthew and Luke had to write their Gospels with a mutilated Mark before them. Early manuscript copies made from Mark had no ending after Chapter 16[8], or had unauthentic verses written specially by others to form a suitable conclusion ; this is indicated at the end of Mark in the Revised Version.

We do not know when the books of the Bible were first brought out in the form of a book or codex. When in roll form, no Church would ordinarily possess more than one Gospel. But in 1931 twelve papyrus codices, incomplete and mutilated, eleven containing the books of the Bible, were discovered in Cairo. One of these codices consisted of the Gospels and the Acts, and this volume has been assigned to the late second century, or even earlier. A papyrus codex or book is a rarity.

When Christianity received imperial support in A.D. 313, a new era dawned for our religion ; then began the free transmission and circulation of the Scriptures made from hidden and preserved manuscripts which had escaped destruction.

How, then, can the original text of the Gospels be reconstructed from these altered texts which appeared after about two centuries of destruction and loss ?

This is the special task of textual Criticism. The magnitude of its task may be gauged by the fact that there are now nearly 1400 Greek manuscripts to be considered, and with them some old versions, besides hundreds of Lectionaries giving the Lessons to be read in Church services, and quotations from the Scriptures made by the Christian Fathers in books written by them in the second and third centuries. Of these 1400 Greek manuscripts, over 1200 date from the eighth century onward, and they can be shown to

have a common descent from an ancestor of the sixth century. They give a text known as the Byzantine text.

The English Versions.

When the Authorised Version was produced in English, the only known text of the Scriptures was this Byzantine text. Erasmus had produced a Greek text from some Byzantine manuscripts known to him, and this was revised by a Paris printer, Stephanus, and accepted as the best text available. It is known as the Textus Receptus or the Received Text. Versions in English had existed in England before the Authorised Version, such as Tyndale's Bible and the Bishops' Bible of 1568 ; and when in the reign of James I a new translation of the Bible was ordered, the translators, when translating from the Textus Receptus, were required to adhere to the Bishops' Bible as much as possible. The new version of 1611, though called the Authorised Version, was never authorised by king, convocation or parliament ; no documentary evidence exists to prove authorisation ; the nearest authority we have is the phrase " Appointed to be read in Churches." This version is a literary classic, and is unsurpassed for the beauty of its language and its rhythm, and for its devotional appeal : it is also hallowed by three centuries of use. But students and in fact all who desire to read the Bible intelligently require the best and most correct translation based on the purest texts. This the Authorised Version could not give, for soon after its appearance came new discoveries of older manuscripts than those which gave the Byzantine text ; and it was soon seen that these newly discovered manuscripts belonged to two families of greater antiquity and of greater reliability than the family of texts known in the days of Erasmus. Gradually there arose a demand for a more reliable version than the Authorised. The scholars

appointed to produce this version had to decide between the claims of three families of texts :

1. The Byzantine, a late text dating from the sixth century. Of this family, a codex, the codex Alexandrinus (or A) of the 5th century was brought to England in 1627 and is now in the British Museum.

2. The Alexandrian, to which belong two famous manuscripts, one known as the Codex Vaticanus (or B), discovered in the Vatican library in Rome where it had lain unnoticed for four centuries, and the other known as the Codex Sinaiticus (or ℵ. This is the first letter, Aleph, of the Hebrew alphabet) now in the British Museum. The text given by these two and other manuscripts was called by the revisers of 1881 the " Neutral Text," because they considered that these manuscripts in particular showed the least signs of deliberate editing by scribes and therefore gave the purest text.   B and ℵ were dated about A.D. 350.

3. The Western, to which family belongs the Codex Bezae (or D) at Cambridge ; this codex has many editorial alterations in it and is dated the fifth century.   To this group belong versions in Syriac, Coptic and Latin, which are older than D.

In choosing between these three families of texts, there was one deciding factor.   The Fathers of the second and third centuries in their quotations from the Scriptures never once quoted from a text in the Byzantine group ; as this text could therefore not have been in existence in the second and third centuries, it could be discarded without hesitation.   Of the other two, the Neutral manuscripts were less edited and therefore were held to be more trustworthy than the Western ; the revisers consequently based their revision mainly on the Codex Vaticanus, supplemented

by the Codex Sinaiticus. A few illustrations of the kind of problems before the revisers may be of interest.

> The Story of the Woman taken in Adultery is omitted by B and ℵ but not by D.
>
> " Father forgive them . . ." is omitted by B and D but retained by ℵ.
>
> The end of Mark as given in the A.V. 16⁹-end, is omitted by B and ℵ but not by D and A.

The revisers had to decide which of these to include and which to omit in the Revised Version.

For purposes of study the Revised Version of 1881 is so substantially accurate that the ordinary student as against the specialist may use it safely. To-day the specialist is, however, confronted by a bigger and more complicated task than that which awaited the revisers of 1881. For since that date further manuscripts have been discovered ; and these are seen to belong to a family other than those three mentioned above, and to occupy a position midway between the Alexandrian and the Western. They give a text known as the Cæsarean Text. This text was used before A.D. 240 by Origen in Cæsarea, hence the name. The main exemplars of this group are the Freer manuscripts bought from a dealer in Cairo in 1906, the Koridethi manuscript discovered in a monastery at Tiflis in the Caucasus in 1913, and the papyrus codices bought by Mr. Chester Beatty in 1931 in Cairo (see p. 7). The Cæsarean text is as accurate as the Alexandrian and as scholarly, and in consequence the authority of the Vatican manuscript B is being questioned, for the Cæsarean does not always give the same text as the Alexandrian. Further, papyri in Egypt of earlier date than B do not belong to the Alexandrian group, and, as a result, the claim of the revisers of 1881 that B is authoritative must be reconsidered.

With this short introduction to the Textual Criticism of

the Gospels and their circulation we will now proceed to the study of the texts of our Gospels as we have them. This is called Documentary Criticism. The solution of many a problem in Documentary Criticism cannot be effected without the help of Textual Criticism, which enables the correct text to be discovered.

Documentary criticism is not destructive criticism. It is a method by which, through a comparison of the texts of the Gospels, the constituent elements of the Gospels can be obtained. It investigates the written words but does not interpret their moral, spiritual or doctrinal significance, which is the province of the theologian and religious teacher. It enables us to resolve such literary problems as contradictions in the story of our Lord's life ; it enables us to understand how our first three Gospels were obtained and how they were composed. It also enables us to enter into the minds of the compilers and authors.

And as we study the three Gospels and compare them critically one outstanding fact will emerge. This fact is the positive certainty both of the main leading events of our Lord's ministry and of the main leading ideas of His teaching. We shall see various writers giving variant versions, which differ in detail and in the time and place of occurrence ; but these variations testify not to the falsity but to the truth of an event and to the substantial accuracy of a saying. For example, there can be no possible doubt of the preaching and imprisonment of John the Baptist, of the Baptism and Temptation of our Lord, His miraculous powers shown by mighty deeds, His tours in Galilee and outside Galilee, His Rejection, Passion, Crucifixion, Death, Resurrection and Ascension. No less attested are His choice and training of the Twelve, their recognition of Him as the Messiah and the Saviour ; further, His teaching on the Fatherhood of God and the Kingdom of God by parable and sermon is as certain as His missionary enthusiasm.

Lastly, His wonderful Personality and overpowering influence are seen dominating the lives of those with whom He came in contact.

The gradual revelation of Jesus of Nazareth as the Incarnate Son of God is as clearly seen by the documentary criticism of the Gospels as is the gradual revelation of the character of God by the documentary criticism of the first five books of the Old Testament.

It might serve a useful purpose if at this stage the student read the short outline of our Lord's ministry as it might be reconstructed from the results of documentary criticism (Chapter XII). For some indication would thus be given of the primary purpose of this book and it would make clear the constructive value of this method of study.

CHAPTER II

THE SYNOPTIC PROBLEM

ACCORDING to the Revised Version, Mark ends at 16⁸ with the words " for they were afraid " ; the conclusion of the Gospel is missing. In the Revised Version, which omits Matthew 17²¹, 18¹¹, 23¹⁴ ; Mark 7¹⁶, 9⁴⁴, ⁴⁶, 11²⁶, 15²⁸ ; and Luke 17³⁶, 23¹⁷, the number of verses in Mark, Matthew and Luke respectively is as follows :

> Mark has 661 verses.
> Matthew has 1068 verses.
> Luke has 1149 verses.

If a reader compares these three Gospels together, even in the English version, he cannot help noticing the considerable number of coincidences in language between them. If, for example, the Sick of the Palsy is compared in the three Gospels (Mark 2¹⁻¹², Matthew 9¹⁻⁸, and Luke 5¹⁷⁻²⁶), or the Feeding of the Five Thousand (Mark 6³⁰⁻⁴⁴, Matthew 14¹²⁻²¹, Luke 9¹⁰⁻¹⁷), or a saying such as the Parable of the Sower in Mark 4, Matthew 13 and Luke 8, he will find that in Matthew and Mark and Luke words and sentences are common to them all, as if the authors copied from one another or copied them from a common source, at the same time making slight alterations or additions as each author thought expedient. On the other hand, there are stories such as the Call of the First Apostles in Mark 1¹⁶⁻²⁰, Matthew 4¹⁸⁻²², and Luke 5¹⁻¹¹, which when compared with

one another give a different impression, for here, while Luke's story of this common theme stands apart, Matthew and Mark are very much alike. We need an explanation first for such resemblances, and secondly for such dissimilarities ; they are to be found in large quantities, and cannot be the result of chance or the result of the respective authors giving independent accounts of the same story or incident or saying.

Further, from figures to be given presently, it will be seen that nearly the whole of Mark is included in Matthew and about half of Mark in Luke, and that more than half the number of actual words of Mark are included in Matthew and in Luke. To use a school expression, it looks as if Matthew had " cribbed " extensively from Mark, and Luke had " cribbed " about half of Mark. But it may also be argued that Mark may have " cribbed " from Matthew and Luke, or all three of them from some other Gospel.

We are thus faced with two kinds of problems in these three Gospels.

(1) The problem of the similarities between Matthew, Mark and Luke, and (2) the problem of the dissimilarities between Matthew, Mark and Luke. Let us call this the Three Gospel problem.

Both these problems also arise when Matthew and Luke are compared together, Mark being left out of the question. For there is much common matter, chiefly sayings, found in Matthew and Luke alone ; in this common matter, there is much that is similar, and much that is dissimilar, even though the two Gospels deal with the same theme. We may illustrate these by the Sermon on the Mount in Matthew, compared with the Sermon on the Plain in Luke, or with the two versions of the Lord's Prayer. They show similarities and dissimilarities. Let us call this problem the Two Gospel problem.

Lastly, there remain the passages which are peculiar to

Matthew and Luke, and found only in each of them. Familiar illustrations are the Infancy stories, the Resurrection appearances, and Parables, in all of which Matthew and Luke make their special contributions independently of each other. Let us call this the problem of Special Sources.

The Three Gospel Problem.

Because similarities exist between Matthew, Mark and Luke, these three Gospels are known as the Synoptic Gospels; these similarities exist in such numbers that nearly all Mark, about half Matthew, and about two-sevenths of Luke can be arranged in parallel columns; this can be done because they give a common view of the life of Christ, deal with common items of subject-matter, and use words and sentences and phrases in common.

The various problems raised by this similarity and resemblance as well as by the dissimilarities and divergences of the contents of these three Gospels are summed up under the phrase " the Synoptic Problem ". How is the existence of these similarities and dissimilarities to be explained? But before this Synoptic Problem is studied in detail, it might be helpful if a general summary of the proposed solution were given in succinct form, as it would serve the double purpose of presenting the nature of the many problems which have to be considered, and of presenting the solutions of these problems which it is proposed to give in this book.

When the subject-matter of Matthew is compared with that of Mark, we find that Matthew reproduces the substance of 606 verses of Mark. This means that only 55 verses of Mark are omitted by Matthew. All these 606 verses, however, are not included in their entirety; some are revised and others are shortened or compressed in Matthew,

with the result that the 606 verses of Mark amount to about 500 verses in Matthew.　But though nearly all Mark is thus found in less than half of Matthew, about 51 per cent. of Mark's actual words, that is more than half his words, is reproduced in Matthew.

When Luke and Mark are similarly compared, it is found that about 320 verses of Mark, that is about half of Mark, are utilised by Luke in about as many verses.　But the proportion of the actual words of Mark in Luke is 53 per cent, which is a larger percentage than in Matthew.　Further, of the 55 verses of Mark omitted by Matthew, 24 are found in Luke.　Thus only 31 verses of Mark are not to be found in either Matthew or Luke.

This synoptic relationship may be stated in the form of equations :

Matthew's 1068 verses = about 500 from Mark
　　　　　　　　　　　　　　　+ over 550 from other sources.
Luke's 1149 verses = about 320 from Mark
　　　　　　　　　　　　　　　+ about 830 from other sources.

The Two Gospel Problem.

These equations can be advanced a stage further.　For when the 550 odd verses from other sources of Matthew are compared with the 830 odd verses from other sources of Luke, about 250 verses, consisting chiefly of sayings and discourses of Christ, show such close parallelism and similarity that it is almost universally agreed that behind Matthew and Luke there is a second common source, and that this source is not oral tradition but a written Greek document. This document is not known to exist ; for many years it was held to be a hypothetical document ; the assumption of its existence was made in order to satisfy the problem of the close parallelism of part of the non-Marcan matter in Matthew and Luke.　This document was designated Q,

from the German *Quelle*, which means *Source*. Q was in all probability written in Antioch in Syria.

It should be emphasised that a hypothesis is not valueless, neither is it fantastic. That Q was a hypothetical document was a valuable step in constructive work, as valuable in its sphere as the Laws of Motion in the science of Dynamics. The Laws of Motion satisfy certain conditions of matter and enable the building up of the science. That is their justification. Similarly, so long as the hypothesis of Q worked satisfactorily, it was a sound basis for further study. But Q is more than a hypothesis. There is evidence that it actually existed originally as an Aramaic document, and that a Greek translation of it was used by Matthew and Luke (see Chapter V).

Our equations may now be stated approximately thus :

Matthew (1068) = Mark (500) + Q (250) +
                        about 300 verses from other sources.
Luke (1149) = Mark (320) + Q (250) +
                        about 580 verses from other sources.

The Problem of Special Sources.

The 300 odd verses which are peculiar to Matthew are of a special Jewish tone and consist of answers to attacks on the Birth and Resurrection of Christ, of denunciations of the Pharisees, of controversial issues between Christians and Jews, and in particular we find in them special ecclesiastical tradition, such as the word " church," which is not found in Mark or Luke. This peculiar matter in Matthew consists of narratives as well as discourses and sayings. Let us for the present designate this matter peculiar to Matthew by the letter M. The nature of the main subject-matter of M suggests Jerusalem as the centre from which it originated. It has been suggested that the sayings in it

formed a written document, and that the narratives came from other sources.

The 550 verses peculiar to Luke include some of the best-known parables in the Gospels, such as the Good Samaritan, the Prodigal Son, the Pharisee and the Publican ; they also include special miracles, such as the Widow's Son at Nain, new matter in the stories of the Passion and of the Resurrection, and stories of the Infancy. Of these, the Infancy stories and the opening preface to the Gospel (Chapters I and II) were probably added later ; this is suggested by the position of the historical data and genealogy in Chapter III, which serve as an introduction to the rest of the Gospel. Let us designate the matter peculiar to Luke after Chapters I and II by the letter L. The sympathetic references in it to Gentiles and Samaritans and women suggest Cæsarea as its place of origin, for in Cæsarea Luke was the guest of Philip and his daughters (Acts 21[8]). Further, the figures of the last equation, where we suggest that Luke obtained more from sources other than Mark, show that Luke's primary source was not Mark ; it is probable that Luke had first produced a Gospel independent of Mark by combining Q and L and then later used Mark to produce the Gospel as we know it, less Chapters I and II. This first Gospel (Q + L) has been called Proto-Luke by Canon Streeter. L and Proto-Luke are hypotheses.

We will now restate our equations in the following form :

Matthew = Mark + Q + M.

Luke = Mark + (Q + L) + Source of Chapters I and II.

The Equations in a New Form.

There is one other formula of great interest, involving the great centres of early Christianity, in which the above equations may be stated. Mark was written in Rome, and the productions of Q, M and L have been assigned to

Antioch, Jerusalem and Cæsarea respectively. We get therefore :

Matthew = a Roman Gospel (Mk) + an Antiochene
document (Q) + Jerusalem tradition (M).

Luke = a Roman Gospel (Mk) + an Antiochene
document (Q) + a Cæsarean Gospel (L) +
Source of Chapters I and II.

The main source of the Gospels probably came from three great centres of Gentile Christianity : from Rome, the capital of the Roman Empire; from Antioch, the third largest city of the Empire ; and from Cæsarea, the seat of government of the province of Judæa. There was only one Jewish source, but it is of great value, and this came from Jerusalem.

Conclusions from Problems.

Four important conclusions follow from these equations. In the first place, the historical value of any narrative or saying is dependent not on the evidence of the Gospels as we know them but on their sources. In other words, the number of witnesses in a Gospel inquiry is not the number of the Synoptic Gospels which refer to an event or saying which is brought up for judgment, but the number of the four sources, Mark, Q, L and M, which happen to contain it. John also in some instances may be dependent on Mark and Luke, and thus John may not be an independent witness. For example, the Feeding of the Five Thousand appears in the four New Testament Gospels ; the evidence for it, however, is not four-fold. We do not possess four authorities in favour of the miracle but only two at the most, for Matthew and Luke obtained the story of the miracle from Mark, and John may or may not have been indebted to Mark. Again, whilst the Baptism of Jesus is supported by Mark, L and M, the details of the Three Temptations given in Matthew and Luke have only the evidence of Q

The second important conclusion is that neither Matthew nor Luke had any scruple in his treatment of Mark or Q. No infallibility was attached to the text of the Gospel or in particular to the words of Jesus as given in Mark and Q. In case after case we shall find Matthew and Luke using the narratives and sayings in Mark and Q with the utmost freedom and in so doing sometimes deliberately altering and adapting even Christ's words, sometimes suppressing them, sometimes paraphrasing them to make an ambiguity clear. We also find that the Gospels do not always agree in matters they recount. We are not justified in starting our studies with any theory of inspiration such as its infallibility. We must let the facts speak for themselves before we attempt to define the meaning of inspiration. But we can say that the writers were inspired to write their Gospels ; they each had a message to deliver and they delivered it, each in his own way.

Thirdly, we shall not expect to find in the Gospels a complete record of our Lord's life and ministry, *i.e.* a biography of Christ. The choice of the material that was preserved was largely influenced by the local history of the individual Churches, their problems and the circumstances ; historical considerations in the main decided what should be preserved in each individual centre of Church life. Also, the Gospels were written by men who each in his own way desired to set before their readers the redemptive rather than the chronological life of One who had changed the whole course of history.

Lastly, by discovering the sources of the Gospels we are given evidence for the events described in the Gospels of an earlier date than the dates of composition of the Gospels. For, as we shall argue, Q and M are to be dated about A.D. 47, and L about A.D. 52 ; and as Mark enshrines much of Peter's reminiscences and other early sources, we are, in the use of those four original sources, brought at least a

generation closer to the time of Christ. Mark may have been composed about A.D. 65, though an earlier date is not impossible, and Matthew and Luke later, but the sources give us first-hand information of an earlier date than A.D. 65. The studies in this volume will thus serve a valuable purpose in strengthening the evidence of the Gospel story by pointing to dates earlier than the dates at which the Synoptic Gospels as we have them may have been composed.

The Main Problems Subdivided.

We will now re-state in detail the various questions involved in the Synoptic Problem, and suggested by our summary :

1. What are the grounds for assuming the priority of Mark, that is to say, for assuming that Matthew and Luke used Mark ? May it not be that Matthew or Luke was primitive, or that they all drew from one source, oral or written, or that Mark was compiled from Matthew and Luke ? (Chapter III).

2. Are there any items in the Synoptic Gospels dealing with common subject-matter which show such dissimilarity that they cannot be assigned to one source ? In other words, are there divergent versions of the same event ? (Chapter IV).

3. What are the probable contents of Q, that is, of the source common to Matthew and Luke only ? What is its purpose ? Did Mark know and use Q ? (Chapter V).

4. What is M and what is its purpose ? (Chapter VI).

5. What is L ? What evidence is there for the hypothesis of a Proto-Luke ? What are the contents of L, and what is its purpose ? (Chapter VII).

6. Did John use Mark and Luke? Does John come within the Synoptic Problem? (Chapter VIII).

7. How did Matthew construct his Gospel? (Chapter IX).

8. Whence did Mark obtain his information? What is its value? (Chapter X).

Further we shall give

9. Short summaries of the meanings of the Kingdom of Heaven, the Messiah and the Son of Man (Chapter XI).

10. An outline of Christ's ministry, based on the results of our inquiries (Chapter XII).

At the end of the volume will be given the probable texts of Q, M and L.

CHAPTER III

THE PRIORITY OF MARK

FIRST consideration in the Synoptic Problem must always be given to what we have termed the Three Gospel Problem ; of this there are two parts : (1) The problem raised by the similarities between Matthew, Mark and Luke. (2) The problem raised by the dissimilarities between Matthew, Mark and Luke.

The present chapter deals with the first of these two divisions. Quite clearly, if, as between the three Synoptics, the indebtedness of Matthew and Luke to Mark can be conclusively proved, it will be superfluous to inquire into any other possible solution, such as that all three got their subject-matter from a common source, or that Mark was a shorter Gospel compiled from the longer Gospels by a process of selection. There are, at least, four lines of argument for asserting that Mark was written before Matthew and Luke, and was used by them, and therefore that Mark is the primitive Gospel ; each of the arguments by itself is not conclusive, but their cumulative effect is such that the one certain and assured result of the study of the Synoptic Problem is that Matthew and Luke reproduced Mark. This does not imply that Matthew and Luke each used Mark in the same way, or that Matthew and Luke used the whole or an equal quantity of Marcan matter. All it means is that one of the sources used by Matthew and Luke was Mark, as we have it.

The four lines of argument for the priority of Mark are these :

1. The common subject-matter.
2. The common wording of the subject-matter.
3. The common outline of events.
4. The revision of Mark's language for (a) reverential, (b) grammatical, and (c) stylistic reasons.

1. The Common Subject-Matter.

In the previous chapter we have given figures which indicate that Matthew contains nearly all Mark, and Luke about half of Mark. This fact alone is no proof of the priority of Mark, but taken together with the three other lines of argument to be next considered, will show that the case for Mark being considered the primitive Gospel is complete. The figures for Luke are discussed in Chapter VII.

2. The Common Wording.

Four illustrations out of many parallel versions will indicate how close is the resemblance between the Synoptics in diction and phraseology.

(i) *The Sick of the Palsy*. (Text on p. 246.)

Mark 2^{1-12}.   Matthew 9^{1-8}.   Luke 5^{17-26}.

The introductions to the incident vary in each of the Gospels ; this is a clear sign that the writers are uncertain of the time or occasion of the incident ; this peculiarity can be frequently observed in the Gospels, and is an indication of the extreme difficulty of constructing an orderly biography of our Lord's ministry. In a large number of cases we simply do not know when and where an incident occurred ; indications of time and place are often not given.

In the versions of the Sick of the Palsy the similarity in words and phrases is obvious, and even the unusual parenthesis " he saith to the sick of the palsy " in verse 10 of Mark is reproduced by Matthew and Luke ; this is one of the last things we expect to find in common unless one writer copied from another.

There is one improvement on Mark's language, an indication that Mark was used by Matthew and Luke ; the Greek word for " bed " in Mark is a vulgar one, and is replaced in the other two Gospels by polite terms, translated " bed " and " couch " in English.

The parenthesis in Mark may be due to one of two reasons : (a) The verses about forgiveness of sins may have been inserted into the miracle in order to bring into one group the various causes which led to the growth of opposition to Jesus (see p. 136). (b) The story of the cure reads as a complete miracle-narrative when verses 3, 4, 5a, 11–12 are read consecutively, the other verses, 5b–10, forming almost a complete sayings-narrative. There may have been two versions of the cure, one giving it simply as a miracle, the other as a sayings-narrative. Mark may have combined them into one narrative.

(ii) *Blessing the little children.* (Text on p. 247.)

Mark 10^{13-16}. Matthew 19^{13-15}. Luke 18^{15-17}.

The stories are clearly similar ; common words and phrases occur in them all. We notice that Matthew and Luke omit for reverential reasons the words about Christ's anger, " he was moved with indignation " ; this is another indication of Mark being the primitive Gospel. Matthew has compressed the story in Mark by omitting verses 15–16a, but verse 15 is utilised by him elsewhere (Matthew 18^3).

(iii) *Giving tribute to Cæsar.* (Text on p. 248.)

Mark 12¹³⁻¹⁷. Matthew 22¹⁵⁻²². Luke 20²⁰⁻²⁶.

The resemblance here extends to the sayings of others than our Lord. This is instructive; for whilst we might have expected a close reproduction of Christ's sayings, we observe that even the words of opponents are carefully copied. Further instances of the reproduction of the words of others than Christ are to be found in Matthew 21²³ and Luke 20² which reproduce Mark 11²⁸; also in the Centurion's Servant.

(iv) *Peter's Confession and the sequel.* (Text on p. 249 f.)

Mark 8²⁷⁻³³. Matthew 16¹³⁻²³. Luke 9¹⁸⁻²².

The three narratives show common dependence in many words and phrases except (1) for the insertion of an important piece of ecclesiastical tradition by Matthew in verses 17–19, and (2) for his omission of the word " rebuked " from verse 33 of Mark, the whole verse being omitted by Luke, through a feeling of reverence for Peter.

We get in this comparison, first, an illustration of Matthew's method of combining two sources, for he has combined Mark's narrative with matter from his special source which we have called M; and secondly, of Luke's (and Matthew's) omission of statements or words which might be thought unworthy of the Apostles.

Examples such as the four we have considered may be multiplied, and it is in passages of this nature, where the resemblances between the narratives are close, that we are justified in saying that Matthew and Luke drew from Mark. Our four studies have also given us illustrations of some of the literary methods of Matthew and Luke, and we have seen how they altered, adapted, and sometimes compressed and sometimes enlarged Mark's narrative; but these

literary methods have not obliterated their indebtedness to Mark. Cases in which the parallel versions diverge so much that dependence on a common source cannot be inferred will be considered in the next chapter, under the head of Divergent Sources. For the present, the evidence of the common subject-matter and their wording, without considering improvements of the language of Mark by Matthew and Luke, gives us two of the arguments for our contention that Mark was written before the two longer Gospels, and was used by the writers of these longer Gospels, each in his own way.

This linguistic evidence, that is the evidence of the diction or choice of words, is a formidable argument for the priority of Mark. This is more evident in the original Greek than in an English translation ; but the common wording can be fairly observed in the Revised Version text of the four examples which have been considered.

We have already stated that Matthew, in utilising the Marcan matter, used just over 50 per cent. of Mark's actual words, and Luke used 53 per cent., or a slightly higher percentage than Matthew, of Marcan matter. This does not mean that these percentages work out exactly in every case which comes under the Three Gospel problem ; the percentages in individual cases of comparison would vary from, say, 30 per cent. to 80 per cent. or more. Again, though Matthew and Luke do not always reproduce the same word, one of them does, with the result that when the actual Marcan words both in Matthew and Luke are counted, the percentage of Marcan words found both in Matthew and Luke will be higher than 53 per cent.

Canon Streeter sums up the evidence in these words : " In any average section, which occurs in the three Gospels, the majority of the actual words used by Mark are reproduced by Matthew and Luke, either alternately or both together." He adds : " This is clear evidence of the greater

originality of the Marcan version, and is exactly what we should expect to find if Matthew and Luke were *independently* reproducing Mark, adapting his language to their own individual style."

3. The Common Outline.

The third line of argument for the priority of Mark is the common order of events. As Mark begins with the story of John the Baptist, we must begin our argument at the same point, and as Matthew follows Mark implicitly after John's imprisonment and death, we need only consider the order of events up to about this point ; in other words, we will confine ourselves to the events between the preaching and the death of the Baptist.

The events in Mark are in the following order :

1. The Preaching of John the Baptist.
2. The Baptism of Jesus.
3. The Temptation of Jesus.
4. The Call of four Apostles.
5. An unclean spirit cast out.
6. Simon's mother-in-law healed.
7. Healing at even.
8. A leper cleansed.
9. Cure of the sick of the palsy.
10. The Call of Levi.
11. Our Lord on fasting.
12. Plucking the ears of corn.
13. The man with the withered hand.
14. The choosing of the Twelve.
15. The Beelzebub controversy.
16. Jesus' Mother and Brethren.
17. The parable of the Sower.
18. The parable of the Mustard Seed.

19. The tempest on the sea.
20. The Gerasene demoniac.
21. Jairus' daughter, and the woman with an issue of blood.
22. The rejection at Nazareth.
23. The mission of the Twelve.
24. Imprisonment and death of John the Baptist.
25. The Feeding of the Five Thousand.

In this list the Parable of the Seed growing secretly, which is peculiar to Mark, as also a few minor editorial insertions, have been omitted. Each item has been numbered from 1 to 25. In comparing the order of events in Mark with the order in Matthew and Luke, we cannot, of course, include non-Marcan matter in those Gospels such as the Genealogies in them, the Sermons on the Mount and on the Plain, the Centurion's Servant, or any miracle or parable found outside Mark.

The order of the Marcan events in Matthew and Luke is given in the second and third columns in the Table on the following page ; Matthew has omitted incident 5 in Mark, and Luke has inserted incidents 15 and 18 much later in his Gospel.

It will be seen that Luke follows Mark more closely than Matthew, who has re-arranged Mark's order considerably. In Luke's order in the Table, Luke has transferred into new positions 24, 22, 4 and 16, and inserted the incidents 15 and 18 much later in the Gospel. When the outlines of Matthew and Luke are compared it will be seen that when Luke departs from Mark's arrangement, as *e.g.* 24 after 1, and 22 after 3, and 4 after 5, 6, 7, Matthew follows Mark, *e.g.* 2 after 1, 4 after 3, and 6, 7 after 4 : whereas Luke gives 15 and 18 much later in his Gospel and gives 17 before 16, Matthew gives, 15, 16, 17, 18 as in Mark. When Matthew gives 10, 11, 21, 14, 23, 12, 13, Luke gives 10,

11, 12, 13, 14. But however Matthew and Luke alter the arrangement, we can from their orders of events get Mark's relative order exactly, as the tabular lists show.

Mark	Matthew	Luke	Mark	Matthew	Luke
1	1	1	—	23	—
—	—	24	12	12	12
2	2	2	13	13	13
3	3	3	14	—	14
—	—	22	15	15	—
4	4	—	—	—	17
5	—	5	16	16	16
—	8	—	17	17	—
6	6	6	18	18	—
7	7	7	19	—	19
—	19	—	20	—	20
—	—	4	21	—	21
—	20	—	22	22	—
8	—	8	23	—	23
9	9	9	24	24	—
10	10	10	25	25	25
11	11	11	—	—	15
—	21	—	—	—	18
—	14	—			

The inference to be drawn from these tables is that the relative order of events in Mark is supported by one or other of Matthew and Luke. When Matthew departs from Mark's order, Luke upholds Mark; when Luke departs from Mark's order, Matthew upholds Mark. In no instance do Matthew and Luke agree against Mark. The sequence of events therefore supports the argument that Matthew and Luke used Mark as a common source.

It will be seen later that the incidents numbered 24, 22, 4, 15, 18, which are placed by Luke in positions which disturb Mark's order considerably, have been chosen from

sources other than Mark, which sources he preferred. These are the sources referred to as Q and L in Chapter II. These five incidents are the Imprisonment of John, the Rejection at Nazareth, the Call of the First Apostles, the Beelzebub Controversy, and the parable of the Mustard Seed. These are, as we shall see later, divergent versions of the same subject-matter, and will be considered in the next chapter. We shall also in Chapter IX attempt an explanation of the reasons which made Matthew alter Mark's order so considerably.

Thus three independent lines of evidence, namely, the common contents, the common diction, and the common arrangement in Matthew, Mark and Luke provide strong arguments for the priority of Mark. Each of the three arguments by itself would not have proved our thesis, but the three arguments together furnish decisive evidence that Mark is the primary Gospel. We may add that if Mark has been compiled from Matthew and Luke, no adequate reason can be found for his omission of the Infancy Stories, of the Sermons on the Mount and on the Plain, of the Lord's Prayer, and of such beautiful parables as the Good Samaritan and the Prodigal Son.

4. Improvements on Mark.

Lastly, the arguments for the primitive character of Mark can be made more convincing still (1) by the nature of the alterations made by Matthew and Luke in order to avoid statements which seemed to them to limit the power of Christ and to be derogatory not only of Christ but also of the Apostles, (2) by the preservation of Aramaic words in Mark which are almost wholly omitted by Matthew and Luke, and (3) by the smoothing down and improvement of Mark's roughness of style. These many improvements are explicable only on the assumption that Matthew and Luke

revised the language of Mark. We will consider these in some detail.

1. There are many instances in Mark where his language seems to place a limit on the power of Christ to heal or to gain obedience, or imply that He was ignorant, or that He was subject to human emotions, or that He was not addressed as He should have been. These words of Mark are either omitted or altered by either Matthew or Luke or by both of them, and though we cannot speak with certainty of the minds of Matthew and Luke and infer their real purpose, yet the whole tendency of the alterations is to magnify Christ's power and Person.

(i) *Mark's Limitation of the Power of Christ.*

(*a*) and (*b*) Two instances may be quoted which refer to Christ's power to heal the sick. Mark in two cases says that Christ only healed " many," which word becomes " all " in Matthew and Luke.

(*a*) Mark 1^{34}. And he healed many that were sick with divers diseases, and cast out many devils.

Matthew 8^{16}. And he cast out the spirits with a word, and healed all that were sick.

Luke 4^{40}. And he laid his hands on every one of them, and healed them.

(*b*) Mark 3^9. For he had healed many.

Matthew 12^{15}. And he healed them all.

Luke 6^{19}. Healed them all.

(*c*) In the Visit to Nazareth, Mark's words suggest inability in Christ to do any wonders, and He is said to have marvelled because of their unbelief. Mark does not state that the want of faith in Christ was the cause of failure. Matthew alters Mark to make Christ do some wonders and definitely attributes Christ's partial failure to lack of faith on the part of the people. Luke omits Mark's statement.

Mark 6[5a, 6a]. And he could there do no mighty work . . . and he marvelled because of their unbelief.

Matthew 13[58]. And he did not many mighty works there because of their unbelief.

(d) In another instance Christ is stated to have been unable to gain a response to His desire for privacy. This is in the story of the Syro-phœnician woman. Luke omits the whole incident ; Matthew gives the incident but omits the disturbing passage.

Mark 7[24]. And he entered into a house, and would have no man know it : and he could not be hid.

(e) and (f) Mark gives two miracles where the cures are only gradual and not instantaneous, and in these miracles means, e.g. spittle, are used. Both these miracles are omitted by Matthew and Luke.

(e) Mark 7[32-37]. The healing of the deaf and dumb man.

(f) Mark 8[22-26]. The healing of a blind man.

(g) In another miracle, that of the lunatic boy, both Matthew and Luke omit nearly all the signs of physical suffering which according to Mark continued to be shown in Christ's presence and, in particular, after Christ had commanded the unclean spirit to come out of the boy. Matthew also adds that the boy " was cured from that hour " and Luke that " they were all astonished at the majesty of God."

Mark 9[20-26] = Matthew 17[15b, 18] = Luke 9[42].

(h) The Cursing of the Fig Tree is omitted by Luke, who gives instead a parable of the Fig Tree. Matthew states that the fig tree withered as soon as Jesus pronounced the curse, whereas Mark implies a gradual withering away.

Mark 11[20]. And as they passed by in the morning, they saw the fig tree withered away from the roots.

Matthew 21[19]. And immediately the fig tree withered away.

(ii) *Statements Derogatory of Christ.*

This group deals with Christ's human emotions, His ignorance, His seeming indifference to the troubles of others, and in two instances with the conception of His personality.

(*a*)—(*c*) Matthew and Luke omit three statements of Mark which might be taken to be a reflection on Christ's behaviour.

(*a*) Mark 3⁵. With anger, being grieved at the hardening of their heart.

(*b*) Mark 3²¹. And when his friends heard it, they went out to lay hold on him : for they said, He is beside himself.

(*c*) Mark 10¹⁴. He was moved with indignation.

(*d*) In the Cleansing of the Leper, the leper acting against Christ's wish makes the cure known. Matthew omits the verse, and Luke so alters it that the desire of Christ seemed to be carried out by the leper.

Mark 1⁴⁵. But he went out, and began to publish it much, and to spread abroad the matter.

Luke 5¹⁵. But so much the more went abroad the report concerning him.

(*e*) and (*f*) Two illustrations may be given of Christ's seeming indifference to the fate of others. In the Storm on the Sea, Mark mentions that there were other boats with Him but says nothing about their coming safely through the storm. Matthew and Luke omit the statement about the presence of these boats. In the Walking on the Sea, an incident which Luke omits, Matthew omits words in Mark which might suggest that Jesus took no notice of the distress of the Apostles.

(*e*) Mark 4³⁶. And other boats were with him.

(*f*) Mark 6⁴⁸. And he would have passed by them.

(g) In the Gerasene Demoniac, the unclean spirit dares to adjure Jesus. Matthew omits the adjuration, whilst Luke changes it into a petition.

> Mark 5⁷. I adjure thee by God, torment me not.
> Matthew 8²⁹. Art thou come hither to torment us before the time?
> Luke 8²⁸. I beseech thee, torment me not.

(h) and (i) There are two illustrations of Christ's Person being called in question in Mark. In one, Mark calls Him the carpenter, which does not find favour with Matthew and Luke; and in the other, Mark's form of Christ's words might impugn Christ's Divinity and therefore Matthew alters Mark's language altogether.

> (h) Mark 6³. Is not this the carpenter?
> Matthew 13⁵⁵. Is not this the carpenter's son?
> Luke 4²². Is not this Joseph's son?
> (i) Mark 10¹⁸, Luke 18¹⁹. Why callest thou me good? none is good save one, even God.
> Matthew 19¹⁷. Why askest thou me concerning that which is good? One there is who is good.

(j) In the Great Commandment, Mark's account suggests that the scribe was patronising Jesus. Matthew omits the words, whilst Luke gives the incident from a variant version in which the words do not occur.

> Mark 12²⁸. Knowing that he had answered them well,

(k) In the Cursing of the Fig Tree, Mark gives a statement which implies ignorance on the part of Jesus. Matthew omits the doubtful words, whilst Luke omits the whole incident.

> Mark 11¹³. If haply he might find anything thereon: . . . for it was not the season of figs.

Thus, as regards our Lord, the tendency of the alterations and omissions by Matthew and Luke, even if many of them

may have had no theological significance, provides evidence that Mark's gospel is the earliest of the three, for no Christian writer would deliberately alter even one favourable trait into unfavourable, whereas the converse process is the more natural one. This argument for the priority of Mark is supported by the editing of statements in Mark which refer to the ignorance, dullness, querulity, mistrust and selfishness of Apostles. In nearly every case failures are omitted or the language so altered that the Apostles are placed in a more favourable light.

(iii) *Statements Derogatory of the Apostles.*

In the cases of dullness and ignorance displayed by the Apostles nearly every instance is omitted ; and in one instance the words are altered by Matthew, whilst Luke finds an excuse for the Apostles.

(*a*) Mark 4^{13}. Know ye not this parable ? and how shall ye know all the parables ?

(*b*) Mark 6^{51b-52}. They were sore amazed in themselves ; for they understood not concerning the loaves, but their heart was hardened.

(*c*) Mark 8^{17b-18}. Have ye your heart hardened ? Having eyes, see ye not ? and having ears, hear ye not ?

(*d*) Mark 9^6. For he wist not what to answer (*cf.* 14^{40}).

(*e*) Mark 9^{32}. But they understood not the saying, and were afraid to ask him.

Matthew 17^{23}. And they were exceeding sorry.

Luke 9^{45}. But they understood not this saying, and it was concealed from them, that they should not perceive it : and they were afraid to ask him about this saying.

(*f*) The Apostles were probably distrustful according to Mark : Matthew and Luke save them from this charge.

Mark 4³⁸.   Master, carest thou not that we perish ?
Matthew 8²⁵.   Save, Lord ; we perish.
Luke 8²⁴.   Master, master, we perish.

(g) The Apostles, in remonstrating against Christ, seem disrespectful.   Matthew omits the words ; Luke puts the inquiry into Christ's mouth, and thus protects the Apostles.

Mark 5³¹.   And sayest thou, Who touched me ?
Luke 8⁴⁵.   And Jesus said, Who is it that touched me ?

(h) The Apostles even argued amongst themselves— Matthew omits the reference.

Mark 9³³⁻³⁴.   He asked them, What were ye reasoning in the way ?   But they held their peace : for they had disputed one with another in the way, who was the greatest.
Luke 9⁴⁶.   And there arose a reasoning among them.

(i) Selfishness was manifested by James and John, says Mark.   This charge is altered by Matthew, who assigns the making of a request not to the two Apostles but to their mother.

Mark 10³⁵.   And there come near unto him James and John, the sons of Zebedee, saying unto him.
Matthew 20²⁰.   There came to him the mother of the sons of Zebedee with her sons worshipping him, and asking a certain thing of him.

(iv) *Jesus as Lord.*

In Mark, Jesus is only once addressed as Lord, and that by the Syro-phœnician woman who could not have used it in a divine sense ; He is generally addressed in Mark as Rabbi or Teacher.   On the other hand, Matthew has Lord 19 times and Luke 16.   The use of the title by Matthew and Luke and not by Mark shows that Mark is primitive,

and gives us an early account of the original view of our Lord's Person held at first by the Apostles.

2. *Aramaic Words preserved by Mark.*

Luke does not retain any of the Aramaic words and phrases found in Mark; Matthew retains only one, the technical term Golgotha, and in the Cry from the Cross, instead of the Aramaic " Eloi, Eloi . . ." gives the Hebrew form " Eli, Eli . . . ." This shows that Mark was revised by Matthew and Luke. Mark's Aramaisms are interpreted for the benefit of his Gentile readers—3^{17} Boanerges; 5^{41} Talitha cumi; 7^{11} Corban; 7^{34} Ephphatha; 14^{36} Abba; 15^{22} Golgotha.

3. *Improvements of the Style of Mark* (see also Chapter X).

Mark's style is that of a writer with limited vocabulary, occasionally harsh and rough and ungrammatical. There is a frequent repetition of stereotyped phrases; many sentences begin with " and " or " and straightway "; " they " is used in a vague, unspecified sense. He is fond of using the historic present, that is, he writes often in the present tense to give vividness to the narrative; of 151 such instances in Mark, Matthew retains 21 and Luke only 1, both preferring some form of the past tense. Mark is also fond of duplicate expressions; and he occasionally uses vulgarisms, such as " pallet " (translated " bed " in Mark 2 $^{4, 9, 11}$) and " scourge " (translated " plague " in Mark $3^{10,}$ $5^{29, 34}$), and " honourable estate " or " rich " for a man in society (Mark 15^{43}). Most of this bad literary style is altered and improved by the more polished style of Matthew and Luke.

Instances of the shortening of duplicate expressions are as follows :

(*a*) Mark 1[32]. And at even, when the sun did set.
     Matthew 8[16]. And when even was come.
     Luke 4[40]. And when the sun was setting.
(*b*) Mark 2[25]. When he had need, and was an hungred.
     Matthew 12[3]; Luke 6[3]. When he was an hungred.
(*c*) Mark 12[44]. All that she had, even all her living.
     Luke 21[4]. All the living that she had.

The four lines of argument which have been examined show that the evidence for the priority of Mark is irrefutable and conclusive. Though the shortest of the Gospels, it is the most important of them all, because it preceded the others in time, and was used by Matthew and Luke, who recognised its great value as an original and trustworthy record. Synoptic criticism has made it the primary Gospel, and its acceptance into the Canon, when its shorter length, its candour and its brevity of teaching and doctrine might have caused it to be overlooked, is a matter for profound thankfulness.

CHAPTER IV

DIVERGENT SOURCES

There are in the three Synoptic Gospels a number of narratives and discourses which, though they refer to the same subject-matter, cannot be assigned to only one common source. The resemblances between the accounts in the Synoptics are here either far from close or the versions differ in some essential particulars, so that we are compelled to conclude that both Matthew and Luke could not have derived their versions from Mark. Indications of the existence of these special sources have already been given in our study of Peter's Confession, where Matthew's special source appeared, and in Chapter III, when referring to Luke's alteration of the arrangement of the subject-matter in Mark (pp. 26 and 30 f.) ; for as regards the latter, Luke's departure from Mark's order of incidents was stated to be the result of his preference for sources in which the incidents causing the dislocation appeared in quite different contexts. Further, if Matthew contains nearly all Mark, and Luke about half of Mark, it is to be expected that, in these divergent versions of the same event, we shall find in most of the cases that it is Matthew who reproduces Mark, and it is Luke who does not reproduce Mark but utilises another source, namely his special source L. The divergent sources will be found chiefly but not exclusively in Luke.

We shall confine our study to those dissimilar items which come under the Three Gospel problem, that is, to those

which are found when we compare Matthew, Mark and Luke. In the next chapter we shall deal with dissimilar versions, in addition to similar versions, found only in Matthew and Luke. In our present study we shall have to refer to the non-Marcan sources of Matthew and Luke, namely Q, the source of similar sayings, and M, the special source of Matthew, and L, the special source of Luke. Further, in order to simplify our inquiry, the special cases to be considered will be placed in two groups ; in the first group the source Q does not come into the problems, whilst in the second group Q does come in.

Group I

The Call and Preaching of John the Baptist. (Text on p. 251.)

Mark 1[4].   Matthew 3[1-2].   Luke 3[1-3].

Luke's account has important variations from the versions in Mark and Matthew. (1) It contains historical data meant to date the time of John's call and preaching ; (2) it has a fuller Old Testament prophecy ; (3) it omits the prophecy of Malachi which in Mark is attributed to Isaiah ; but this prophecy is found in Matthew 11[10] and in Luke 7[27] in a non-Marcan context ; (4) Luke alone, in words recalling those of the Old Testament prophets, gives the call of John, which is said to have occurred in the wilderness. In addition, Luke gives the locality of John's preaching as " all the region around about Jordan," whereas Mark gives it as " the wilderness," and Matthew as " the wilderness of Judea." Thus in Luke, John's call took place in the wilderness, and his preaching in the region round about Jordan ; (5) Lastly, Luke does not include, as Matthew docs, the interesting description of John's clothing and desert fare. These variations point to an independent source for Luke's version.

The sole objection to this discrimination is that Mark and Luke agree against Matthew on the theme of John's preaching.

Mark and Luke. " The baptism of repentance unto remission of sins."

Matthew. " Repent ye ; for the kingdom of heaven is at hand."

There are, however, two considerations which point to Matthew's deliberate editing of Mark's text, for, if Matthew 3^{1-6} is compared with Mark 1^{2-6} it will be seen that Matthew has used Mark as his source. In the first place, Matthew may have desired to represent John as being the fore-runner of Jesus even to the very message proclaimed, for in Matthew 4^{17} we read of Jesus, " From that time began Jesus to preach, and to say, Repent ye ; for the kingdom of heaven is at hand." This probability is strengthened by Matthew's care in answering an existing attack or in providing against a possible attack on our Lord's divinity (compare especially Matthew 19^{16-17} with Mark 10^{17-18}). Had Matthew copied Mark's version of the theme of John's preaching his Jewish readers might have concluded that Jesus had been baptised with a baptism of repentance unto remission of sins, and that therefore Jesus was not sinless. That Matthew realised the possible implication of Mark's version as impairing belief in the sinlessness of Jesus is assured by the insertion of an argument between the Baptist and Jesus which is given by Matthew alone (Matthew 3^{14-15}). John would have hindered Jesus, but at the request of Jesus suffered Him to be baptised, not for remission of sins but in order to fulfil all righteousness. Thus, by changing the subject-matter of John's preaching and by inserting a discussion between the Baptist and Jesus, Matthew is particularly careful to safeguard the divinity of Jesus, attacks on which he also meets in his accounts of our Lord's Infancy and of His Resurrection.

Thus it is extremely probable, if not certain, that general tradition held that John's theme was " the baptism of repentance unto remission of sins." As his work was preparatory to the coming of the expected Deliverer, it was not for John to proclaim that the kingdom of heaven was at hand ; that was to be the special message of the Deliverer, called by him the " One mightier than I " whom he had to announce. John's theme would be constantly repeated to all who came to hear him ; a short pithy statement of that kind by a new prophet who had revived the prophetic rôle would not be forgotten. Thus Mark and Matthew and Luke would know the theme, and it would not be necessary to assume that Luke borrowed from Mark. Here, therefore, we have an instance of the overlapping of Mark and L, that is to say, there are two versions of the Call of John given in Mark and L.

Matthew's story of the Call of John is based on Mark ; Luke's version is from his independent source L.

The Baptism of Jesus. (Text on p. 252.)

Mark 1$^{9-11}$. Matthew 3$^{13-17}$. Luke 3$^{21-22}$.

Here, as in the case of the call and preaching of John, there is ample evidence that Luke's source is not Mark. (1) Luke's account leaves a clear impression that it was not Jesus only who saw the sky rent asunder and heard the voice ; the bystanders also saw and heard. That is to say, the experience of Jesus was not internal, as in Mark and Matthew, but external. (2) This is supported by Luke's words that the Spirit did not descend " as a dove " but " in a bodily form, as a dove." This materialistic representation of a spiritual experience is characteristic of Luke's treatment of our Lord's Resurrection experiences obtained from L ; in the source L, Christ walks and sits down to meat, breaks bread and distributes it, and also in particular eats

a piece of broiled fish. (3) Again, there is no mention in Luke of the journey of Jesus from Nazareth in Galilee to the Jordan. (4) In Luke alone, it is said that the baptism of Jesus took place after all the people had been baptised. (5) The message of the voice is in some texts of Luke given as " Thou art my Son, this day have I begotten thee," which is the reading quoted by Justin Martyr about A.D. 150. This reading is probably original, and may have been altered by a scribe to the form given in Mark as a safeguard, for the original version of Justin Martyr could be quoted as evidence by those Gnostic heretics who believed that in the words " this day have I begotten thee " they had ground for their belief that Jesus became the adopted Son of God at His Baptism and not before it.

The Names of the Twelve. (Text on p. 252 f.)

Mark 3^16-19.   Matthew 10^2b-4.   Luke 6^14-16.

The uncertainty in the name of one of the Apostles is remarkable. Luke gives one of the Twelve as " Judas the son of James " ; we cannot conclude that this Judas is to be identified with Thaddæus. Also the order of the names varies in each of the Gospels, as well as in Acts 1^13 and in John 21^2. If Matthew and Luke had reproduced Mark both the lists of names and their order would have been preserved.

The order in John 21^2 is illuminating and there is a new name mentioned. Peter first, then Thomas, then Nathanael, and then " the sons of Zebedee."

The divergent readings of the manuscripts are also instructive. The Byzantine text in Matthew (given in our A.V.) reads Lebbæus who is called Thaddæus ; and in Mark, Thaddæus. B and ℵ read Thaddæus in Mark and Matthew. D gives Lebbæus in Mark and Matthew. Origen states that Matthew gave Lebbæus, thus showing

that the Byzantine text is an attempt at harmonising Matthew and Mark. An old version substitutes Judas Zelotes for Lebbæus in Matthew.

The only conclusion to be drawn is that in Mark and Matthew and Luke we have three different traditions and that therefore Q, the source used by Matthew and Luke, did not contain a list of the names of the Twelve.

The Great Commandment. (Text on p. 253.)

Mark 12$^{28-31,\ 34}$. Matthew 22$^{34-40,\ 46}$. Luke 10$^{25-28}$.

Whilst Matthew is undoubtedly based on Mark, Luke's version shows evidence of being drawn from another source. Matthew and Mark place the incident amongst the four discussions in the week of Christ's Passion ; Luke omits this discussion in the events of that week and places it in an earlier stage of the ministry, where it leads up to the parable of the Good Samaritan. Also, the lawyer's question in Luke is " what shall I do to inherit eternal life ? " and not as in Mark and Matthew, where the lawyer or scribe inquires which is the first or great commandment. Lastly, in Luke it is the lawyer, and not our Lord, who quotes the *Shema*, " Thou shalt love the Lord thy God," etc.

Luke therefore is based on L and is not dependent on Mark.

We have given four illustrations of divergent versions but there are many others. For example, Matthew's dependence on Mark may be seen in :

The Call of the Apostles ; Mark 1$^{16-20}$, Matthew 4$^{18-22}$.

The Rejection at Nazareth ; Mark 6$^{1-6}$, Matthew 13$^{53-58}$.

The Imprisonment of John ; Mark 6$^{17-18}$, Matthew 14$^{3-4}$.

The Anointing ; Mark 14$^{3-9}$, Matthew 26$^{6-13}$.

But if the versions of these four stories are read in Luke, and compared with Mark, the student will realise two facts : first, the independence of Luke, whose versions are totally different ; and secondly, that Luke's versions are given in different contexts, *e.g.* the visit to Nazareth is placed by Luke immediately after the Temptation, whereas Mark and Matthew place it much later. We therefore assign these four events to Luke's special source L ; they are found in Luke 5^{1-11}, 4^{16-30}, 3^{19-20}, 7^{36-50} respectively.

GROUP II

(This includes the source Q)

The Temptation.   (Text on p. 255.)

Mark 1^{12-13}.   Matthew $4^{1-2, 11}$.   Luke $4^{1-2, 13}$.

We are concerned with the fact of the Temptation, and not with the three temptations which are described in Matthew and Luke alone and by their similarity show that the details of the temptations are from Q.

The variations in the narratives are more striking than the agreements. Mark makes no mention that Jesus fasted in the wilderness ; the suggestion in Mark is quite otherwise, for angels ministered (*i.e.* kept ministering) to him. Also in Mark the reader's interest is not drawn to any fast but concentrated on the wild beasts and angels ; and lastly, in Mark the temptation by Satan is said to have been continuous during the forty days. On the other hand, according to Luke, Jesus was not " driven forth " but was " led " by the Spirit ; also Jesus ate nothing in those forty days when " being tempted of the devil," and the first detailed temptation came at the end of the period of fasting ; further, in Luke there is no mention of the ministry of angels (a point which Luke ordinarily is fond of) as in Mark and Matthew ; and lastly, Luke has a special note to the effect that " when the devil had completed every temptation he

departed from him for a season ". Luke therefore is not indebted to Mark but to L ; the details of the temptations he found in Q. Matthew's version differs in a few details from both ; according to him, and not to Mark and Luke, Jesus was " led up " into the wilderness for one purpose—to be tempted ; Matthew also implies that the temptation followed the fast ; His fasting, according to Matthew, may not mean that " He ate nothing in those days " as Luke says. Matthew's source is not Mark but independent tradition.

The Beelzebub Controversy. (Text on p. 255.)

Mark 3$^{22-27}$.   Matthew 12$^{22-30}$.   Luke 11$^{14-23}$.

Matthew and Luke introduce the Controversy with a miracle, the cure of a dumb demoniac ; also they have three verses each which show close parallelism and which are not in Mark, namely Matthew, verses 27, 28, 30 = Luke, verses 19, 20, 23. Thus the cure of the dumb demoniac and these three verses held in common belong to Q. Also Matthew and Luke in these verses have words and phrases not elsewhere found in Mark's Gospel.

On the other hand, in verses 24–26 and 29 in Matthew, whilst close verbal resemblances are found between them and verses 22–27 in Mark, there are words borrowed from Luke in them ; also verse 22 in Luke, which corresponds to verse 27 in Mark and verse 29 in Matthew, is peculiar to Luke. Thus, in verses 24–26 Matthew has combined Mark and Luke, but not utilised verse 22 of Luke. Again Matthew and Mark follow the Controversy with the Blasphemy against the Holy Spirit, which Luke deals with later in 12^{10}. Matthew has thus used both Mark and Luke.

We shall see later that there is good reason for assuming that Luke gives Q in a more connected and reliable form than Matthew. If therefore Luke's version of the Controversy is that of Q, we conclude that Matthew has conflated his two

versions Mark and Q. This conflation or the interweaving of versions of the same subject-matter is a special characteristic of Matthew. Mark and Q had parallel and different versions of the Controversy; Matthew drew from both.

The circumstance that varying versions of the Controversy are found in Mark and Q is evidence not that Mark knew Q but that Mark and Q overlapped.

Blasphemy against the Holy Spirit. (Text on p. 257.)

Mark 3^{28-30}.   Matthew 12^{31-32}.   Luke 12^{10}.

The phenomena observed in the Beelzebub Controversy are to be noticed here. Matthew draws from Mark and Q and thereby conflates Mark and Q (Matthew 12^{32} = Luke 12^{10} = Q). As Mark and Q give divergent versions of the Blasphemy, this is another instance where Mark and Q overlap.

The Parable of the Mustard Seed. (Text on p. 258.)

Mark 4^{30-32}.   Matthew 13^{31-32}.   Luke 13^{18-19}.

Another case of conflation by Matthew, who has obtained from Luke " which a man took," " became a tree," " lodged in the branches thereof," and the casting of the seed into the man's own field. If Luke is Q, Matthew has conflated Mark and Q, and Mark once again overlaps Q.

The Mission of the Twelve. (Text on pp. 259 ff.)

This is a complicated example of conflation and agglomeration by Matthew, for he has both interweaved and collected into one mass not two sources but three, Mark, Q and M. Further, in Luke there are two missions, the mission of the Twelve (9^{1-6}) from Mark, and the mission of the Seventy (10^{1-12}) from L and Q; and in the mission of the Twelve, Luke has borrowed a few words from Q and inserted them into his source Mark. $10^{1,\ 17-20}$ is L.

In our study we shall deal with the narratives in two parts, first to illustrate how far Matthew and Luke drew from the common source Mark, and secondly to bring in the source Q which is drawn on by Matthew and Luke only. The special source M is found in Matthew 10^{2-4}, and will be omitted for the present.

Mark 6^{7-13}.   Matthew $10^{1, 5-15}$.   Luke 9^{1-6}.

The indebtedness of Matthew and Luke to Mark is clear. The Revised Version does not bring out that the Greek word translated " money " in Mark is the same as the Greek word for " brass " in Matthew, and means copper money ; also that Luke's Greek word for " money " is silver money. Further, Mark and Matthew have the same Greek word for purse, which is not the same word in Luke 10^4. Matthew gets his words " gold " and " silver " by assimilation from " brass ". Matthew also enlarged his version by repeating ideas involved in the words " enter," " peace " and " worthy " in verses 11 and 13. Apart from this assimilation and repetition, nearly every word in Matthew is found in Mark. Matthew obtained " for the labourer is worthy of his hire " from Q (Luke 10^7) ; he has thus conflated Mark and Q.

The second part will compare Matthew's version with the two missions in Luke in order that the relationship between them may be seen. We shall omit verses 2–4 from Matthew 10 ; they give the names of the Twelve, and these verses, we concluded, came from M (see p. 44).

Matthew 9^{37}–10^{15}.   Luke 9^{1-5}.   Luke 10^{1-12}.

Luke 9^{1-6} we saw is based on Mark ; Luke 10^{2-12} is from Q. We notice in Matthew the special source M in the limitation of the mission to the lost sheep of Israel (verses 5–8). When we compare Matthew with Luke's two accounts it is easy to see that Matthew has combined Mark and M

4

and Q dexterously, and rearranged the order of the sentences in Q.

We might follow up Matthew's verses to the end of the chapter; he continues to utilise his three sources with great skill, choosing verses and passages from his sources and fitting them together to make a well-connected whole, within the framework of Mark.

16a. Q (Luke 10³).

16b. M.

17–22. Conflation of Mark 13⁹⁻¹³ and Q (Luke 12¹¹⁻¹²).

23. M.

24. Q (Luke 6⁴⁰).

25. M.

26. Mark 4²².

27–35. Q (Luke 12³⁻⁹, ⁵¹⁻⁵³).

36. M.

37–38. Q (Luke 14²⁶⁻²⁷).

39. Q (Luke 17³³).

40. Mark 9³⁷, or possibly divergent.

41. M.

42. Mark 9⁴¹.

The charge to the Twelve as given in Matthew is an instance of " agglomeration," that is to say, of a collection of passages from various non-Marcan sources and various contexts joined together to make a larger discourse fitted into the context of Mark. The 7 verses of Mark have become 42 in Matthew. This is one of Matthew's methods, and is to be found in the construction of long discourses in his Gospel. Compare also Matthew 13 with Mark 4, and Matthew 18 with Mark 9³³⁻⁴⁸. Matthew's other great method, as we have seen, is " conflation," which is the interweaving of two or three parallel and overlapping versions of the same incident or saying; one version is taken as a basis, and words and phrases from the other versions are inserted into the basic version.

CHAPTER V

Q

WHEN the Marcan portions, amounting approximately to 500 verses out of 1068 in Matthew, and to 320 verses out of 1149 in Luke are removed, we are left with the major portions of the two Gospels, and in them we find the same two kinds of phenomena as we met with in our previous studies. These phenomena are (1) the existence of close parallelisms in items of Matthew and Luke which can be explained by assuming a source Q, and (2) the existence of divergent versions of the same subject-matter which cannot with certainty be assigned to Q, and therefore may be allocated to the special sources of Matthew and Luke.

The problems which awaited solution in the Three Gospel problem, *i.e.* in the use of Mark by Matthew and Luke, have forewarned us of many dangers in any attempt to reconstruct Q. (1) As Matthew and Luke did not use all of Mark they probably did not use all of Q, and therefore there may be verses of Q of which no trace is found in Matthew and Luke. (2) As Matthew and Luke altered and adapted Mark, they probably treated Q likewise. (3) As Matthew and Luke did not always choose the same items of Mark, there will probably be verses peculiar to Matthew and Luke which came from Q. (4) As Matthew collated or interweaved his sources, fitting them together to give a co-ordination of ideas, whilst on the other hand, Luke generally, as we shall see in Chapter VII, took blocks of matter from

his sources, Mark and L, any reconstruction of Q must be based on Luke and not on Matthew, for we shall expect to find blocks of Q in Luke.

Q is a hypothesis which had been made to explain the fact that in Matthew and Luke there are nearly 250 verses whose diction and phraseology are very much alike. Oral tradition cannot account for this large amount of close identification of language, though it may account for divergences of tradition.

That Q is more than a hypothesis may be assumed from the circumstance that occasionally the same saying occurs in Matthew and Luke in two forms, *e.g.* Luke 8^{17} = Mark 4^{22} = Luke 12^2 = Matthew 10^{26}, where Luke's two references give the same saying. If Luke obtained one of his sayings from Mark, a written source, it is possible that he obtained the other from another written source, such as Q.

We may go further, for Dr. Burkitt argues that a little point in the parable of the Master and Servant (Matthew 24 $^{45-51}$ = Luke 12^{42-46}) " clinches " the argument for the real existence of Q as a written Greek document. Both Gospels contain a Greek mistranslation of an Aramaic word, for both say of the forgetful slave that the master " shall cut him asunder " and then set him among the unfaithful. " This is absurd, for a slave who has been so treated would not need to be ' set among the unworthy '. Obviously ' cut him asunder ' is a Greek mistranslation of some original Aramaic word meaning to ' segregate '. But, as both Matthew and Luke have this mistranslation they must have been using a Greek text, the same Greek text, which contained it. Q therefore, as used by Matthew and Luke, was a Greek document, a Greek translation of a still more original Aramaic collection of sayings of Jesus."

Q is therefore a written Greek document. It is also a trustworthy document, for it was used by Matthew and Luke and even used occasionally in preference to Mark

when there was a parallel version in Mark.   Q is as reliable as Mark.

Parallel Versions in Matthew and Luke.

We will first consider a few cases which illustrate closeness of similarity.   The resemblance in the rest of the 250 odd verses is generally as close as in the cases to be quoted.   At the same time, it should be observed that this common matter is not found in the same contexts in Matthew and Luke, nor is it arranged in the same sequence in both these Gospels.   " Subsequent to the Temptation story," says Streeter, " there is not a single case in which Matthew and Luke agree in inserting the same saying at the same point in the Marcan outline."

Jesus' Reply to John the Baptist.   (Text on pp. 263 ff.)
    Luke 7$^{24-28}$.   Matthew 11$^{7-11}$.

" *I thank thee, O Father.*"
    Luke 10$^{21-22}$.   Matthew 11$^{25-27}$.

" *Consider the Lilies.*"
    Luke 12$^{27-28}$.   Matthew 6$^{28-30}$.

" *O Jerusalem, Jerusalem.*"
    Luke 13$^{34-35}$.   Matthew 23$^{37-39}$.

" *Two Masters.*"
    Luke 16^{13}.   Matthew 6^{24}.

The variations in the context of these illustrations are noticeable.   Whilst Matthew places the items on the Lilies and on the Two Masters in the Sermon on the Mount, and the lament over Jerusalem in the week of the Passion, Luke

places the three items after the Sermon on the Plain. Matthew places Jesus' reply to John after the Charge to the Twelve and long after the Sermon on the Mount, whilst Luke inserts it between the Sermon on the Plain and the Anointing. Matthew places the words of Thanksgiving after the Charge to the Twelve, to which he added matter from the Charge to the Seventy, whilst Luke places it after the return of the Seventy.

Passages such as those just given can be assigned without difficulty to a common source. The problem becomes acute in cases where the versions differ very greatly, and it is partly because of these variant versions that scholars are not agreed in their reconstructions of Q. We have no right to pre-suppose that all the sayings of Christ would be recorded in one source (*cf.* Acts 20³⁵); neither have we a right to expect the saying or discourse to be given in identical terms in various sources. The marvel is not that divergent versions exist, but that so many should exist with such close parallelism after a generation of oral tradition. We have every reason to expect to find some overlapping of sources in cycles of tradition connected with the great centres of Christianity.

Divergent Versions in Matthew and Luke.

The Beatitudes. (Text on p. 266.)

Luke 6¹⁷⁻²⁶. Matthew 5¹⁻¹².

The Beatitudes form the opening sentences of two sermons, the Sermon on the Mount in Matthew, and the Sermon on the Plain in Luke. The inquiry before us is the literary connection between them.

The following contrasts are to be noticed:

(1) Luke's Sermon was delivered when Jesus came down from a mountain and " stood on a level place "; Matthew's

Sermon was delivered when Jesus "went up into a mountain".

(2) Luke's Sermon follows the choice of the Twelve, and was meant for the Twelve (6^{20}); Matthew's Sermon precedes the choice of the Twelve, and was spoken with a view to the audience (Matthew 5^{1-2}).

(3) Luke has four Beatitudes and four Woes, all in the second person plural; Matthew has nine Beatitudes, of which only one, the last, is in the second person plural, and eight are in the third person plural. There are no Woes in Matthew.

(4) Luke's Beatitudes are ascetic in tone, the blessed being those who are poor and hungry and weep; that is to say, the reference is to actual poverty and hunger and tears. Matthew's corresponding Beatitudes are for the poor in spirit, for those that hunger and thirst after righteousness, for those that mourn; and he also refers to the meek, the merciful, the pure in heart, etc. Matthew emphasises the character of those who enter the kingdom of heaven.

There is one point of agreement; the last Beatitude and the Rejoice show resemblances which point to a common source Q. Thus in the actual Sermon, we conclude that Matthew obtained from Q and edited four verses, 3, 6, 11 and 12; of the rest of the section, verses 1–2, 4–5, 7–10 came from his special source M.

The setting of each of the Two Sermons displays a special purpose of its own. In Matthew, the new Law is to be given on a mountain, which is the new Sinai; the Twelve have not yet been elected, and there are only four disciples who have been called by Christ. In Luke, Jesus retires to a mountain all night to pray; in the morning He selects the Twelve whom He designates Apostles (6^{12-13}) and "lifting up His eyes" on them delivers a charge; at 6^{27} Jesus speaks to the multitudes assembled.

The Lord's Prayer. (Text on p. 267.)

Luke 11^{2-4}.   Matthew 6^{9-13}.

Luke does not contain " our," " which art in heaven," " Thy will be done, as in heaven, so on earth," and " but deliver us from the evil one " ; he also has " day by day " as against Matthew's " this day," " sins " as against " debts," and " for we ourselves also forgive every one that is indebted to us " as against " as we also have for-given our debtors ". Further, some manuscripts and authorities give instead of Luke's " Thy kingdom come," the phrase " Thy holy Spirit come upon us and cleanse us ". Again, the Lord's Prayer in Luke is in the midst of material from his special source L, as Matthew's is in the midst of material from his special source M. Lastly, Matthew's version contains two Greek words characteristic of Matthew, namely, " be done " and " evil ". We have therefore no ground for deriving the two versions from Q but are com-pelled to assign them to the two sources L and M.

The Centurion's Servant. (Text on p. 268.)

Luke 7^{1-10}.   Matthew 8^{5-13}.

The resemblance in the request of the centurion " Lord, I am not worthy, etc." and our Lord's response " I say unto you, I have not found so great faith, no, not in Israel," is very close ; very striking is the fact that the long state-ment of the centurion's faith is preserved, for it is not a saying of Jesus. That Luke 7^{6-9} and Matthew 8^{8-10} are from Q is certain.

The rest of the narratives, that is the introductions and the concluding verses in each Gospel, is far from similar. In Matthew the centurion himself comes to Jesus, and Jesus offers to return with him but is dissuaded ; and in the sequel, the servant is healed in the very hour the words of

healing are uttered. In Luke, on the other hand, the centurion sends elders of the Jews to Jesus, they make an earnest plea for the centurion, and Jesus actually sets out for the centurion's abode ; the centurion somehow hears of the Healer's approach and sends a second body, not of elders but of his friends, to meet Jesus on the way ; no word of cure is pronounced by Jesus, but only words of commendation of the centurion's faith ; and the friends on returning find the servant whole.

Two explanations are possible ; (1) L and M may have contained the initial and final verses of Luke and Matthew respectively, together with a middle section each of which was not quite as full as Q. This middle section was then discarded for Q by each editor. (2) The initial and final verses may be fuller editorial additions to an incident retained in Q for the value of the words of the centurion and of Christ. The sayings in Q probably began as follows, if we use the common words in Matthew and Luke : " He entered into Capernaum, and a centurion, whose servant was sick, came to Jesus and said, ' Lord, I am not worthy,' " etc. In either solution, Q had a story of the centurion's servant.

The Lost Sheep. (Text on p. 269.)

Luke 15$^{3-7}$.   Matthew 18$^{12-13}$.

On reading Luke's version of this parable with the two parables which are associated with it and which are peculiar to Luke, namely, that of the Lost Coin and that of the Prodigal Son, we realise that they form a triad, with teaching in each one which supplements the others. This association suggests that Luke's version of the Lost Sheep is from L as his other two parables are. This suggestion is supported by the differences in the two versions ; in Luke we find " lost," " wilderness," " righteous," " and

need no repentance," as against the " going astray " (repeated three times), and " the mountains." In Luke, verses 6 and 7 are not found in Matthew and verse 5 differs somewhat from verse 13 in Matthew. The identification is only in such details as would appear in any story of one sheep out of a hundred being lost.

That Luke's version is L is also indicated by the rejoicing of the neighbours in the Lost Sheep and the Lost Coin.

Matthew's source is probably M. Its insertion among sayings on children is strange.

The Strait Gate.   (Text on p. 270.)

Luke 13$^{24-27}$.   Matthew 7$^{13, 22-23}$.

As we assume that Luke gives Q, we conclude that Matthew has inserted verse 22 from M into Q matter (Luke, verses 24 and 27 = Matthew, verses 13 and 23), the said verse replacing two verses from Q. Matthew has conflated M and Q.

The versions which have been considered bear evidence both of the intermingling of sources by Matthew and of the over-lapping of the sources M and Q. They also show us that Q consists mainly of sayings, discourses, and parables, and that where a miracle is mentioned it is only as an introduction to the saying which is the chief interest of Q. Again, in many of our studies we have had good examples of Matthew's editorial methods, which show that Matthew drew his matter from various sources and inter-weaved them and massed them together. Luke is more direct in his use of sources, for he takes whole blocks of them, and we shall therefore find it expedient to base any attempt at reconstructing Q on Luke and not on Matthew, though, at the same time, we remain conscious that there are likely to be passages in Matthew alone which ought to be assigned to Q.

The Reconstruction of Q.

We shall take a few complete sections of Luke in which most of the verses, as they are closely similar to verses in Matthew, are from Q, and examine the other verses in each section in order that we may decide whether on reasonable grounds the whole section may be said to be from Q.

Later on in this Chapter the probable contents of Q are given in full, and to them reference should be made in what follows.

The Sermon on the Plain.   Luke 6^{20-49}.

In verses 20–26 the four Beatitudes are from Q, and the four Woes which follow, which are not in Matthew but only in Luke, balance the Beatitudes so admirably that they must go together.   Verses 27–32 are paralleled in Matthew $5^{44, \ 39, \ 40, \ 42}$, 7^{12a}, 5^{46} and are Q.   The teaching of verses 33–36 is summed up in Matthew $5^{47, \ 42, \ 45, \ 48}$; Matthew has adapted verses 37 and 38 in his 7^{1-2}.   The rest of the Lucan section from verse 39 is found in Matthew in different contexts;   39 in Matthew 15^{14}, 40 in Matthew 10^{24-25}, 41 and 42 in Matthew 7^{3-5}, 43 and 44 in Matthew $7^{18, \ 20, \ 16}$ (cf. 12^{33}), 45 in Matthew $12^{35, \ 34}$, 46–49 in Matthew $7^{21, \ 24-27}$.   The Sermon on the Plain is therefore all Q.

Various Sayings.   Luke 11^{9-52}.

Verses 27–28, 36–38, 40–41 and 45–46 are the only verses which have no close parallels in Matthew.   Of these verses 27 and 28, which include " Blessed is the womb that bare thee," follow the Unclean Spirit ; a similar sequence, but with a reference to our Lord's Mother, is given by Matthew in 12^{43-50}, where the Unclean Spirit is followed by the incident of Jesus' Mother and Brethren, which is somewhat similar in general teaching to Luke 11^{27-28}.   Thus verses

27 and 28 are from Q. As to verses 36–38, which are
omitted in Matthew, there is a longer passage on the same
theme in Matthew 15^{2ff}, which he obtained from Mark
7^{1ff}; and the teaching of verses 40 and 41 is given in
Matthew 23^{26}. Verses 45 and 46 begin the Woes on the
Lawyers, which is continued to verse 52, and therefore
cannot be separated and must make a complete unit; this
means that though 45 and 46 are not in Matthew, they
cannot be separated from the later verses which are from
Q. We conclude that Luke 11$^{9-52}$ is all Q. See pp. 77 f.

Various Sayings. Luke 12$^{22-59}$.

The only verses peculiar to Luke, and therefore needing
consideration, are in two groups : (1) verses 35–38 on Watchfulness, but the same teaching is given in the parable of the
Ten Virgins in Matthew 25$^{1-13}$, which ends with the lesson
" Watch therefore, for ye know not the day nor the hour " ;
(2) verses 47 and 48, but the concluding portion of 48 has
its parallel in Matthew 13^{12}; the rest of 47 and 48 may
have been retained by the editor from Q but omitted by
Matthew. Thus Luke 12$^{22-59}$ may be all Q.

The Contents of Q.

(The references are to Luke's Gospel.)

3 $^{7-9}$. The Preaching of John the Baptist.

$^{16-17}$. John's saying about the Mighty One.

4 $^{3-12}$. The Temptations of Jesus.

6$^{20-49}$. The Sermon on the Plain.

7^{6b-9} . The Centurion's Faith.

$^{18-23}$. The Message of John the Baptist and our Lord's
          Reply.

$^{24-28}$. Sayings of Jesus regarding John.

$^{31-35}$. On Children at play.

Why was Q Written?

The nature of the contents of Q, with its emphasis on missions and on the place of Gentiles in the Church, with its advice to those who would be disciples of Christ and its admonitions against over-anxiety to those who were disciples already, with its call to combine faith with works and the necessity of confessing their faith even unto death, point to Antioch in Syria as the city where Q was written. Q cannot be understood apart from the history of the Church in that city. Antioch and Antioch alone is the only possible place of origin. No other great centre suits the conditions; neither Jerusalem nor Cæsarea nor Ephesus nor Rome is possible, for Antioch was the great centre of the struggle for Gentile Christianity in the days of the Apostles, and from Antioch the first great missionary enterprise to the Gentiles set forth.

Q contains the barest of references to narratives, but gives a cycle of the sayings and discourses of Jesus. Stories about Jesus are more easily remembered than unconnected discourses and sayings; if anything needed to be preserved, it would be the words of Jesus rather than narratives of them. Further, a young Christian Church would require definite guidance on their special problems from the teaching of its Founder; but in the case of a vigorous and aggressive Church from which the first great missionaries, Barnabas and Saul, were sent out into the Roman Empire with the sanction and approval of the whole Christian community, the necessity for authoritative guidance would be even more pressing and urgent.

Christianity was taught in Antioch soon after the scattering of the Church in Jerusalem consequent on the persecution which followed the martyrdom of Stephen. Antioch was the third largest city in the Roman Empire and was situated on the river Orontes; it was a city of

such evil and unsavoury reputation that it was popularly said that the Orontes had flowed into the Tiber and polluted even that river on which Rome of unenviable reputation was built. To Antioch there came certain men of Cyprus and Cyrene, whose evangelistic work was confined to the God-fearers, or Gentiles who were attached to the synagogue for social and religious instruction with a view to conversion to Judaism. So successful were these missionaries that the Apostles in Jerusalem sent Barnabas to report ; on his arrival he saw the grace of God, rejoiced at it, and exhorted the believers (Acts 11[23]). The Church grew in numbers and Barnabas therefore fetched Saul from Tarsus to be his colleague. It was a critical time in Church history, for Gentiles were being admitted into the Christian Church without circumcision. " The disciples were called Christians first at Antioch " wrote the historian of the Acts ; no longer was a distinction made between the circumcised and uncircumcised. Antioch had revolted against Judaism.

Meanwhile Agabus, a prophet from Jerusalem, had arrived with warnings of an impending famine in Judæa, and the Church at Antioch sent relief to their brethren in distress.

The continued growth of the Gentile Church necessitated some organisation ; we are given the names of five of its prophets and teachers, Barnabas, Symeon Niger, Lucius of Cyrene, Manaen, the foster-brother of Herod the tetrarch, and Saul. No longer was Jerusalem to be the centre of missionary enterprise ; its place was taken by Antioch. The waters of the Orontes were not to pollute but to cleanse and purify and to be for the healing of the nations. But before this glory was to enfold the Church, Antioch was honoured by a visit from Peter, one of the Twelve, the only Apostle mentioned by name in Q. His visit ended unfortunately ; at first he had eaten food with the Gentiles, but on the arrival of certain men from James he had

withdrawn from such social intercourse. Saul even withstood
Peter to his face because he stood condemned for his vacil-
lation (Gal. 2^{11}). This *contretemps*, however, did not adversely affect the policy of the Antiochene Church, for
we read in the Acts that as they ministered to the Lord and
fasted in a special act of worship with a definite intention,
the Holy Ghost, probably through one of the prophets,
said " Separate me Barnabas and Saul for the work whereunto I have called them." At the end of their missionary
tour which followed this call (A.D. 48), Barnabas and Saul
returned to Antioch to render an account of their stewardship (Acts 14^{27}).

The liberal attitude of the Antiochene Church, which had
resulted in the separation of the Gentiles from the synagogue, raised the question of the legitimacy of Gentile
Christianity. Certain men of the party of the circumcision,
claiming the authority of James, came from Judæa to
Antioch and proclaimed that no salvation was possible
without circumcision. There arose dissension and questioning and much searching of heart. The solution was sought
by a Conference in Jerusalem, where Barnabas and Saul and
Peter, who argued for freedom of entry, won the day.
The problem of circumcision was settled once for all so
far as Antioch was concerned.

With this outline of history in mind we may turn to
Q. Has Q the teaching needed by a community with such
a history ?

1. Was a Gentile Church in accordance with the teaching
of their Founder ? Was Antioch justified in separating
from the Jewish synagogue ? The answer was, Yes ;
Christ had so taught. In a Gentile centurion He had found
exceptional faith, such as He had not found in Israel (7^{9}),
and He had foreseen the time when many would come from
the east and west, from the north and south, and would
sit down in the kingdom of God (13^{29}). Again, the old Law

was superseded, " for the law and the prophets were until John " (16¹⁶).

2. What about Jewish opposition ?   Christ had warned His disciples to expect opposition and not to be overborne by Jewish arguments (11³⁷⁻⁵²) or by their calumnies (11¹⁴⁻²⁶) ; they were not to fear hostility (17²²⁻³⁷) and were to love their enemies (6²⁰⁻³⁸).   There was to be no bitterness or hatred if they lived according to Christ's teaching.

3. What then about Peter's conduct ?   He had ceased to eat with the Gentiles !   How was the Church to act towards him ?   Christ had solved even a case like this. The Christian Church was to forgive even if a rebuke had been administered to Peter by Saul (17³⁻⁴).   A greater social honour awaited them, for when Christ came He would invite the faithful " to sit down to meat " and would Himself serve them.   It was, said Q, when Christ had thus spoken that the self-same Peter had asked, " Lord, speakest thou this parable unto us, or even unto all ? "   Much had been given Peter and much would be required of him (12³⁵⁻⁴⁸).

4. What about helping a needy people ?   Christ had so enjoined.   " Sell that ye have and give alms " (12³³⁻³⁴). Works should accompany great faith (17⁵).

5. Was Christian Baptism necessary ?   Would not the baptism of John the Baptist suffice ?   These questions were of importance and were not confined to Antioch (Acts 19¹⁻⁶).   The answer given by Q was to refer to John's own preaching.   John spoke of a greater baptism than his own, and pointed to a Mighty One who would baptise with the Holy Ghost and with fire.   Further, John in prison had sent disciples to Jesus to get guidance from Him.

6. What about missionary effort ?   Christ gave definite and clear instructions on this matter.   Not only did He send out His Apostles as missionaries, but He gave them

detailed guidance. The Church's duty was plain; the Gentiles must hear the Gospel. The generation in which the Christians lived would not be easy to convert; they would ask for signs, but no sign should be given them (11^{29-32}).

7. What about those seeking admission into the community? Such had come to Christ, and He had tested them (9^{57-62}, 14^{26-27}).

8. The Antiochene Christians were living in the midst of a hostile and immoral world. What guidance had He left them? The Christian was to be a light in the world (11^{33-36}), to have one master (16^{13}), to face temptation as Christ did, to trust God's providential care ($12^{4\,ff.}$). He was also to confess Christ before men (12^9), to be fearless when accused before rulers (12^{11}), and to be steadfast unto death (12^4). Nay more, the Christian whilst holding family life sacred (16^{18}) was to show a love for Christ greater than that bestowed on parents, wife and children (14^{26}) and to be constantly on the watch for His coming (12^{35-40}).

Date of Q.

Q was a guide to Christian life and conduct, specially written to meet the needs of the Antiochene Church at a time of crisis. It was authoritative, for it gave the words of their Founder and Saviour. Q was a Gospel Manual for a Gentile Church. Quite clearly it did not contain all the teaching of Jesus, but only as much as was necessary to meet the special problems and circumstances of a special Church at a special stage in its history. It could only have been written before the Apostolic Council (A.D. 50). A date before the first Mission of Barnabas and Saul, *i.e.* nearer A.D. 47 is probable. Its uniformly broad-minded and charitable tone towards the Gentiles is more impressive than another sayings-document probably issued about the

same time in Jerusalem ; this is M, the special source of
Matthew, which is Jewish in tone and not as definitely pro-
Gentile.   Also Q has no polemic against the Pharisees such
as is characteristic of M, and its spirit is akin to that of
Luke's special source L.

Other Points in Q.

Apart from meeting the needs of a special Church, there
are other points of importance to be noticed in Q.

1. There are references in it to a ministry of Christ of
which little or nothing is known.   Bethsaida and Chorazin
had heard Him and seen many wonderful works, but their
peoples had turned a deaf ear.   Jerusalem had been visited
" often " ; Mark only speaks of one visit but John of more
than one.   Not only in this particular does Q support
John, for there is included in Q a saying of Jesus which
implies as deep a Christology as we find in John (Luke
10^{21-24}).

2. Q gives no chronology and no guidance as to time and
place.   It hints at Christ's active ministry of healing in
His reply to John 7^{22}, and in the introductory words which
occasionally precede a few of the sayings.   Q assumes a
knowledge of stories about Jesus.   There are no long parables in Q ; three verses are given to the Mustard Seed and
Leaven and their inclusion is made for their teaching.
A few miracles are referred to, but only for the sole purpose
of leading up to some pronouncement of Christ, e.g. the
healing of the centurion's servant ($7^{6\ \mathrm{ff.}}$), the cure of a
dumb man (11^{14}), the cure of the man with dropsy ($14^{2\ \mathrm{ff.}}$).
For its teaching Q is a document as important as Mark
for its narrative ; the one supplements the other.   But Q
preceded Mark.   Narratives of journeys and miracles do
not dictate policy nor decide issues of critical importance.
Only the attested words of Christ could do that.   The time

for preserving a fuller record of Christ had not yet arrived : Apostles and other eye-witnesses were still alive.

3. For such a short document as Q, the wealth of references to nature, the animal world, to home life, and to details of daily interest is most striking. We find mention of the following : (1) wheat, harvest, grass, lilies, mustard seeds, reeds, figs, thorns, brambles, trees, sycamines, grapes ; (2) foxes, serpents, vipers, birds of the air, ravens, lambs, sparrows, nests, wolves, eagles, moths, hens, chickens ; (3) lightning, storms, clouds, winds, showers, scorching wind, streams, sand pits, rocks ; (4) weddings, feasts, dinners, meals, loaves, fish, eggs, leaven ; (5) axes, lamps, purses, mill-stones, houses, barns, bushels, sawdust, beams, cellars, house-tops, money, ovens, threshing, sandals, coats, clothes, wallets, cups and platters, chaff ; (6) children's games, gifts to children, music on pipes.

The Author of Q.

The author of Q is unknown. It has been suggested that the *Logia* mentioned by Eusebius in a quotation from Papias may be Q and may have been written by Matthew.

But if a guess might be made, it was probably written by a member of the Church in Antioch who was in a position to do so because of his standing and of his knowledge of the circumstances of the Church. The interest in the Gentiles and in missions suggests a writer of wide vision imbued with the spirit of the Acts. Now Luke was a native of Antioch ; Eusebius says definitely that Luke was born in Antioch and so does Julius Africanus who lived a hundred years earlier. Luke's interest in Antioch is very noticeable in the Acts, and he gives such details as would be of special interest to natives of that city, *e.g.* that Nicholas was a proselyte of Antioch (Acts 6[5]), that men of Cyprus and Cyrene first preached in that city

(Acts 11²⁰), and the names of the leaders of the Church there. Lastly, the Bezan text of Acts 11²⁸ reads, " And when we were collected together one of them named Agabus . . ." ; the first person plural implies that Luke was a member of the Antiochene Church. May he not have made the collection of sayings ? And later when he was in Cæsarea he would obtain fuller details of Christ's ministry to enable him to supplement Q and produce Proto-Luke (see p. 108).

The tone of Q is the tone of L, and both are alike in senti-ment and in spirit.

Did Mark use Q ?

If Mark did not use Q but was independent of Q, the value of Q is increased, for then Q is proved to be an authentic source as independent and as trustworthy as Mark. The question—Did Mark use Q ?—arises from the contacts between the sayings found in Mark and Q which deal with the same subject-matter. The points of contact arise in the following cases :—

Mark 1⁷⁻⁸.   The Coming of the Mighty One.
3²²⁻²⁷.   The Beelzebub Controversy.
3²⁸⁻³⁰.   The Sin of Blasphemy.
4²¹⁻²⁵.   Sayings about the Lamp, etc.
4³⁰⁻³².   The Mustard Seed.
6 ⁷⁻¹¹.   The Mission of the Twelve.
8¹².   Jesus refuses to give a Sign.
8³⁴.   Taking up the Cross.
8³⁸.   Being ashamed of Christ.
9⁴².   Causing a little one to stumble.
9⁵⁰.   Salt.
10¹¹⁻¹².   Divorce.
10³¹.   The Last shall be First.
10⁴²⁻⁴⁴.   Overlordship of the Gentiles.

Mark 11$^{22-23}$. Faith to remove mountains.

　　　12$^{38-40}$. Condemnation of the Scribes.

　　　13^{21}.　　" Lo, Here is Christ."

Of this list, we have seen that the longer passages, such as the Beelzebub Controversy, the Sin of Blasphemy, the Mustard Seed, and the Mission of the Twelve, are instances not of Mark's use of Q but of overlapping of divergent versions (Chapter IV).

The saying on the Mighty One is part of John's preaching, in which, if we take Luke to represent Q, we find that Matthew and Mark have variations from Q ; for in Matthew we read that John spoke of Him " Whose shoes I am not worthy to bear " as against " the latchet of whose shoes I am not worthy to unloose " in Q, and " the latchet of whose shoes I am not worthy to stoop down and unloose " in Mark ; also in Matthew we find " unto repentance " after " baptize you with water ". Matthew seems to have conflated Q with matter from another source. Mark's account is shorter ; he does not mention the words " and with fire," and he uses " stoop down " after " worthy ". Mark is therefore a variant tradition of Q ; there are bound to have been varying versions of the substance of John's preaching as against his main theme or " text " of his sermon.

The passage on Divorce and Adultery is a long one in Mark, and there is a longer one in Matthew. Luke only gives one verse (16^{18}), which he got from L and preferred to use even though it was so short (see Chapter VII). Thus Matthew is based on Mark and there is no question of Q involved here.

The list of sayings in Mark 4$^{21-25}$ is a collection which can be paralleled by sayings in other contexts than Q. They are found in various parts of Matthew (see p. 124), and twice in Luke, namely 8$^{16-18}$ which gives Q, and in

11^{33}, 12^2, 14^{35b}, 6^{38b}, 12^{31b}, 19^{26}. The sayings were evidently well known in other sources than Q.

As for the individual verses where Mark and Q are in contact, they are of the kind of sayings which would circulate in various forms amongst Christian believers. In fact, there is evidence of this circulation in different forms, for the saying about taking up the Cross is found both in Q (Matthew 16^{24} = Luke 9^{23}) as well as in Matthew 10^{38}, and the saying about being ashamed of Christ is found in Q (Matthew 10^{32-33} = Luke 12^{8-9}) as well as in Luke 9^{26} in a slightly different form. Thus Matthew and Luke give these two sayings twice over, each giving one in a different context—clear evidence that each writer found similar sayings in two different sources.

The number of verses in Mark which bear a resemblance to Q is just over 40. Had Mark known Q, he would have made more use of Q than that : it is difficult to account for Mark's small use of Q and his omission of the Sermon or the Mission of the Seventy, or other valuable sayings in Q, had he known the document. The available evidence is in favour of Mark and Q being independent but overlapping.

We may draw certain inferences from Mark's independence of Q.

1. As Mark and Q corroborate one another where they overlap, Q is a trustworthy document ; in fact Matthew and Luke by using Q showed that they thought it as trustworthy as Mark.

2. Mark probably obtained the sayings from a sayings-collection to which he had access. It was not Q but a collection similar to Q which may have existed in Rome. Other sayings in Mark probably came from this collection (see Chapter X).

CHAPTER VI

M

WHEN the passages which Matthew reproduced from Mark and Q are removed from his Gospel, we are left with a residue of over 300 verses, which has been temporarily designated M. This residue consists of (1) passages found in Matthew alone and in no other Gospel, and (2) divergent versions of certain subject-matters which have parallels in Mark or Q, such as the list of the Twelve, the Lord's Prayer, the Strait Gate, and some of the Beautitudes (see Chapter V).

This residue is made up of sayings and narratives. If this special matter existed, in whole or in part, as a document or collection, it may have existed as a Gospel consisting both of sayings and narratives or as a sayings-document only, the narratives then being drawn from independent sources. On the other hand, all of it may be oral, not documentary. Of these various hypotheses, the most likely, according to some scholars, is the second. Those who favour the view that M existed as a document argue that this hypothesis of a sayings-document may be justified on two grounds. We have had instances, they argue, of conflation or inter-weaving of Mark with matter from another source, as in the Mustard Seed and the Sin of Blasphemy : the non-Marcan passages which were thus conflated with Marcan were at one time assigned to a hypothetical document Q, and this document is now recognised to be more than hypothetical. If, in the same way,

there are complete sections in Matthew of which only a part is found in Mark (the other part not being in Q) or Q, we may infer that the remaining part came from a document other than Mark or Q ; in other words, that Matthew inserted into Mark or Q matter from another document. Instances of this other document may be seen in the Mission of the Twelve (p. 48), in Peter's Confession (p. 26), and the Strait Gate (p. 58) ; also, in the saying on Divorce in Matthew 19$^{3-12}$, which is based on Mark, there are three verses, 9–12, which must have formed part of a fuller section on Divorce in another source or document. The second ground for postulating a written sayings-document is the presence in the sayings of a certain definite character or tendency which runs through them. That this tendency exists is indisputable, but as an argument for a written source it is precarious. M may be a body of tradition, and in dealing with this matter peculiar to Matthew, we shall, for purposes of study, separate it into sayings (M) and narratives. We shall omit from our references many such passages as are editorial insertions, general accounts of healings often leading to words which show astonishment on the part of the spectators, general statements summing up the effect of the discourses on those present and marking the conclusion of the discourses, and also the Old Testament prophecies which may have existed as a collection of proof-texts or *Testimonia*.

M or the Sayings peculiar to Matthew.

At the Baptism of Jesus, 3$^{14-15}$. John's hesitation to baptise, and our Lord's reply.

The Sermon on the Mount.

This sermon, like the Mission Address, is an " agglomera-tion," by which term is meant that Matthew has collected

from various sources passages of a suitable character in order to make up a larger discourse than he originally found in Q's Sermon on the Plain. Now Matthew in constructing his Gospel, used Mark as his framework, and his insertion of this Sermon into the Marcan framework is worthy of notice. He found the first mention of Christ's teaching in Mark 1^{21}. That gave him his position; he inserted his constructed sermon there where teaching was first mentioned and ended up the sermon with the next verse, Mark 1^{22}. "And they were astonished at his teaching: for he taught them as one having authority, and not as the scribes."

This sermon will repay study verse by verse in order that the passages which can be allocated to M may be determined.

The various sources of this sermon are as follows:

5^{1-2}. M.

^{3}. Q (Luke 6^{20}).

$^{4-5}$. M.

^{6}. Q (Luke 6^{21a}).

$^{7-10}$. M.

$^{11-12}$. Q (Luke 6^{22-23}).

^{13a}. M.

^{13b}. Conflation of Mark 9^{50} and Q (Luke 14^{34}).

^{14}. M.

^{15}. Conflation of Mark 4^{21} and Q (Luke 11^{33}).

$^{16-17}$. M.

^{18}. Q (Luke 16^{17}).

$^{19-24}$. M.

$^{25-26}$. Q (Luke 12^{58-59}).

$^{27-28}$. M.

$^{29-30}$. Mark $9^{47, 43}$ (see also Matthew $18^{9, 8}$).

^{31}. Mark 10^4 (see also Matthew 19^7).

^{32}. Conflation of Mark 10^{11-12} and Q (Luke 16^{18}).

$^{33-39a}$. M.

5^{39b-40}. Q (Luke 6^{29}).

^{41}. M.

^{42}. Q (Luke 6^{30}).

$^{43-47}$. Conflation of M and Q (Luke 6$^{27-28,\ 35b,\ 32,\ 33b}$).

^{48}. M.

6$^{1-8}$. M.

$^{9-13}$. M.   Divergent version of Luke 11$^{2-4}$.

$^{14-15}$. M.   Divergent version of Mark 11^{25}.

$^{16-19}$. M.

$^{20-33}$. Q (Luke 12$^{33-34}$; 11$^{34-35}$; 16^{13}; 12$^{22-31}$).

^{34}. M.

7$^{1-5}$. Q (Luke 6$^{37f,\ 41f}$).

^{6}. M.

$^{7-12a}$. Q (Luke 11$^{9-13}$; 6^{31}).

^{12b}. M.

$^{13-14}$. Conflation of M and Q (Luke 13$^{23-25}$).

^{15}. M.

^{16}. Q (Luke 6^{44}).

^{17}. M.

^{18}. Q (Luke 6^{43}).

$^{19-20}$. M.

$^{21-23}$. M.   Divergent version of Luke 6^{46}; 13$^{26-27}$.

$^{24-27}$. Q (Luke 6$^{47-49}$).

This analysis will show the skill of the writer of Matthew's Gospel. From various sources he has gathered sayings of our Lord and fitted them into an incomparable and unique sermon of intense value and great beauty—a sermon which is a call to holiness of life rather than a code of ethics.

It was meant to be committed to memory; hence its arrangement in threes—the Beatitudes in three triads, the new Law in two triads (5$^{17-48}$), three precepts of righteousness (6$^{1-18}$), three warnings (6^{19}–7^{6}), three commands (7$^{7-23}$).

When all the parallels in Q are removed but the divergent

and overlapping passages are retained, we get a coherent discourse in M which begins like Luke's (or Q's) Sermon on the Plain with a number of Beatitudes. Matthew's Sermon on the Mount, we notice, is an agglomeration of matter from Mark, Q, and M; in other words, of a Sermon in M, of a Sermon in Q, of other Q matter, and of matter from Mark. In the Sermon on the Mount, the following verses can be allotted to M:

$5^{1-2,\ 4-5,\ 7-10,\ 13a,\ 14,\ 16-17,\ 19-24,\ 27-28,\ 33-39a,\ 41,\ 43,\ 48}$.

$6^{1-19,\ 34}$.

$7^{6,\ 12b,\ 15,\ 17,\ 19-20,\ 21-23}$.

" *I desire mercy.*" 9^{13a}.
The List of the Twelve. 10^{2-4}.
The Charge to the Twelve. $10^{5-8,\ 16b,\ 23,\ 25b,\ 36,\ 41}$.

These verses read consecutively give the impression of being a short charge or part of a fuller charge. It is not anti-Gentile in character, though it seems so (p. 81).

" *Come unto Me.*" 11^{28-30}.
On the Sabbath. $12^{5-7,\ 11-12a}$.
On the Importance of Words. 12^{36-37}.
On the Sign of Jonah. 12^{40}.
Four Parables in 13^{24-52}.

$^{24-30,\ 36-43}$. The Tares. M.

$^{31-32}$. The Mustard Seed; conflation of Mark and Q.

^{33}. The Leaven. Q.

^{34}. Is from Mark 4^{33-34}.

^{35}. O.T. quotation.

^{44}. The Hidden Treasure. M.

$^{45-46}$. The Pearl of Great Price. M.

$^{47-50}$. The Drag-Net. M.

$^{51-52}$. Conclusion. M.

Thus all but verses 31–35 is M.

On the Pharisees being Offended. 15$^{12-13}$.
The Syro-phœnician Woman. 15$^{23-25}$.
On Signs from the Weather. 16^{2b-3}.
On the Leaven of the Pharisees and Sadducees. 16^{11b-12}.
" Thou art Peter." 16$^{17-19}$.
On Children. 18$^{3-4,\ 10,\ 14}$. (*The Lost Sheep*, vv. 12-13.)
On Discipline in the Church. 18$^{15-18}$.
On Common Prayer. 18$^{19-20}$.
On Forgiveness. 18$^{21-22}$.
The Parable of the Unmerciful Servant. 18$^{23-35}$.
On Divorce. 19$^{9-12}$.
" In the Regeneration." 19^{28a}.
The Parable of the Labourers in the Vineyard. 20$^{1-16}$.
During the entry into Jerusalem. 21$^{10-11}$.
The Children in the Temple. 21^{15b-16}.
The Parable of the Two Sons. 21$^{28-32}$.
Warning to the Pharisees. 21^{43}.
The Parable of the Marriage Feast. 22$^{1-14}$.

This includes another parable, the Wedding Garment, in verses 2, 11-14; and this latter is peculiar to M. A divergent version of the Marriage Feast is Luke's Great Supper (Luke 14$^{15-24}$). Thus 22$^{1-14}$ is M.

The Two Commandments. 22^{40}.
Woes on the Pharisees. Matthew 23.

We will follow the verses through the chapter.

$^{1-3}$. M.

^{4}. Q (Luke 11^{46}).

^{5}. M.

$^{6-7a}$. Q (Luke 11^{43}).

$^{7b-10}$. M.

^{11}. M.   Divergent version in Matthew 20^{26}.

^{12}. Q (Luke 14^{11}).

^{13}. Q (Luke 11^{52}).

^{14}. Is omitted in the Revised Version.

$^{15-22}$. M.

   ^{23}. Q (Luke 11^{42}).

   ^{24}. M.

   ^{25}. Q (Luke 11^{39}).

$^{26-28}$. M.   Divergent version of Q (Luke 11$^{40-41, \, 44}$).

$^{29-33}$. M.   Divergent version of Q (Luke 11$^{47-48}$).

$^{34-39}$. Q (Luke 11$^{49-51}$; 13$^{34-35}$).

Thus to M are assigned verses 1–3, 5, 7b–11, 15–22, 24, 26–33.

Comparing Matthew 23 with Luke 11$^{37-52}$, both of which contain Woes on the Pharisees, we notice that there are seven Woes against the Pharisees in Matthew as against three Woes against the Pharisees and three against the Lawyers in Luke. There are also, as may be seen above, differences in their order, structure and phraseology. Matthew has conflated M and Q.

On False Prophets. 24$^{10-12}$.

Three Parables in Matthew 25.

These are attached as a pendant to the eschatological discourse of Chapter 24.

   $^{1-13}$. The Ten Virgins.   M.

$^{14-30}$. The Talents.   M.   Luke gives a divergent parable, that of the Pounds, in Luke 19$^{11-27}$.

$^{31-46}$. The Sheep and the Goats.   M.

The Final Commission. 28$^{18-20}$.

The Contents of the Sayings.

M has two sermons, one to the disciples and the other to the Twelve following Christ's choice of them. These sermons, with the parables, the ecclesiastical sayings, and the Woes on the Pharisees, form the major portion of the sayings and give us an insight into the main theme of M. To these must be added the scattered verses which are (a) anti-Pharisaic, and (b) seem anti-Gentile. It will

help us if the teaching of M is gathered under various heads.

The Sermon to the Disciples.

The Beatitudes describe the character of those who would join the Kingdom of God ; they were the salt of the earth and the light of the world. Jesus came to fulfil the law and the prophets, to give a new law, stricter than the old law ; the teacher of this new law was great in the kingdom : the standard of observance required of members of the kingdom was higher than that of the scribes and Pharisees. The members were not to act as the hypocritical Pharisees in almsgiving, prayer and fasting, or make vain repetitions as the Gentiles did ; they were always to remember that God was their Father. They were not to give anything holy to the dogs or to cast pearls before swine, and were to beware of false prophets of the Pharisees.

The Mission Address to the Chosen Twelve.

The Twelve were to go on a mission ; they were not to go into any way of the Gentiles, nor enter into any city of the Samaritans ; they were rather to go to the lost sheep of the house of Israel. Before they had gone through the Jewish cities, Jesus would come to them (10^{23}). The restriction was repeated, probably by one of the Twelve using Christ's words, in a Gentile land to a Gentile woman : " I was not sent but unto the lost sheep of the house of Israel " (15^{24}).

The Church.

The Apostles were to proclaim the Gospel to Jews only (10^{23} ; 15^{24}), and from them Christ would get His believers, and on the faith of Peter's confession He would form a

Church or community of these believers. Power to bind
and loose was given to the whole Church (18^{18}), but it was
first given to Peter, to whom was also given as a special
gift the power of the Keys (16^{17-19}). In case of any wrong
done by a brother, the final arbiters were the Church, and
if the sinner refused to listen to the Church he was to be
treated as a Gentile or a tax-gatherer; we might recall
that Jesus was taunted as being a friend of publicans and
sinners.

The Pharisees.

As for the Pharisees who stood outside the community,
they would be rooted up like plants (15^{13}) and the kingdom
of God would be taken away from them and given to a
nation which brought forth fruit (21^{43}). They could not
discern the signs of the times (16^3); and the tax-gatherers
and harlots were entering the kingdom before them (21^{31}).
The Christian Jew was to beware of the leaven of the
Pharisees and Sadducees (16^{11}); it was not the old Israel of
God, but those who followed Christ who in the regeneration
would sit on the throne of His glory and judge the twelve
tribes of Israel (19^{28a}).

The Parables.

These bring out the salient teaching of the preceding
summary. First, as to the new Israel; membership in
it was worth every sacrifice and effort, for it was like a
Treasure and a Pearl of great price. Then, as to the exclusiveness of this special community; those who stood
outside were like the weeds in the Tares or the useless fish
caught in the Drag-net, and they could be compared to
those who showed failure or disloyalty or heedlessness in
the parables of the Two Sons, the Vineyard, the Wedding
Garment, and the Marriage Feast. These warnings were

repeated in the three eschatological parables—the Ten
Virgins, the Talents, the Sheep and the Goats—in the last
of which, in particular, Jesus taught that in the final judgment God would inevitably separate the new Israel from
those who deliberately had turned a deaf ear to His teaching.

Problems in M.

The Gentiles and the Church.

The Jewish character of the Church is clearly taught in
M : the Church was the new Israel.   But we should be
false to the teaching in M and to the teaching and practice
of Jesus if we concluded that in M membership of this new
Israel was to be limited exclusively to Jews.   The exclusiveness of the new Israel was essentially not that of nationality
but of witness and life.

The limitation of membership to the Jews was only
preliminary and necessitated by circumstance.   When the
Apostles were sent out on a mission confined to the lost
sheep of the house of Israel, they were untrained and
untested men with no experience of the method of conversion and with no appreciation of the truth of the Messiahship of Jesus.   Their mission was a mission to proclaim
the same message as their Master proclaimed, namely the
near advent of the kingdom.   The proclamation to Gentiles
and Samaritans would come in time.   That certainly was
Christ's intention, as shown in M, when He, after Peter's
confession, warned the Pharisees that another nation might
prove more worthy of the kingdom than they (21^{43}).   Once
the kingdom could be proclaimed as already here, and the
Messiahship was an accepted fact, and the rôle of Jesus as
Saviour realised, then would come the time for the proclamation of the Gospel to the Gentiles.   The new Israel,
the Church, was to be open to all : disciples were to be

made of all nations and baptism was not to be the sole right of Jews (28^{19-20}).

This view of M's teaching is borne out by the teaching in Mark and Q and L. For example, the fact that Jews might miss a blessing which Gentiles might accept was taught early in Christ's ministry in Nazareth itself (Luke 4^{24-27}), and Jesus saw that in the future many would come from the east, and the west, and from the north, and the south, and would sit down in the kingdom of God. In His own tours, Jesus went to the Samaritans, to Tyre and Sidon, to the Decapolis. In His parables the same view of a world-wide Church is taught : He spoke of the birds of the heaven (a term for Gentiles in 1 Enoch) sheltering under the mustard tree ; that is, after the seed had been sown among the Jews and the shoot had grown up.

What then did Jesus mean by the words in Matthew 10^{23}, " Ye shall not have gone through the cities of Israel, till the Son of man be come " ? Was this an eschatological saying ? It is more than doubtful. Jesus at first did not speak of Himself as the Son of Man—a Messianic phrase : he did so later in His ministry. The evidence of Mark and Q is that He spoke of Himself as the Son of Man only after Peter's Confession. There is, further, evidence that the writers of the Gospels, looking back on the words of Jesus, often substituted the phrase " The Son of Man " for Christ's " I " (Chapter XI). This has happened here. The disciples were being sent on a mission to the Jewish cities ; they were likely to be persecuted and compelled to flee from one city to the other. But before they completed the tour, Jesus, probably after a visit to Jerusalem, would join them. " Ye will not have made a missionary tour through the cities of Israel before I arrive " is clearly what Jesus said.

The Ecclesia or the Church. (Matthew 16¹⁷⁻¹⁹.)

Two questions are raised by the words which are peculiar to M. Did Jesus found a Church ? Why is such a prominent place assigned to Peter ? The second question will be dealt with later in this chapter, and we shall therefore confine our remarks here to the first.

Did Jesus use the word " Church " ? Was not the Church founded only after Pentecost ? If the word " Church " is used in its later interpretation, when in course of time it was identified with the kingdom, objection might be raised to the word having been used by Jesus. The identification need not be made here, as indeed it is not. The Greek word for Church is *ecclesia*, and this word is found in the Septuagint, i.e. the Greek version of the Old Testament, as a word which simply means a community. The disciples were a community, and on Peter's Confession Jesus said He would build this community. This community needed discipline and leadership in addition to faith in Him as the Messiah. The leader was Peter, who was the first to grasp the truth that He was the Messiah.

The Purpose of M.

The Sayings peculiar to Matthew whether they form a body of tradition or an incomplete document, more incomplete than Q, are pervaded by a single dominant tone or tendency, for the main theme is that Jesus founded a new Church with a new law on a new mountain and it was to be at first an exclusively Jewish Church : it was the new Israel of God. In His attitude towards the old Israel, Jesus is represented as anti-Pharisaic.

In M, there are two sermons, one to the disciples and one to the Twelve, the latter being a mission address preparatory to their mission. These sermons with the ecclesiastical sayings, the parables, and the Woes on the Pharisees form

the major portion of the sayings, though there are beautiful gems to be found in the residue, especially the " Come unto Me " saying.

As we read M, the impression grows on us that it is the voice of a rigorist that we hear, a rigorist to whom the success of the kingdom is the predominant issue, and the character of its adherents is of its very essence. The new Israel was to be a model for all time and to set a standard of highest purity, steadfast courage and loyal endurance. As the old Israel had a law given on Mount Sinai, the new Israel had a law given on an unknown mountain in Galilee : this new Israel was to show a Sonship worthy of God who was their Father. The new Israel was an exclusive body, exclusive in that the members of it were to live under a new law which demanded much more than the Mosaic law. If the Pharisee of old lived under the discipline of tradition, the " Churchman " was to live under the rigorous and stern discipline of an awakened conscience. Not only had thought to be controlled, not only must every word be carefully weighed before utterance, but every organ of sense was to be kept in subjection. The disciple must surrender himself whole-heartedly and offer himself, body, soul and spirit as a living sacrifice. He must be as the salt of the earth and as the light of the world. To be a member of the new Israel meant more than being moral ; the call of Christ was a call to a holy life. Holiness is the key-word of the Sermon on the Mount.

As for the Pharisees who stood outside the Church, they were to be placed amongst the untouchables : they were like unto whited sepulchres ; to appeal to them was to cast pearls before swine. Their observance of the law was outward only. Inwardly they were full of hypocrisy and iniquity and uncleanness ; they were like unto dead men's bones. Let the new Israel beware of their leaven.

This new Israel could confidently await the coming of the

Son of Man, for in the regeneration it was not the old Israel but the new that would sit on thrones judging the twelve tribes of Israel. In the final judgment, there would be a separation between the wheat and the tares, the sheep and the goats—a separation between the new Israel and those who stood aloof from it.

The Gentiles would in time be admitted to this Church; it must first be built up on sure foundations before appeal was made to all nations; the Jewish Church was to be a missionary Church before it could be Catholic.

The pride of Christ in His Kingdom shines forth in the pages of M. The Church is His own creation, and it can cause no surprise that a Christian Jew saw in it the very body of Christ of which He was the Head. This pride of Christ may explain the animus against the Pharisees, if the stern language was His own; the bitter condemnation may be designed to make clear to the new Israel the urgency of the times and the invaluable grandeur of their opportunity, and to awaken in them the realisation that they hold the key position of the kingdom of God on earth.

The Value of M.

The historic value of the sayings in M is in its preservation of traditions, ecclesiastical and didactic, which are of great importance. In only one respect does it lay itself open to a charge, namely, the polemic against the Pharisees—a polemic so unlike the restrained criticism which we find in Mark and L. The language, however, may be that of the author, and not of Jesus. If so, it is one thing to represent Christ as criticising calmly and dispassionately the ostentation and display of religious observances; it is another thing to represent Him as inveighing bitterly against a whole sect, amongst whom He had personal friends. Yet this polemic may serve a useful purpose; it bears evidence

of being urged in the heat of some conflict when passions were roused and party spirit kindled to a white heat—a conflict when one party could recall our Lord's limitation of the Gospel to Jews as supplying a valuable anti-Gentile argument, and when another could find an argument in words which gave a supremacy to Peter, and a third could advance sayings which proved that the new Israel was to be a Separatist party, whose aim should be to show more righteousness than the scribes and Pharisees.

M is a valuable source : as valuable as Mark or Q or L, provided we make allowance for its bias against the Pharisees. As an illustration of the lack of impartiality in this particular matter of the attack on the Pharisees, we may compare a statement in it with one in Mark. Christ is represented in Matthew 23^{2-3} as saying, " The scribes and the Pharisees sit on Moses' seat : all things whatsoever they bid you, these do and observe : but do not ye after their works ; for they say, and do not." Here Jesus, whilst denouncing the acts of the Pharisees, encourages the observance of what they bid, namely their tradition. But in Mark 7^{5-13} Christ is represented as rebuking the Pharisees because they had rejected the commandment of God to keep their tradition and had even repealed the word of God in favour of the tradition kept and observed by them ; here the commandment of God is held by Jesus to be more important than tradition. Christ could not have contradicted Himself on such a vital subject. Mark is known to be a reliable source, and M must therefore be used with caution in this matter of the Woes on the Pharisees.

The Author and Date of M.

The collector of M was an unknown disciple of Jerusalem. He was a lover of peace and of his Church. He aimed at reconciling, in the interests of the new Israel, not only two

parties in the Church who were divided on the matter of supremacy, but also two conflicting views held in Jerusalem on the matter of the legitimacy of Gentile Christianity. As regards the conflict of parties, we have the classic example of Corinth to prove the existence of rival bodies, and there, too, as here, Peter's name was being quoted as the leader of one party. It would seem that in Jerusalem the Petrine party desired to champion the cause of Peter against those who supported James. The Acts is silent on the circumstances which led to James being accepted as Head of the Church in Jerusalem and President of the Apostolic Council in preference to Peter the acknowledged leader of the Church in the days of Pentecost. The collector's desire was to set forth the facts. It was true that the power to bind and loose was given to Peter first (16^{17-19}), but it was also given to the whole community (18^{16-20}); to Peter was specially given the power of the Keys. True, the Church was founded on Peter's Confession; that was not supremacy, but distinction. As regards Gentile Christianity, it was true that the Apostles were sent on a mission to the cities of Israel and forbidden to go to the Samaritans and Gentiles; but this was in the early stages of the life of the Church, before the Apostles had been trained and had accepted Jesus as the Messiah, and when the Apostles were only sufficiently far advanced in faith to proclaim that the kingdom of heaven was at hand. They could not be asked to do more at first. The view of Jesus could not be less broad than the views of the prophets and apocalyptists, whose teaching was in line with the prophet who wrote of the Suffering Servant, or the righteous remnant of Israel, whose duty it was to be missionary-hearted and bring Gentiles into the kingdom. In point of fact, says M, Jesus in His last words before the Ascension had given His final commission that the Church was to make disciples of all nations.

Lastly, with regard to the bitter denunciations of the Pharisees, the Churchman must strive to show more righteousness than they did; the members of the new Israel must out-James James, who was the ideal of a righteous man.

There is one period of apostolic history when the circumstances render the argument of M opportune. When was James and not Peter the leader of the Church in Jerusalem? When was the Gospel first preached to Samaritans and Gentiles by Peter and others, in obedience to our Lord's final commission? When was the legitimacy of Gentile Christianity a burning question? When were Jewish observances and traditions openly questioned? When was the Church divided in two on the question of Church membership?

The probabilities are in favour of an early date just prior to the Apostolic Council, and every consideration favours Jerusalem as the city where M was current. A date about A.D. 47 would satisfy the conditions.

It was about this time that Q, a small pro-Gentile volume of sayings, was produced in the Gentile Church of Antioch. Was Q meant to support more vigorously the argument of M with its less clear presentation of the case for Gentile Christianity?

The Narratives.

Apart from Chapters I and II, which give the genealogy of Jesus back to Abraham and stories of His infancy, the narratives peculiar to Matthew are mainly to be found in the final chapters of the Gospel. Incidents recorded in the body of the Gospel are few. They are

$4^{1-2,\ 11}$. The fact of the Temptation (v. p. 46).
9^{26-34}. The healing of the two blind men and the healing of a dumb man, which are meant to take the place

of similar cures in Mark. These Marcan miracles
were passed over by Matthew because they were
not instantaneous cures (*v.* p. 33).

We are left therefore with only two which are in any
sense peculiar to Matthew.

14$^{28-31,\ 33}$. Peter walking on the sea.

17$^{24-27}$.   The Coin in the mouth of the fish.

In the final chapters which deal with the Passion and
the Resurrection the passages are of two kinds. First,
there are details inserted into the Marcan text. These
include the following :

26^3. The plot to kill Jesus was planned at the court of
       Caiaphas.

26^{15}. The price of the betrayal was thirty pieces of silver.

26^{25}. Judas asks, " Is it I ? "

26^{50}. Jesus says to Judas after the kiss of betrayal,
       " Friend, do that for which thou art come."

The second group consists of short narratives complete
in themselves and also inserted into the Marcan framework :

26$^{52-54}$. Peter asked to sheathe his sword.

27$^{3-10}$.   The death of Judas.

27^{19}.   Pilate's wife's dream.

27$^{24-25}$. Pilate washes his hands.

27^{51b-53}. The Resurrection of saints.

27$^{62-66}$. The earthquake and the descent of an angel
       from heaven.

28 $^{9-10}$. The appearance to the two Maries.

28$^{11-15}$. The guard bribed to spread a rumour.

28$^{16-17}$. The appearance to the Eleven in Galilee.

The two Introductory Chapters are unique in Matthew, for
they are the only instance in the Gospel of a complete section which is independent of any of his usual sources ; only
here do we find that Matthew's information stands apart

from sources used elsewhere ; only here do we find two whole chapters as a complete unit based on special knowledge accessible to the final editor.　The grouping of the genealogy in sets of fourteens, *i.e.* in multiples of seven, points to the information having been arranged by the editor himself, for it is the editor who has grouped sayings in threes, fives and sevens ; its Jewish outlook points to a Jewish source, and the fact that we read so much of Joseph in the narratives of the Infancy implies that the information came either from Joseph or his Jewish circle.　We are justified in saying that the first two chapters are not drawn from the same source which gave the other special stories, complete in themselves, which we find in the matter peculiar to the Gospel (see Chapter IX).

These short complete stories found only in Matthew are from their nature for the most part legendary and are on the border-line of the Apocryphal Gospels—particularly the stories of Peter's walking on the sea, the Coin in the mouth of the fish, the dream of Pilate's wife, the Resurrection of saints, and the descent of the angel.　The stories are evidently Jerusalem gossip.　What historical basis they possess we do not know.　As regards the Resurrection appearance to the Maries, the editor had only the incomplete Mark before him, and he seems to have completed Mark's narrative : in Mark, the message to the Apostles was that they were to go into Galilee, and so Matthew mentions that Jesus appeared in Galilee ; in Mark the women went to the tomb, and so Matthew completes the visit by an appearance to the Maries.　His Gospel also needed an ending, and this the editor obtained from M ; that this ending came from another source is clear, for it does not follow naturally after the last words of verse 17, " but some doubted."　We expect these words to be followed not by the final charge given in M but by some such appearance as the appearance to the Ten with Thomas (John 21).

There is a purpose, however, in the insertion of the short stories into the Resurrection narrative. Matthew is defending an attack on the truth of the Resurrection ; there was a rumour that the body of Jesus was stolen by the disciples and that this theft was the cause of the tomb being empty. Two facts stand behind these stories, rumour or legend though they be. These two facts are (1) The tomb was empty, and (2) Jesus was seen alive after His death and burial. The purpose of these Resurrection narratives is thus apologetic.

The short narratives as a whole are not as valuable as the sayings, and they do not possess that trait of exclusiveness and insistency characteristic of the sayings. Matthew used Mark and M, obtained Chapters I and II from a special source, and inserted some short stories from the current talk of Jerusalem.

CHAPTER VII

L

WE now turn to Luke's Gospel. That Luke was composed of Mark, Q and matter peculiar to the Gospel is assured. This special matter raises the same question that was considered when we dealt with the matter peculiar to Matthew. Did it exist as a written source, or as oral tradition ? But we have now an extra aid in the inquiry which was not available before ; we can learn something of Luke's editorial methods from his second book, the Acts of the Apostles, and in his introduction to the Gospel reference is made to other written records which he used. Thus, from the very beginning of our inquiry, we have some reason for thinking that behind the special matter in Luke there may be a written document. In short, we are justified in examining the hypothesis that L was a written document ; further, we must ask how much of the Gospel is neither Mark nor Q, and how did Luke utilise the non-Marcan matter.

The whole problem of Luke's methods of composing his Gospel has been raised afresh by Canon Streeter (see p. 18). Streeter's view has gained support from some New Testament scholars, and it is the view adopted in this book. It is reasonable and justifiable. The general point of view, which will be considered presently, is as follows :

In tracing Q and M, the literary methods of Matthew and Luke had to be considered. Matthew, we saw, had two principal methods ; he " conflated " sources which

gave variant versions of the same incident or saying, and
he " agglomerated " or massed together sayings from
various sources and contexts into long or short discourses
within the framework of Mark, for Mark was used by him
as his foundation. Luke adopted different methods, and
these were as follows : (1) He, too, used Mark, but he did
not make Mark his foundation or primary source ; he used
his non-Marcan sources as his main sources and introduced
Marcan matter into them. (2) He did not, except in the
Passion narrative, conflate his sources as Matthew did, but
took whole blocks of matter from them and arranged these
blocks alternately ; occasionally he inserted items from one
source into another. (3) Whilst Matthew built up his
Gospel from Mark, Q, M, and narratives from other sources
in one stage and one only, Luke built up his Gospel in three
stages. These stages were (i) the joining together of Q and
his special source L into a Gospel, called Proto-Luke ;
(ii) the addition of matter from Mark to Proto-Luke, thus
giving us Luke 3^1 to the end ; (iii) the addition of the
Preface and the Infancy stories to Proto-Luke + Mark.

There are 1149 verses in Luke, of which 132 belong to
Chapters I and II. Of the remaining 1017 verses, there are
two sections which have been called " the lesser interpola-
tion " (6^{20}–8^3), and " the great interpolation " (9^{51}–18^{14}),
because they formed two large blocks of non-Marcan matter
which, it was held, were " interpolated " into Mark. Now,
if the non-Marcan matter had consisted only of these two
blocks, which total 433 verses, Mark would have given 584
verses, and therefore would have been the primary source
of Luke into which the two said non-Marcan blocks had
been inserted. But there are, as we shall see, three other
non-Marcan blocks, making five in all. These five blocks,
with other non-Marcan matter, total about 693 verses, and
therefore are longer than the whole of Mark. This means
that Luke used only about half of Mark, that is about 320

verses (1149–132–693). Hence Mark was not his primary source but his secondary source; the Marcan matter was added to the non-Marcan, and not *vice-versa*. To speak of the lesser and the great " interpolations " into Mark is therefore a misnomer.

Luke's arrangement of his sources may be stated in tabular form:

		Number of Verses.	
		Non-Marcan.	Marcan.
Chapters 1 and 2.	Special source	(132)	—
Chapter 3^1–4^{30}.	Non-Marcan	68	—
4^{31}–6^{11}.	Marcan in main	11	53
6^{12}–8^3.	Non-Marcan	90	—
8^4–9^{50}.	Marcan	—	103
9^{51}–18^{14}.	Non-Marcan	351	—
18^{15-43}.	Marcan	—	29
19^{1-27}.	Non-Marcan	27	—
19^{28}–22^{13}.	Marcan in main	10	109
22^{14}-end.	Non-Marcan in main	136	30 about
	Total 1149 =	132 + 693	324

Of the 1149 verses, therefore, 132 are from a special source, about 693 are non-Marcan (Q + L), and about 324 Marcan.

Proto-Luke also most probably included a narrative of Christ's last days in Jerusalem; this was discarded for the story as given in Mark when Luke produced Luke 3^1 to end, that is to say, Luke obtained 19^{28}–22^{13} mainly from Mark, and a few verses from L. Proto-Luke might well have included a version of this part of the Passion narrative and been about 695 + 100 verses in length, *i.e.* about 800 verses.

The Great Omission.

Before we consider the Marcan and non-Marcan blocks in some detail, there is a problem to be dealt with. Why did Luke omit a whole block of Mark, *viz.* 6^{53}–8^{10}, known as the Great Omission? That Luke omits verses or small para-

graphs can cause no surprise ; that he omits the unedifying
story of Salome is natural in one to whom courtesy to
women was a second nature ; but the omission of a long
section such as this, which Matthew retains, needs to be
explained. (1) One suggestion is that Luke's copy of
Mark was mutilated and lacked the section ; such a mishap
is possible but not probable, as the section, unlike the lost
end of Mark, would be in the middle of a roll, and therefore
the least likely part of the roll to be damaged. (2) Another
suggestion is that this section of Mark not only contained
stories of a kind already found in previous chapters of that
gospel, *e.g.* the Feeding of the Four Thousand, the cure of
a deaf and dumb man, and sayings of Christ on the tradition
of the elders, but also that the Walking on the Sea savoured
of the Docetic view that Christ's body was not real, and
that the Syro-phœnician Woman might have been treated
by Luke as an instance of Christ's opposition to evangelistic
work among the Gentiles. (3) A third suggestion is that
Luke had to keep within the limits of a papyrus roll of
about 30 feet. He had to omit something, and chose to
omit this section. (4) Another suggestion is that Luke was
dissatisfied with its vague geographical references. For the
geographical details in this section, Mark 6^{30}–8^{10}, are complicated and involved :

Feeding of the Five Thousand in a desert place followed by a
voyage of the disciples who set out to go to Bethsaida. Jesus
later joins them and they cross over to Gennesaret (6^{53}) not
Bethsaida ; there follows a long tour through the Borders of
Tyre and Sidon (7^{24}) through Decapolis (7^{31}) to the Sea of Galilee
where Four Thousand are fed, thence by boat they go to the parts
of Dalmanutha (8^{10}) and at last they come by boat to Bethsaida
(8^{22}).

Whatever be the reasons for the omission, the only safe
suggestion is that it was deliberate, and this is strengthened
by a similar treatment of the non-Marcan source L. For
the non-Marcan matter which Luke has used as his primary

source reads as a complete Gospel except at one stage, namely, that it lacks the series of events from the desire of the priests and scribes to destroy Him to the institution of the Last Supper. The events of this period are wholly drawn from Mark. Luke 20^1–22^{13} = Mark 11^{25}–14^{16}. It is impossible to assume that L lacked information on these final days in Jerusalem ; some account must have followed the verses in L which ended at Luke 19^{47-48}. " And he was teaching daily in the temple. But the chief priests and the scribes and the principal men of the people sought to destroy him : and they could not find what they might do ; for the people all hung upon him, listening." What was this wonderful teaching to which the people listened so earnestly ? Some account of it must have followed 19^{48} ; the next verse in L could not have been the next quotation from L, namely 22^{14}, " And when the hour was come, he sat down, and the apostles with him," words which are introductory to the Last Supper. These three verses of L require a story between them, and we know that the Passion story was one of deepest interest to the Christians. 19^{48} is not final but can only be introductory to a story in L.

If then Luke, as it seems, deliberately omitted a complete section of L and preferred Mark's version, which Luke saw was probably more authentic since it was based on the knowledge of Peter and Mark himself (see Chapter X), he might have deliberately omitted a complete section of Mark to find room for the non-Marcan matter he had collected.

The Contents of L.

When the Marcan and Q materials are removed from Luke, we get the contents of Luke's special source L. These are given under headings below, with the omission of Chapters I and II ; the Q material is indicated alongside

in order that Proto-Luke may be easily constructed. The skeleton outline will also show a remarkable circumstance ; the Q material is found not in the Marcan blocks but only in the non-Marcan blocks, and in the long non-Marcan blocks Q and L alternate in minor blocks. This is one of the indications for the early existence of a complete Gospel, Proto-Luke. In the final section, Luke 22^{14}–end, the probable Marcan passages which have been conflated with L are indicated.

L   Q

3^1–4^{30}. NON-MARCAN.

3^{1-6}.	The Call of John.	
3^{10-14}.	The Preaching of John.	3^{7-9}
3^{18-20}.	The Imprisonment of John.	3^{15-17}
3^{21-22}.	The Baptism of Jesus.	
3^{23-38}.	The Genealogy of Jesus.	
$4^{1-2,\ 13}$.	The Temptation of Jesus.	4^{3-12}
4^{14-15}.	The Departure to Galilee.	
4^{16-30}.	The Rejection at Nazareth.	

4^{31}–6^{11}. MARCAN in the main. The non-Marcan
                passage is

5^{1-11}.	The Call of Simon.	

6^{12}–8^3. NON-MARCAN.

6^{12-16}.	The Choice of the Twelve.	
6^{17-19}.	Miracles of Healing.	
$7^{1-6a,\ 10}$.	A Centurion sends Elders to Jesus.	6^{20-49}
7^{11-17}.	The Raising of the Widow's Son at Nain	7^{6b-9}
7^{36-50}.	The Woman who was a Sinner.	$7^{18-28,\ 31-35}$
8^{1-3}.	The Ministering Women.	

8^4–9^{50}. MARCAN.

9^{51}–18^{14}. NON-MARCAN.

9^{51-56}.	The Samaritan Village.	9^{57-62}
10^1.	The Appointment of the Seventy.	10^{2-16}

18^{15-43}. MARCAN.

19^{1-27}. NON-MARCAN.

   19^{1-10}.   Zacchæus.

   19^{11-27}.   The Parable of the Pounds.

19^{28}–22^{13}. MARCAN in the main. The non-Marcan passages are

   19^{37-40}.   The Rejoicing at the Mount of Olives.

   19^{41-44}.   The Weeping over the City.

   19^{47-48}.   Daily Teaching in the Temple.

		Marcan.
22^{14}–end.	NON-MARCAN in the main.	
22^{14-38}.	The Last Supper.	$22^{18, 19a, 19b-20}$ ($^{19b-20}$ probably scribal), $^{22, 34}$.
22^{39-46}.	The Agony in the Garden.	22^{42}.
22^{47-53}.	The Arrest.	$22^{50b, 52b-53a}$, 22^{54-62}.
22^{63-65}.	The Mocking.	
22^{66-70}.	The Hebrew Trial.	
23^{1-24}.	The Roman Trial—before Herod.	22^{71}, $23^{3, 17}$, (^{17} probably scribal), $^{25, 26}$.
23^{27-31}.	The Daughters of Jerusalem.	
23^{32-54}.	The Crucifixion.	$23^{34b, 38, 44-45}$, $^{49, 50-53}$.
23^{55-56}.	The Women prepare Spices.	
24^{1-11}.	The Women visit the Tomb.	24^{12} (probably scribal).
24^{13-35}.	The Appearance to the two Disciples going to Emmaus.	
24^{36-49}.	The Appearance to the Eleven.	24^{40}.
24^{50-53}.	The Ascension.	

The Marcan Sources of Luke.

$$\begin{aligned}
\text{Luke } 4^{31-44} &= \text{Mark } 1^{21-39}. \\
5^{12}-6^{11} &= 1^{40}-3^6. \\
8^4-9^{50} &= 3^{31}-4^{25} ; \ 4^{35}-6^{44} ; \ 8^{27}-9^4 . \\
18^{15-43} &= 10^{13-34, \ 46-52}. \\
19^{28-36} &= 11^{1-8}. \\
19^{45-46} &= 11^{15-17}. \\
20^1-22^{13} &= 11^{25}-14^2 ; \ 14^{10-16}.
\end{aligned}$$

The Non-Marcan Sources.

(*a*) Luke 3^1–4^{30}. In Chapter IV we considered many of the items in this section, and allotted the Call of John and part of his preaching (3^{10-15}) and his Imprisonment to L ; to the same source were assigned the Temptation (p. 46), and the Rejection at Nazareth (p. 45). We are left (1) with the Genealogy, which is peculiar to Luke and is L ; and (2) the Departure for Galilee. Of this last, there are only two words common to Mark 1^{14} and Luke 4^{14a}, namely " Jesus " and " Galilee," and these alone are insufficient to prove that here Luke borrowed from Mark. Luke 4^{14b-15} is peculiar to Luke. Now Luke in 4^{16} mentions that Jesus went to Nazara, and this rendering of Nazareth is not found any-where else in the New Testament except in Matthew 4^{13} ; this suggests Q and not Mark as a source for the name. In any case, Luke 4^{14-15} is non-Marcan, probably L or L + Q. To Q belong $3^{7-9, \ 16-17}$ and the details of the Temptation.

(*b*) Luke 6^{12}–8^3. The only points of contact with Mark are the Choice of the Twelve, which was assigned to L (p 44), and the Anointing (p. 45), which was also seen to be L.

(*c*) Luke 9^{51}–18^{14}. This is commonly called " The Peræan Section," but it is a mistake to do so. Luke's indications are that the tour described in 9^{51}–18^{14} was a tour through Samaria to Jerusalem, and that in no part of

the tour did Jesus go "beyond Jordan" (*i.e.* Peræa), as stated by Mark. There are in this block the Great Commandment, which we saw is L (p. 45) ; also the Beelzebub controversy (p. 47) and the Mustard Seed (p. 48), which are from Q.

(*d*) Luke 19[1-27]. The Parable of the Pounds is a divergent version of the Parable of the Talents, and is peculiar to L.

(*e*) Luke 22[14]–end. Luke preferred the Passion story in L to that in Mark, but interweaved into it certain verses from Mark varying in number from 24 to 30. These have been given above.

In these blocks we may see evidence that Proto-Luke had been composed before Luke utilised Mark. He has preferred to retain certain incidents and sayings in the context in Proto-Luke, even when, on his coming across Mark, he found the said incidents and sayings in a different context in Mark. Quite clearly the variant versions of John's Call and Preaching and the Baptism and Temptation of Jesus would come at the beginning of any document which deals with the ministry of Jesus. But after these, we find that the documents give no guide as to the time and place to which many an incident or sayings may be referred. For example, we see that the Imprisonment of John, the Rejection at Nazareth, the Anointing, and the Great Commandment are some of the items which disturb the order of Mark's Gospel, and in them there are no indications of time and place. Now the versions of these four items in Luke are not the same as the versions in Mark, and they are not in the same context as in Mark. Why did Luke keep the order he did ? Evidently because when he used a block from Proto-Luke he found these said incidents there and retained them, even though they did not occupy the same relative position in Mark. This is clear from the circumstance that everything else in the order of Mark is

reproduced except these variant versions. This same argument would apply to the Beelzebub Controversy and the Mustard Seed (Q). If, then, we allow the existence of Proto-Luke we find a simple explanation for the disturbance of Mark's order of the narratives and sayings caused by the incidents just mentioned.

In Luke's narrative of the Passion there are twelve variations in order as compared with the order in Mark, and the majority of them are due to the insertion of Mark's verses.

1. Luke 22$^{15-23}$. Reference to betrayal after the Institution.

   Mark 14$^{18-25}$. Reference to betrayal before the Institution.

2. Luke 22$^{17-20}$. A cup before bread followed by " I will not drink."

   Mark 14$^{22-25}$. A cup after bread followed by " I will not drink."

3. Luke 22$^{21-23}$. Intimation of betrayer precedes questioning.

   Mark 14$^{19-21}$. Intimation of betrayer follows questioning.

4. Luke 22$^{33-34}$. Denial of Peter foretold before the departure from upper room.

   Mark 14$^{26-31}$. Denial of Peter foretold after the departure from upper room.

5. Luke 22$^{56-71}$. Denials related before the examination by the high priests.

   Mark 14$^{55-72}$. Denials related after the examination by the high priests.

6. Luke 22$^{63-71}$. Mockery before the examination.

   Mark 14$^{55-65}$. Mockery after the examination.

7. Luke 23$^{35-38}$. Superscription after the reviling by the soldiers and before the taunts of malefactors.

Mark 15²⁶⁻³². Superscription before the reviling by the soldiers and before the taunts of male-factors.

8. Luke 23³⁶.   Mockery by soldiers before vinegar is offered.

Mark 15¹⁶⁻²⁰. Mockery by soldiers in the Prætorium.

9. Luke 23⁴⁵.   Veil rent before Christ's death.

Mark 15³⁷⁻³⁸. Veil rent after Christ's death.

10. Luke 23⁵⁰⁻⁵⁴. Time of burial mentioned after the request for Christ's body.

Mark 15⁴²⁻⁴⁶. Time of burial mentioned before the request for Christ's body.

11. Luke 23⁵⁶.   Preparation of spices before the mention of the Sabbath.

Mark 16¹.   Spices mentioned after the mention of the Sabbath.

12. Luke 24¹⁻¹⁰. Names of women mentioned after visit to the tomb.

Mark 16¹⁻⁸.   Names of women mentioned before visit to the tomb.

Evidence in favour of Proto-Luke.

Proto-Luke is the non-Marcan matter of Luke from 3¹ to the end of the Gospel, and includes L and Q, that is to say, the special Cæsarean source L and the Antiochene sayings-document Q. The reasons for assuming that Q and L had formed a Gospel before the editor had known Mark and used Mark may be summarily stated.

1. The first and last blocks of Luke from 3¹ to the end are non-Marcan ; the Marcan matter comes between.

2. The non-Marcan and Marcan matters are arranged in blocks alternately.

3. The non-Marcan matter totals nearly 700 verses

(and probably 800) as against the 325 approximately of Marcan, and makes a Gospel slightly larger than that of Mark.

4. In the Passion story, Mark's contributions are small and subsidiary, and their insertion has led to variations in the order of the Passion narrative as between Mark and Luke.

5. The Marcan matter by itself would not give a complete narrative, but only a fragmentary one.

6. The assumption explains Luke's preference for the non-Marcan version as a whole.

7. Where divergent versions of the same theme occur, the non-Marcan version is preferred, even if the context is altogether different. This fact holds even if the non-Marcan version is shorter, as in the statements on Divorce, where Luke gives one verse from L (Luke 16^{18}) in preference to the eleven of Mark (Mark 10^{2-12}).

8. The versions which Luke has chosen from L in preference to Mark break up Mark's order of events ; it is reasonable to infer that the Lucan order of events was that of a complete narrative which he preferred as a whole.

9. The preference of Luke for his non-Marcan sources extends to Q, and Q is only found in the non-Marcan blocks. This suggests that Q and L had been worked up into one narrative before Luke came across Mark.

10. The nature of the Marcan material, *e.g.* 24 hours in our Lord's life, points in the Galilæan ministry, and miracles, are just those details which are lacking in L and Q. Luke evidently used Mark to supply this deficiency in Proto-Luke, just as he collected L to supply narratives which were remarkably wanting in Q.

11. The hypothesis explains why the Chronology and the Genealogy occur in Chapter III. The Chronology finds its fitting position at the beginning of a complete story. The Genealogy, if it had been inserted by the final editor of Luke's Gospel, would have been at the beginning ; this is what we find in Matthew. But, if the Genealogy stood in Proto-Luke, a complete Gospel, its position there could be explained, for it immediately follows the first mention of the name Jesus.

12. The hypothesis is consonant with Luke's methods as seen in Acts. There he first made his notes—the " we-sections " and then used them with material obtained later. So in the Gospel, L would have been written at Cæsarea and later joined to Q before L + Q was combined with Mark.

13. The hypothesis gives point to Luke's Preface where he speaks of " many " who had written records of Jesus but says he would only use those which he could guarantee as accurate, being based on the evidence of eyewitnesses or ministers of the word such as Peter, Philip, Philip's daughters, and Mark. He would be referring to Mark, L, and Q.

Conclusion.

Even if the hypothesis of Proto-Luke is not justified on the strong grounds stated above, we reach a conclusion of fundamental importance for the study of the Gospels. We have behind our Synoptic Gospels four independent sources, Mark, Q, L and M, all of which existed prior to the date of composition of Matthew and Luke. If also, on the analogy of the composition of the Acts, L was collected at Cæsarea in or about A.D. 52, the three sources, Q, L and M, would all date within about twenty years after Christ's

death.   Proto-Luke would have been compiled later than
A.D. 52, say about A.D. 60.

The primary sources of the Gospels, that is, for the life
and teaching of Jesus, are Mark, Q, L and M.

The Value of L.

This Cæsarean Gospel is akin to the Roman Gospel Mark.
Both contain narratives and sayings, unlike Q and M which
give sayings only.   For our study, therefore, of the external
history of our Lord's ministry we possess two main sources,
just as for a study of the teaching of Jesus we possess two
main sources.   These are not exclusive, for Mark and L
possess sayings, and incidental references of a narrative
character are given in Q and M.

L is essentially the Gospel of the perfect humanity of
Jesus, whose life was devoted to reclaiming the lost sheep
not only of Israel, but also of the Gentiles and Samaritans.
To this work, Jesus devoted Himself from the very first ;
in Nazareth He had spoken of Gentiles who in the person of
the widow of Zarephath and Naaman the Syrian had in the
past received blessings which the Israelites had not had.
In a Samaritan, there was to be found sympathy which a
priest and a Levite lacked ;   Jesus had rebuked the im-
petuous desire of James and John to call down fire on a
village of the Samaritans ;   it was a Samaritan leper who,
out of ten that were cured of leprosy, had returned to give
thanks to the Healer.   As to the publicans, there was
Zacchæus, the chief publican, and also a sinner, with whom
Jesus lodged, and who gratefully put right the wrongs
he had done ;   and there was the publican at prayer who
was more earnest and humble than the Pharisee.   L is also
the Gospel of the under-dog as against the types of men
represented by the rich fool and Dives ;   the poor, the
hungry, the weeping are blessed, said Jesus, in His sermon

on the plain ; the beggar at the gate of the rich man was received after death into Abraham's bosom, whilst the rich man went to Hades ; hospitality should be shown to the poor, the maimed, the lame, and the blind, though they could not return an invitation ; if the rich refused an invitation to a supper, as they might on various pleas, the poor and the crippled and the outcasts might be invited.

Jesus is not only, says L, the friend of all men, but He is also the courteous and lovable friend of women. L is the Gospel of womanhood. It relates incidents of the widow who lost her only son, the woman who was a sinner, the woman who received justice from an unrighteous judge, the woman with a spirit of infirmity ; women had ministered to Him, Martha and Mary had received Him as a guest, the daughters of Jerusalem had wept on His painful journey to Golgotha. Jesus was a friend of women.

L is also the Gospel of home-life. The quiet entertaining of a friend, the unexpected midnight visitor, invitations to feasts and the problem of hospitality, and the one dish that was sufficient for His own reception at a meal in Bethany, form a contrast to the sad events of home-life when brothers quarrel about an inheritance, a sheep is lost, a coin is lost, a son is lost.

L is the Gospel of prayer-life ; Jesus prays before the Twelve are chosen ; it is after the disciples see Him at prayer that they ask for instruction on prayer. He prayed for Peter that his faith fail not ; He prayed in the Garden so earnestly that His sweat became as it were great drops of blood ; He prayed on the Cross for those who were crucifying Him.

The human Jesus is also the great Revealer of God as Father. L is the Gospel of the Fatherhood of God ; under various symbols, such as the Shepherd, the Host, the Father of the prodigal son, and the Nobleman, the love and mercy and grace of God are taught.

The Author of L.

There is in L a great deal which links it with the Acts.
(1) The interest shown in Samaria and the Samaritans in
parable, in miracle, and in the incident connected with
James and John (9^{51-56}) may be compared with the evangelistic work of Philip in Samaria and with the mention of
Samaria in the Preface to the Acts ; (2) the importance
attached to Gentile Christianity in L may be compared with
the conversion of the God-fearers and the Samaritans, and
with the missionary zeal of the Church at Antioch and its
results ; (3) the salvation offered to all people of all classes
in L may be compared to the salvation offered to the prose-
lytes, Jews, and priests, as well as to the Gentiles ; (4) the
sympathy for women so prominent in L, *e.g.* the widow of
Nain, the sinful woman, the infirm woman, the ministering
women, the importunate widow, the daughters of Jerusalem,
and Martha and Mary, may be compared with many a reference in Acts, *e.g.* the women awaiting Pentecost, Dorcas,
the daughters of Philip, Lydia, etc. ; (5) the world-wide
commission of Luke 24^{47} may be compared with the scope
of the history of the Acts (1^8), ending with S. Paul's work
in Rome itself.

These various considerations suggest S. Luke, the author
of the Acts, as the author of L as well as of Proto-Luke, if
not of Q. In other words, S. Luke is the author of the
Gospel which bears his name in every stage of its composition. He stayed at Cæsarea for two years, and for a
time in the home of Philip the evangelist, who had four
daughters who prophesied (Acts 21^{8-10} ; 25^4). From that
family, who were at least ministers of the word, he might
have gained authentic information of Christ's life, and
collected special incidents referring to Christ's influence
with women. L is essentially the Gospel of women as well
as the Gospel of the outcast, and the poor, and the unfor-

tunate. The author was a man of sympathy, patience and mercy; there is no denunciation of the Pharisees, no bitterness, no railing, but only gentle rebukes for their love of money, their ostentation, and their exclusiveness. Christ died for all, for the Pharisee and the publican, the prodigal son and his elder brother, the rich man and Lazarus, the Samaritan and the Galilæan, the Jew and the Gentile. The tone and tendency of the Acts, of L, and of Q, is at one; they form a unity of spirit, they bear the impress of one personality. It may well be that the source of this unity is the great-souled Luke.

CHAPTER VIII

JOHN AND THE SYNOPTICS

THOUGH John is not one of the Synoptic Gospels, we propose to inquire into the indebtedness of John to them. John contains narrative, but the narrative is often merely introductory to the teaching of Jesus ; and the teaching is so closely knit with the author's own interpretation and meditation on our Lord's Person and ministry in the light of experience, that it is at times impossible to distinguish where Christ's words end and the writer's words begin. But though, in conception and in symbolism, John stands apart from the Synoptics, there is a connection between them on the literary side. This indebtedness cannot, from the nature of the Gospel, be of the same kind as that of Matthew and Luke to Mark, who, as we have seen, used respectively nearly all and about half of Mark, but its nature may be realised if we state our inquiry in a more definite form, thus : Had John read Mark and pondered over his reading in such a way that his Gospel bears evidence of a first-hand acquaintance with the Marcan Gospel ? So also with Matthew and Luke, or rather with their non-Marcan sources.

John and Mark.

A few illustrations will show that John had read Mark and was familiar with its language.

(1) *John the Baptist.*

John 1.	Mark 1.
26. I baptize you with water: in the midst of you standeth one whom ye know not,	7. There cometh after me he that is mightier than I, the latchet of whose shoes I am not worthy to stoop down and unloose.
27. even he that cometh after me, the latchet of whose shoe I am not worthy to unloose.	8. I baptized you with water; but he shall baptize you with the Holy Ghost.
33. . . . the same is he that baptizeth with the Holy Spirit.	

Accounts of John the Baptist's preaching are found in all three Synoptics, but John agrees with Mark and Luke in using a phrase about loosing the latchet of the shoes against Matthew's bearing or carrying the shoes ; also John agrees with Mark against Matthew and Luke in not adding " with fire " after " with the Holy Ghost."

This point of contact with Mark is remarkable, for Mark, as against Q, the sayings-document used by Matthew and Luke, contains relatively little about the teaching of John the Baptist. The fact that in a saying of the Baptist, John should agree with Mark and not with Q is very striking.

(2) *A Saying of Jesus.*

John 4[44].	Mark 6[4].
For Jesus himself testified,, that a prophet hath no honour in his own country.	And Jesus said unto them A prophet is not without honour, save in his own country, . . .

The contexts vary, but the sayings are almost identical. Matthew has repeated Mark ; Luke has a variant version of it drawn from L. John is evidently recalling Mark.

(3) *In different Miracles.*

<table>
<tr><td>John 5.</td><td>Mark 2.</td></tr>
<tr><td>(At the Pool of Bethesda.)</td><td>(The Sick of the Palsy.)</td></tr>
<tr><td>8. Jesus saith unto him, Arise, take up thy bed, and walk.</td><td>11. I say unto thee, Arise, take up thy bed, and go unto thy house.</td></tr>
<tr><td>9. And straightway the man was made whole, and took up his bed, and walked.</td><td>12. And he arose, and straightway took up the bed, and went forth before them all.</td></tr>
</table>

Not only is the wording similar, but John uses the same vulgarism for " bed " that Mark uses ; this word Matthew and Luke replaced by a polite term.

(4) *The Feeding of the Five Thousand.*

<table>
<tr><td>John 6.</td><td>Mark 6.</td></tr>
<tr><td>7. Philip answered him, Two hundred pennyworth of bread is not sufficient for them, that every one may take a little.</td><td>37. And they say unto him, Shall we go and buy two hundred pennyworth of bread, and give them to eat ?</td></tr>
</table>

Though Matthew and Luke drew on Mark for their accounts of the miracle, John and Mark are the only two of the four Gospels which mention "two hundred pennyworth." John, we notice, gives the name of the Apostle who spoke to Jesus ; he is therefore supplying information which was

not given in Mark.   John also mentions the " grass " which is found in Mark and Matthew but not in Luke (John 6¹⁰, Mark 6³⁹).

(5) *Jesus Walking on the Sea.*

John 6.	Mark 6.
19. When therefore they had rowed about five and twenty or thirty furlongs,	47. . . . the boat was in the midst of the sea, . . . 48. And seeing them distressed in rowing,

John agrees with Mark, as against Matthew, that the disciples were rowing.   Luke omits the incident.

John, with Mark, does not mention Peter's walking on the sea, found only in Matthew's special source.   Matthew, in the Authorised Version (14²⁴) reads that the boat was many furlongs from the shore, but this detail is not to be found in the Revised Version, which repeats Mark's " in the midst of the sea."   Thus John, in giving the approximate distance, is supplementing Mark and not Matthew.

(6) *The Anointing.*

John 12.	Mark 14.
3. Mary therefore took a pound of ointment of spikenard, very precious, and anointed the feet of Jesus, and wiped his feet with her hair : and the house was filled with the odour of the ointment.	3. And while he was in Bethany in the house of Simon the leper, as he sat at meat, there came a woman having an alabaster cruse of ointment of spikenard very costly ; and she brake the cruse, and poured it over his head.

8

John 12.	Mark 14.
4. But Judas Iscariot, one of his disciples, which should betray him, saith,	4. But there were some that had indignation among themselves, saying, To what purpose hath this waste of the ointment been made ?
5. Why was not this ointment sold for three hundred pence, and given to the poor ?	5. For this ointment might have been sold for above three hundred pence, and given to the poor.

John and Mark alone use the phrase " of ointment of spikenard." John is also supplementing and correcting Mark's narrative, for he identifies the woman of Mark's story with Mary, the sister of Lazarus, and gives Judas Iscariot as the one who protested against the waste ; he corrects Mark by saying that Mary anointed Christ's feet and not His head. This correction John obtained from L (Luke 7^{36-50}) ; here the woman who was a sinner came into a Pharisee's house with an alabaster cruse of ointment and " began to wet his feet with her tears, and wiped them with the hair of her head, and kissed his feet, and anointed them with the ointment."

In one small particular John agrees with Matthew against Mark. Matthew states that the disciples murmured against the waste, whereas Mark gives vaguely " some " ; John supports Matthew in giving the name of the disciple.

In John's story of the Anointing, the incident is located in Bethany. John 12^2 reads thus, " So they made him a supper there : and Martha served." This reference to Martha as serving at supper is explicable if John knew Luke or L, for there, in a different incident, Martha is mentioned with special reference to serving, but the name of the village is not mentioned. " Now as they went on

their way, he entered into a certain village : and a certain woman named Martha received him into her house. . . . But Martha was cumbered about much serving " (Luke 10$^{38-40}$). John in 12^2 is identifying the " certain village " of Luke 10^{38} with Bethany.

(7) *A Saying.*

John 14^{31}.	Mark 14^{42}.
Arise, let us go hence.	Arise, let us be going.

The quotations are identical and used at the same point in the story of the Passion ; they are not found in Luke. Matthew is based on Mark.

(8) *Peter's Denials.*

John 18^{18}.	Mark 14^{54}.
Now the servants and the officers were standing there, having made a fire of coals ; for it was cold , and they were warming themselves : and Peter also was with them, standing and warming himself.	And Peter had followed him afar off, even within, into the court of the high priest ; and he was sitting with the officers, and warming himself in the light of the fire.

John, with Mark and Luke, mentions the fire in the court but only John and Mark state that Peter was warming himself. Matthew omits all reference to the fire. Also John, with Mark (and Matthew who used Mark), separates the mention of Peter's entry into the court of the high priest from the denials, whereas Luke tells the story of the entry and denials in one piece.

(9) *Art Thou the King of the Jews ?*

All the Synoptics agree with John.

8 *

(10) *Barabbas.*

	John 18.	Mark 15.
39. Will ye therefore that I release unto you the King of the Jews ?	9. Will ye that I release unto you the King of the Jews ?

John and Mark agree against Matthew in the form of Pilate's question. Matthew has " Whom will ye that I release unto you ? Barabbas, or Jesus which is called Christ ? "

There is no parallel question in Luke.

(11) *At the Crucifixion.*

John mentions that vinegar was offered just before the end as in Mark and Matthew ; Luke places it earlier. Also John has Golgotha with Mark and Matthew ; Luke omits the word.

(12) *The Appearance to the Women.*

Mark's ending is missing. Matthew relates an appearance to women, and John an appearance to Mary Magdalene.

(13) *Cures where means are used.*

An interesting little point is that unlike Matthew and Luke, John and Mark give instances where means are used. John 9^{6-7} ; Mark 7^{32-34} ; 8^{22-26} (see p. 32). In these instances, it is to be noted that agreements with Matthew's special sources are very few. There are only two such contacts and they are of a minor character ; in the Anointing the murmuring of the disciples in Matthew is a possible inference from Mark, whilst in the Appearance to the Women, Matthew is clearly completing the lost story of Mark by following up Mark's narrative where it ends.

Other points of contact between John and the Synoptics may be seen in the following :

The Cleansing of the Temple placed by the Synoptics in the week of the Passion but by John early in the ministry.

The mention of the " Twelve " by John ($6^{67, \ 70-71}$; 20^{24}) where John assumes that their names were well known to his readers from knowledge of other documents.

The Triumphal Entry.   John 12^{12-14}; Mark 11^{1-10}.

Knowledge of the Betrayal.   John 13^{11}; Mark 14^{18}.

Two sayings in different contexts.   John 12^{25}; Mark 8^{35}. John 13^{20}; Mark 9^{37}.

Prophecy of Peter's denials.   John 13^{38}; Mark 14^{30}.

The Mocking.   John 19^{2-3}; Mark 15^{16-20}.

The Crucifixion.   John 19^{17-24}; Mark 15^{22-27}.

The Empty Tomb.   John 20^{1-2}; Mark 16^{1-8}.

Also in the allusions to John's imprisonment, Andrew as Simon Peter's brother, the title " Cephas " given to Peter, the demand for a sign (John 6^{30-32}), the withdrawal beyond the brook Kedron, the Hebrew trial, and the taking down of Christ's body from the cross.

John's knowledge of Mark is assured ; there are many parallelisms between the two Gospels and many phrases common to them which are not found in the parallel passages in Matthew and Luke, e.g. John $5^{8 \ f.}$; 6^{7}; 12^{3-5}; 14^{31}; and $18^{18, \ 39}$. This degree of resemblance is remarkable, especially in the sayings, for Mark's sayings are small in number when compared with Matthew and Luke. As for John's knowledge of Matthew, there are, as we have seen above, two points of very minor importance in passages peculiar to Matthew, but these are not sufficient to show that John knew Matthew.

John and Luke.

In addition to the points of contact between John and Luke (or L) noted above, namely, in the story of John the

Baptist, the Anointing, and in Martha serving, there are others which show that John was acquainted with Luke or L. We shall realise this from the following list :

1. The action of Judas in betraying Jesus was due to Satanic influence. John 13^2; Luke 22^3.

2. The fact that it was the right ear of Malchus that was cut off. John 18^{10}; Luke 22^{50}.
   John also supplements Mark and Luke by supplying the names of Peter and Malchus. Mark 14^{47}.

3. The repetition of the cry " Crucify him " by the mob ; Mark gives the cry only once. John 19^6; Luke 23^{21}.

4. The three-fold declaration of the innocence of Jesus. John 18^{38}, 19$^{4, 6}$; Luke 23$^{4, 14, 22}$.

5. The tomb was one in which no man had been laid. John 19^{41}; Luke 23^{53}.

6. The tomb was visited by Peter. John 20^4; Luke 24^{12} (if not a scribal addition).

7. The tomb was found empty by " certain " visitors to it and by the women. John 20$^{2-8}$; Luke 24^{24}.
   John here supplements L and also agrees with L as against Mark and Matthew that two angels were there.

8. The words " Peace be unto you," spoken by Jesus to the Apostles. John 20^{19}; Luke 24^{36} (if not a scribal addition).

9. Jesus showed the Apostles the marks on His body. John 20^{27}; Luke 24^{40} (if not a scribal addition).

10. The first Appearance was in Jerusalem and not in Galilee, as in Mark and Matthew.

Thus we have at least ten points of contact between John and Luke or L, allowances being made for the possible scribal insertions.

If John did not know Luke but knew L, we reach a con-

clusion of value. For we find that John used Mark and L just as Luke did. John therefore comes within the range of the Synoptic Problem.

These many and varied points of contact between John on the one hand, and Mark and Luke or L on the other hand, together with John's desire to identify places, incidents, and persons not specified in Mark and Luke, are evidence that John was drawing on his knowledge of the said Gospels, at times supplementing them, at times correcting them.

CHAPTER IX

MATTHEW

THE author of the first Gospel is unknown. He was not the Apostle. He was a Jew, and wrote for Jews. He painted for them a portrait of the Messiah as the Saviour of all men (24^{14}; 28^{19}) in an Old Testament setting of prophecies.

In constructing his Gospel, he made use of at least three sources, Mark, Q and M, and in his treatment of them he followed the methods of the Old Testament editors who composed the Pentateuch from records already existing, for he took passages from his sources, edited them, fitted them together and made complete narratives or groups of sayings ; as there were five books in the Pentateuch, he arranged the sayings in five blocks, ending each of them with a common formula at 7^{28}, 11^1, 13^{53}, 19^1, 26^1. He was a redactor, not an original writer. He was content to get as much matter as he could of his sources into one Gospel, the length of which was probably influenced by the restrictions of a papyrus roll. He was therefore compelled to omit a number of complete verses, about fifty, in Mark and to compress some of the Marcan matter. He decided to make Mark his foundation Gospel, and within its framework to insert sayings from Q and M and narratives from other sources. His main interest was, however, in Q, which was a collection of sayings and discourses, and this made a rearrangement of Mark's order necessary. Once he had utilised Q he could follow Mark's order carefully. As a

Jew writing for Jews, he realised that some adaptation of Mark's outlook and " theology " would be necessary ; as a teacher, he had a fondness for numbers as an aid to memory, and he saw the value of re-grouping his materials in threes, fives, and sevens, within the framework of Mark's Gospel ; as an editor, he impressed his own style and views and personality on his production by editing Mark for stylistic, doctrinal, apologetic and other purposes ; as a peace-maker he sought to reconcile the Jew, for whom he wrote, to the Gentile, for whom he pleaded.

The Marcan Omissions.

Did Matthew omit certain verses of Mark, 55 in number, because he had an earlier and shorter edition of Mark known as *Urmarcus* (*Ur* means original in German), or had he other sound reasons for doing so ? The first explanation, which had at one time the support of some scholars, is now held to be unwarranted, for we find in the Gospel that Matthew did not " omit " all the verses, but only a few, for which good reasons could be given, and that references to the other " omissions " exist. The 31 verses not found in Matthew and Luke are :

1^1; 2^{27}; 3^{20-21}; 4^{26-29}; 7^{3-4}; 7^{32-37}; 8^{22-26}; 9^{29}; 9^{48-49}; 13^{33-37}; 14^{51-52}.

The 24 verses found in Luke but not in Matthew are :

1^{23-28}; 1^{35-38}; 4^{21-24}; 6^{30}; 9^{38-41}; 12^{40-44}.

Of the 55 verses, 24 are found in Luke. These 55 verses include three miracles, the Demoniac ($1^{23\ ff.}$), the Dumb Man ($7^{32\ ff.}$), the Blind Man at Bethsaida ($8^{22\ ff.}$), of which Luke gives the first ; all three contained statements which sug-gested a limitation of supernatural power, in that the cures were not immediate and instantaneous (see Chapter III). But verses or phrases from the narratives are found in other

contexts, *e.g.* Mark 1^{24}; 5^7; 8^{23} are in Matthew 8^{29} and 9^{29}. Also Matthew in 15^{30} gives a general summary of such miracles. The parable of the Seed growing secretly (Mark 4^{26-29}) is replaced by the more vivid parable of the Wheat and the Tares, whose growth is mentioned. Two passages in Mark, both consisting of sayings (Mark 4^{21-24} and 13^{33-37}), are inserted in other contexts in Matthew. Two verses omitted have a special interest; in Mark 9^{38-39} Jesus rebukes John for his attitude to one who, though not a follower, had cast out devils in Jesus' name. This remark of Jesus might have been quoted by Gnostics in support of their views; therefore Matthew, who in 24^{12} had given warning of the spread of antinomianism, resulting in the cooling of the love of many, purposely omitted the dangerous passage. Matthew 10^{42} is another version of Mark 9^{41}. The story of the young man in Mark 14^{51-52} was of no general interest; and the attempt to take Jesus away in Mark 3^{20-21} because people were saying, " He is beside himself," was far from reverential. Omitting odd verses, the only other passage to be considered is the Widow's Mite (Mark 12^{40-44}), for the omission of which the editor's Jewish character may be responsible.

Mnemonic Aids.

Matthew's grouping of material runs right through the Gospel. The Genealogy has three divisions with " begettings " in fourteens (2×7) in each; there are seven petitions in the Lord's Prayer; seven parables in Matthew 13; forgiveness should be given not until seven times but until seventy times seven (18^{21-22}). There are five great discourses ending with a special formula: these are 5^1-7^{27} and chapters 10, 13, 18, 24–25, closing with formulæ in 7^{28}; 11^1; 13^{53}; 19^1; 26^1; also five illustrations of fulfilling the law in the Sermon on the Mount. Of the number

three, there are over twenty instances, *e.g.* three Infancy stories, three temptations, three illustrations of right conduct (6^{1-18}), three negative counsels ($6^{19}-7^{6}$) followed by three positive counsels (7^{7-20}) in the Sermon on the Mount, three groups of three miracles each (8^{1-15}; $8^{23}-9^{8}$; 9^{18-34}), three sayings beginning " Fear not " (10^{26-31}), three parables of sowing seed (13^{1-32}), three sayings about little ones (18^{6-14}), three questions (22^{15-40}), three eschatological parables ($24^{43}-25^{30}$), and three denials of Peter, etc.

Enlargement and Compression of Sources.

Matthew both enlarged and compressed Marcan narratives and sayings. In the enlargements he utilised matter from M and Q as in the Preaching of John, the Baptism of Jesus, the Temptation, the Syro-phœnician woman, Peter's confession ; he also drew on some of the popular talk in Jerusalem circles, most of it of doubtful value and some bordering on the standard of the apocryphal gospels, *e.g.* Peter's Walking on the Sea, the Resurrection of Saints, and the Descent of an Angel. By his method of " agglomeration " he inserted, within the framework of Mark, sayings from non-Marcan sources to illustrate an incident or enlarge a saying in Mark's particular context ; for example, the seven verses of Mark's charge to the Twelve became 42 in Matthew, the twelve verses of Mark $9^{33-37, \ 42-48}$ became 35 in Matthew 18, three parables of Mark 4 were increased to seven in Matthew 13, and the apocalyptic sayings of Mark 13 had appended to them three parables of judgment. Other examples on a smaller scale of this method may be seen in Matthew 17^{20} and 19^{28} where single verses from non-Marcan sources are inserted into a Marcan incident and saying respectively ; also Mark's saying on Divorce is enlarged by three verses (p. 73).

On the other hand, Matthew occasionally took a complete

group of sayings in Mark and fitted them into other contexts.   A good illustration is given in the following :

Mark 4.	Matthew.
21. And he said unto them, Is the lamp brought to be put under the bushel, or under the bed, and not to be put on the stand ?	5^{15}. Neither do men light a lamp, and put it under the bushel, but on the stand ; and it shineth unto all that are in the house.
22. For there is nothing hid, save that it should be manifested ; neither was anything made secret, but that it should come to light.	10^{26}. . . . for there is nothing covered, that shall not be revealed ; and hid, that shall not be known.
23. If any man hath ears to hear, let him hear.	11^{15}. He that hath ears to hear, let him hear.
24. And he said unto them, Take heed what ye hear : with what measure ye mete it shall be measured unto you : and more shall be given unto you.	7^{2b}. . . . and with what measure ye mete, it shall be measured unto you.
	6^{33b}. . . . and all these things shall be added unto you.
25. For he that hath, to him shall be given : and he that hath not, from him shall be taken away even that which he hath.	13^{12}. For whosoever hath, to him shall be given, and he shall have abundance : but whosoever hath not, from him shall be taken away even that which he hath.

Examples of compression may be seen in the following : the 325 words of Mark's Gerasene Demoniac(s) became

136, the 374 of Jairus' Daughter became 135, the 235 of the Feeding of the Five Thousand became 157, the 270 of the Lunatic Boy became 132.

Correction of Mark's Inaccuracies.

Matthew in 12^4 omitted Mark's " when Abiathar was high priest " (Mark 2^{26}), in 15^{39} wrote " borders of Magadan " in place of Mark's " parts of Dalmanutha " (Mark 8^{10}), in 26^2 omitted Mark's " and the unleavened bread " (Mark 14^1), in 26^{17} omitted Mark's " when they sacrificed the passover " (Mark 14^{12}), in 27^{32} omitted " coming from the country " from Mark 15^{21}. But some of these errors in Mark may be scribal interpolations into Mark's narrative.

The Sources of Matthew.

Matthew, as we have seen, is made up of Mark, Q, M, the special source of chapters 1 and 2, and Jerusalem legends and stories.

The Re-arrangement of Mark's Order.

Our intention is to attempt to discover the mind of Matthew in re-arranging Mark's Gospel ; we shall base this attempt on his desire to use Q and M, his partiality for grouping in threes, fives and sevens, his special interest in sayings, and his method of agglomeration. What reasons may have influenced him to construct his Gospel in the order in which we find it ?   He follows Mark's order from his chapter 14 onwards, and our inquiry therefore will only extend to the end of chapter 13.

Matt.		Mark
3^1–4^{22}.	In the Preaching of John the Baptist, Matthew inserts Q material (3^{7-10}) and in the Baptism of Jesus adds verses from M	1^{1-20}

Matt.   Mark

to safeguard His Person (3^{14-15}). In place
of the Temptation in Mark, he inserts the
fact from M and adds details from Q (4^{3-11}),
and to the Preaching in Galilee he adds an
O.T. prophecy. Matthew 3^1-4^{22} is Mark
1^{1-20} with additions from Q and M.

$4^{23}-7^{29}$ In Mark 1^{21} Matthew comes across the 1^{21-22}
first reference to teaching, and in 1^{22} the
marvellous effect of that teaching. Now
in 4^{13} he had already mentioned Capernaum,
so he omits 1^{21a} from Mark, and deals with
1^{21b} to lead up to the Sermon, the corner-
stone of his structure ; in place of Mark
1^{21b} he inserts three verses of his own composition (Matthew 4^{23-25}) to bring a multitude together on a new Mount Sinai for
proclaiming the new law, which, we have
seen, was built up from Q, M and Mark.
At the end of the Sermon (Matthew 7^{28-29})
he inserts Mark 1^{22}.

8^{1-17} The basis of the Sermon on the Mount 1^{23-45}
was Q's Sermon on the Plain, which was
followed by the Centurion's Servant. Also
in Mark 1^{23} there is the first mention of a
miracle ; and Matthew finds three miracles
in Mark 1^{23-45} : the three are The Unclean
Spirit, Peter's Mother-in-law, and The
Leper. Matthew does not like the first,
for the behaviour of the unclean spirit
showed resentment in obeying Christ's
command. He therefore drops it altogether
in favour of the Centurion's Servant from
Q, and uses the two miracles left from
Mark 1^{23-45}. Thus Matthew gets his first

Matt.   Mark

triad of miracles, ending his account with
words from Mark 1$^{32-34}$, and adds an O.T.
prophecy ; he omits Mark 1$^{35-39}$, as they
have no place in a series of miracles. This
takes us to Matthew 8^{17} and Mark 1^{45}.

8$^{18-22}$ The next section in Mark is from 2^1–4^{34},   2^1–4^{34}
which is the crux of the problem. It is a
series without any common factor except its
controversial interest or its didactic aim ;
even the miracles contain more teaching and
are plainly included for their teaching. The
contents of this section of Mark, which
Matthew holds in reserve, are :

> The Sick of the Palsy.
> Matthew's Call and Feast.
> Discourse on Fasting.
> Plucking the Ears of Corn.
> The Withered Hand.
> Choice of the Twelve.
> The Beelzebub Controversy.
> Jesus' Mother and Brethren.
> Three Parables.

Matthew does not want to miss any of this
Reserve section from Mark, and he is not
ready for controversial issues. He notices
in Mark 4^{35} that Christ has arranged to
cross the lake to the east side · he therefore
inserts Matthew 8$^{19-22}$ from Q, and follows
up the crossing with the two miracles from
8$^{23-34}$ Mark 4^{35}–5^{20}, viz.: the Tempest and the   4^{35}–5^{20}
Gerasene Demoniacs, which stories bring the
visit to the east of the lake to an end ; but
in Mark 5^{21} Jesus is on the west side.

9^{1-8}

Matthew wants a third miracle to complete his group (8^{22-34}). To get it, he turns to Mark 2^1-4^{34}, but then Christ was on the west side of the lake. So he inserts 9^1 to correspond with Mark 5^{21}, makes Christ return to the west side into " his own city," and gets the third miracle from his Reserve section, Mark 2^1-4^{34}, *viz.* the Sick of the Palsy (Matthew 9^{2-8}). This gives him his second group of three miracles.

5^{21}

9^{9-34}

Mark's Sick of the Palsy was followed by the Call and Feast of Matthew, and the discussion on Fasting. These Matthew inserts (9^{9-17}). We are still at Mark 5^{21}. He notices that Mark 5^{22-43} is a miracle, Jairus' Daughter, on the west side : he wants two more to make his three. He gets them from M, or more probably bases them on Mark—the Two Blind Men and The Dumb Man (Matthew 9^{18-34}). This is the third group of three miracles each. We are now at Mark 5^{43}.

$9^{35}-11^1$

After following Mark's story of Jairus, Matthew notices two references to teaching (Mark $6^{1-2, \ 6b}$). He temporarily passes over Mark 6^{1-6a} and sees after 6b a charge to the Twelve. He seizes his opportunity to insert teaching. He borrows a list of the names of the Twelve from M, which he prefers to the list in the Reserve section (Mark 2^1-4^{34}), and follows it with a long charge to the Apostles, which charge he builds up from Mark's charge to the Twelve, the charge to the Seventy from Q,

6^{1-13}

Matt.   Mark

matter from M, and other material, and adds
suitable passages at its beginning and end.
(Matthew 9³⁵–11¹.)

11²⁻³⁰   Mark followed his charge to the Twelve   6¹⁴
with the account of John's death (6¹⁴⁻²⁹).
Matthew is thus reminded of John's message
in Q, which followed Q's Centurion's
Servant. He finds this an ideal place for
inserting John's message and our Lord's
reply. If, in His reply, Jesus had referred
to miracles wrought by Him, Matthew had
given triads of miracles already. Further,
the warning note of opposition to Jesus
Himself inherent in the reply serves as a
preparation to stories of the growth of
12¹⁻⁵⁰   opposition to Jesus. Matthew had noted
illustrations of this opposition in his Reserve
section ; he utilises them now—the Plucking
the Ears of Corn, the Withered Hand,
with a suitable prophecy added, the Beelzebub Controversy, and Jesus' Mother and
Brethren.

13¹⁻⁵³.   There remain the three Parables of the
Reserve section, and Mark 6¹⁻⁶ to be
included. There are, Matthew observes,
parables in Q and M. He has to make a
choice to get one of his special mnemonic
numbers. So he takes from Mark's Reserve section the Sower and the Mustard
Seed, chooses the Wheat and the Tares
from M in place of Mark's Seed growing
secretly, borrows the Leaven from Q, and
the Hid Treasure, the Pearl, and the Drag-
net from M, and makes his group of seven.

Matt.   Mark

13^{54-58} The only passage left untouched was
            Mark 6^{1-6}; Matthew inserts it here.

            From this point Matthew follows Mark
            implicitly (Matthew 14^{1-12} = Mark 6^{14-29}).

The Infancy Stories.

There are two accounts of our Lord's birth and childhood in the special sources of Matthew and of Luke.
These two accounts are independent of each other; the
writer of one Gospel was not aware of the account in the
other. This means that in spite of varying versions of
the birth and childhood of Jesus, beliefs were current in
Jerusalem, a Jewish Christian Church, and in Cæsarea, a
Gentile Church, and elsewhere, that there was something
miraculous in our Lord's birth. The existence of two
independent witnesses is a fact of importance.

The witnesses do not always agree. For example, we
cannot find room in Luke's story for the flight into Egypt;
according to Luke, Joseph and Mary stayed in Bethlehem
till just before the Purification, and after visiting Jerusalem
for the Purification they returned to Nazareth. Again, in
Matthew we may see a desire on the part of the writer to
draw parallels with the story of Moses, and in Luke we may
see in the Magnificat a piece of poetry modelled on the Song
of Hannah, and composed by the author himself. Further,
the genealogy in Matthew is clearly artificial and traced
through Joseph, and not always accordant with that of
Luke.

Yet, behind these sources, in spite of their differences in
outlook and incidents, we are presented with common
features which witness to some mystery connected with
the birth, reflected in the hesitation of Joseph to take Mary
as his wife and in the willingness of a Virgin to accept

motherhood before a marriage was consummated. This mystery is not one attached to the actions of Joseph and Mary, but one connected with the Being and Person of Christ.

This mystery involves (a) the Virgin Birth, (b) the Incarnation ; of these two, the fundamental doctrine is that of the Incarnation. It is from the standpoint of the Incarnation that we should approach the Virgin Birth ; the Virgin Birth will not lead us to believe in the Incarnation ; the Incarnation may help us to understand the Virgin Birth. That Jesus is God does not depend on the Virgin Birth : that Jesus is God is a truth expressed in the words that Jesus, the Messiah of the Gospels, the Saviour and Lord, " was made man," that is, was incarnate.

CHAPTER X

MARK

The Second Gospel was written anonymously; the author did not reveal himself in the record nor publish his name. He wrote not for the public but for a special church for its own special use. Though anonymous and meant for private circulation in Rome, copies of his record were later transmitted to other churches; its value, too, was recognised in spite of the early loss of its conclusion, for the authors of Matthew, Luke and John used Mark, each in his own way, in their respective Gospels. This very circumstance, however, that three other Gospels utilised Mark, coupled with other factors such as the absence in Mark of Infancy Stories and of Resurrection Appearances, together with its poverty of doctrine and teaching (it did not even include the Lord's Prayer), affected its status in other centres than Rome; it was neglected for a while; it was placed not second but fourth in the usual order of arrangement in some Latin MSS., in the Codex Bezæ, and in the Freer Manuscripts, where the order reads Matthew, John, Luke, Mark. Yet in Rome it held its own to the early second century, and at last, because of its connection with the Church there and of the association of the name of Peter in its production and origin, it was recognised as canonical by Irenæus in A.D. 180.

The Author and his Sources.

S. PETER.—The tradition that John Mark of the Acts
wrote the second Gospel, and wrote it in Rome, is well
attested. No less attested is the fact that Peter was the
informant of a great deal of its contents. The main evidence is found in Eusebius's " Ecclesiastical History," in
which a fragment of the writings of Papias is quoted
(Papias wrote about A.D. 150). " John the Elder also
said this : Mark, who became the interpreter of Peter, wrote
down accurately, but not, however, in order the sayings
and deeds of our Lord, as far as he remembered them ; for
he had neither heard nor followed our Lord, but was later,
as I said, a follower of Peter who used to adapt his teachings
to the needs (of his hearers) but not as if he were drawing
up a connected history of our Lord's words. Wherefore
Mark has not erred in writing some things as he remembered them, for he was particularly careful in one thing,
to leave out nothing of the things he heard and to include
nothing false in them."

This is good evidence that Mark wrote the second Gospel ;
it also tells us that Mark was being adversely criticised
in comparison with another Gospel, possibly Matthew or
John. Papias is defending it, and while he admits that the
Gospel is not written chronologically he affirms that its
contents are accurate, for they contained the actual teaching of Peter ; he also affirms that Mark, though not a
disciple of Jesus Himself, was a companion of Peter and
was his interpreter, by which Papias probably meant that
Mark knew the mind of Peter well enough to interpret his
thought correctly and was able to reproduce his reminiscences of Christ accurately.

The connection of Mark with Peter is evidence of its
Roman origin, and this is substantiated by Irenæus (*circa*
A.D. 180) who states that Mark, the disciple and interpreter

of Peter, wrote his Gospel " after the deaths of Peter and Paul," that is after A.D. 64.

The indebtedness of Mark to Peter is therefore well established. It is shown in a very particular way in the Gospel ; for there, as we read the record, we almost hear Peter giving his " testimony "—a phenomenon observable in any revivalist or evangelistic campaign. Peter speaks of his failures in the past without reserve and Mark as faithfully reproduces them. Peter the convert may be frequently heard to say, " Look at what I was and compare it with what I am now, no longer dull, cowardly, traitorous, but a steadfast witness to Christ's power and grace." The defects of Peter and his fellow apostles are candidly proclaimed in the Gospel, and Peter is very severe on himself (8^{27} ff.; 9^{5-6}; 10^{28-31}; $14^{29-37, \, 66-72}$). Papias's opinion that Mark was accurate is more than justified in his delineation of the attitude of Peter and the apostles before their " conversion." And this unfavourable estimate is also evident in regard to other " converts," notably the members of Christ's own family, which included James, the Lord's brother and head of the Church in Jerusalem ($3^{21, \, 31-32}$; 6^{4}). They, too, had become changed men and women. We may compare this depreciatory and self-condemnatory attitude with that of Paul revealed to us in his own accounts of his conversion.

There is one other point in the statement of Papias which is instructive. Peter is said to have adapted his speaking to his audience. We are reminded of two stages in missionary enterprise. The first is the proclamation of the good news about Jesus and Salvation by stories of Him drawn from incidents of His work, Passion and Resurrection ; there is definite evidence of this stage in the reminiscences of Peter in the Gospel. The second stage is the building up of the converts into an organised and instructed Church ; teaching rather than narrative

would be necessary now. Here we see Mark at work in his Gospel, making use of one or more sayings-collections, if not forming them in Rome, or recalling the teaching of Peter. The community would want to know Christ's views on points of interest, such as fasting, the sabbath, forgiveness, baptism, the Messiahship, etc., and in particular the Christian attitude in face of persecution and death. It was a similar desire for instruction that had produced Q in Antioch. We recall the reverence in which Christ's own words are referred to by Paul, to whom they were final and authoritative (1 Thess. 4^{15}; 1 Cor. $7^{10-11, 25, 40}$; 9^{14}; 11^{23}). Each Church would have its own special problems; and the selection by Mark of matter for his Gospel was to some extent doubtless guided by conditions peculiarly affecting the Church in Rome.

OTHER SOURCES.—Peter therefore was not the only source of Mark's information. Mark may have had a Passion narrative at his command; the section 8^{27}–10^{45}, with its thrice repeated prediction of the Passion (8^{31}; 9^{31}; 10^{33}), reads like a collection of sayings which served as an Introduction to such a narrative. Peter would have supplied details; the story of his denial bears evidence of being his own reminiscences. Also Mark, a resident of Jerusalem, may have supplied some details himself; if he was, as it is very possible, the young man present at the arrest of Jesus (Mark 14^{51-52}), he may have heard Christ's prayer in the Garden and supplied some details of the Passion, such as the secret preparation for the farewell supper.

As to the sayings-collections referred to above, their existence was stated to be a possibility when we studied the question whether Mark knew Q (pp. 69 f.). In Mark, there are catenæ of sayings which may be assigned to such a collection. For example, Mark 4^{21-32}, with its catchwords " lamp," " light," " measure," and " seed," seems to

have been put together as a mnemonic to help the memory ; another such artificial group may be seen in 9^{41-50}, with its catchwords " little ones," " stumbling," " fire," and " salt." Further, there are groupings of stories with a topical interest. The most striking of these is the group of five narratives in 2^1-3^6, which deal with the growing opposition to Jesus ; the narratives show the opposition becoming more intense as we proceed. The opposition watches Jesus in the first incident (2^6), complains to the disciples in the second (2^{16}), reasons with Jesus in the third (2^{18}), objects to the action of the disciples in the fourth (2^{24}), determines to accuse Jesus, and ends up by taking counsel with the Herod-party to destroy Him in the fifth ($3^{2, 6}$). Other groupings are to be found in the four parables of chapter 4, the series of questions associated with the Passion ($11^{15}-12^{40}$), and the apocalyptic chapter 13. All these may have come from one sayings-collection or document, but we are not certain whether there was only one such collection.

Lastly, two at least of the narratives, notably the Death of John the Baptist and the Gerasene Swine, may have been based on hearsay ; the way the scene shifts in the latter is almost dramatic—the sea-shore, the mountain side, the city, the sea-shore, Decapolis. They were very probably " bazaar rumours."

The Choice of Subject-Matter.

The choice of the subject-matter of the Gospel was, as we have stated, probably influenced by other reasons than the preservation of stories and sayings used by Peter in preaching and teaching. We have seen in our study of Q and M that they cannot be understood apart from the life of the Christian communities in Antioch and Jerusalem respectively, and that in the case of L the influence of the home-circle of Philip the Evangelist in Cæsarea had

probably been responsible for its contents. A similar line of approach enables us to get an insight into Mark's contents. We may see in this Gospel traces of (1) the Church in Rome under persecution ; (2) the problems affecting its life ; and (3) the influence of the age of the early Apostolic Church.

(1) *The Persecution under Nero.*—Archdeacon Rawlinson has brought this out. After calling attention to the bearing of the apocalyptic chapter (Mark 13) on the events of the time, he continues : " The Gospel is full of the echoes of martyrdom. The central section of the book—the journey of Jesus to Jerusalem (8^{27}–10^{45})—is already in principle a *Via Dolorosa*. The Lord goes up to Jerusalem as to a city predestined to reject Him—and so it comes to pass. Meanwhile the way of discipleship is set forth as itself also the way of the Cross ($8^{34ff.}$). The death of Jesus is the Absolute Martyrdom, which avails as a *ransom for many* (10^{45}). But those who would follow Jesus in the way must themselves also be prepared for the possibility of martyrdom. The solemn question of Jesus to the two sons of Zebedee (10^{38}) confronts all would-be disciples—*Are ye able ?* " The sayings in 9^{41-50} similarly contain such echoes of martyrdom.

(2) *Church Life.*—We see also in Mark's choice of narratives and sayings many an answer to problems of interest in an early Church. What was the teaching of Jesus on fasting, on the observance of the Sabbath, on the law of Moses, on the payment of Roman taxes, on divorce, on children, on missionary effort, on the admission of Gentiles, on social life, on the powers of evil, on the Resurrection, on His coming again ? Were Gentile Christians bound by the Jewish fasts, the Jewish Sabbath, and the Jewish food regulations ? Of the events of the Passion we have almost a diary ; to the early Church, as to the world in general at the time, the way of salvation was a matter of momentous

importance. Hence the large proportion of space given to the Passion as compared with the Resurrection. The problem of suffering is the universal problem, and in Mark we realise that it had a poignant interest to the Roman Church.

(3) *Ætiological*.—In one special instance Mark shows the influence of ætiology, the desire to explain the origin or source of things. He attributes to John the Baptist knowledge of the " Holy Spirit," whereas this knowledge of the Third Person of the Trinity came later in Christian theology. John's words, as the context suggests, were probably that Jesus would baptise with fire. The Baptist could not have known of the Third Person in the Trinity, and could not have spoken of Christian baptism. Mark is trying to represent John as anticipating a knowledge of Christian baptism (Acts 19^{1-6}). So also in the Sin of Blasphemy (3^{29}), we cannot conclude that the reference is to the Holy Spirit as we know Him ; Jesus evidently meant that speaking evil of anything that is holy in a man cannot easily be forgiven by the one slandered. Another anticipatory statement is in Mark 13, where events which preceded the fall of Jerusalem are ante-dated ; for example, there is a reference to a theory later than the days of Jesus in the phrase " the abomination of desolation standing where it ought not." Mark's word for " standing " is masculine, and he thus shows that at the time at which he was writing his Gospel he had someone definite in mind (*cf.* 2 Thes. $2^{2, 4}$) ; he throws this knowledge back into the past and inserts it in the sayings of chapter 13. Again, differences between the Christian and Jewish fasts may have influenced the wording of 2^{20} ; the phrase " in that day " is probably meant to justify one of the Christian fast days, namely Friday, which day was observed only after the Crucifixion. Further, the verses dealing with " forgiveness of sins " may have been purposely retained in order to support the

Church's power of absolution. Lastly, the note added by Mark himself on the ceremonial observances of the Jews in $7^{2-4,\ 11}$ is exaggerated, possibly in the interests of Gentile controversies with the Jews. It has also been suggested that Mark's dating of the Last Supper as the Passover was done to support the Roman Church view of regarding it as the substitute for the Jewish Passover.

(4) *Scribal Insertions.*—A few of the mistakes in Mark may be due to the work of scribes, *e.g.* the quotation from Malachi in 1^2, wrongly assigned to Isaiah, the words " when Abiathar was high priest " in 2^{26}, and the following inter-polations, " as long as they have the bridegroom with them . . ." (2^{19b-20}), " all the Jews " (7^3), " and the gospels " (8^{35}), " because ye are Christ's " (9^{41}), and " for the gospel's sake " (10^{29}). Further, Mark was written in Rome and not in Palestine, and written about thirty years after the events described in the Gospel ; these circumstances would cause errors to creep in through mere forgetfulness.

External History.

The value of Mark lies not in its chronology but in its emphasis on the significance of Jesus. For example, before the Confession of Peter, the interest of Mark is in the gradual unfolding of the meaning of the kingdom of heaven ; after the Confession there is a change, for now we realise that Jesus concentrates on His inner circle, the Twelve, and is unfolding to them not the mystery of the kingdom but the mystery of His Person as the Messiah about to suffer. But there is a historical framework in Mark, and this is seen in the three sections in which Christ's ministry is set, the narrative of the death of John the Baptist (6^{13-29}) serving as a kind of link to prepare for Christ's departure from Herod's territory of Galilee. The three sections are these :

(1) Ministry in Galilee. 1^{14}–7^{23}.

(2) Outside Galilee. 7^{24}–9^{50}.

(3) On the way to (10) and in Jerusalem (11–16).

Mark gives no indication of time except by his reference to the Passover in the events connected with the Crucifixion. We are thrown back on two references to seasons of the year. In 2^{23} the disciples pluck the ears of corn ; the corn therefore has not been cut and the time of year will be the spring, about May : in 6^{39} at the Feeding of the Five Thousand, the multitude sit on the green grass, which will be the early spring, about April. If the two events are in order of time, there must therefore be a year between them. But there is no guarantee that Mark is written chronologically ; he has grouped five miracles in 1^{21}–2^{12}, and followed it up with five instances of hostility 2^{1}–3^{6}, including the mention of the Herodians in 3^{6}, who are not mentioned again till 12^{13}, in both cases in conjunction with the Pharisees. Though the hostility appears too early, yet the criticism of the apostles for breaking the Sabbath is probably an early episode of the ministry.

After the Feeding of the Five Thousand, there is a tour through Tyre and Sidon and the Decapolis to Cæsarea Philippi and thence to the scene of the Transfiguration, where on the mount Peter proposes to build three booths— a possible reference to the Feast of Tabernacles (September –October). The tour must have taken some months, and would fall between May and October. There is enough time for the events between the Transfiguration and the Crucifixion at the time of the Passover, *i.e.* between September and April of the following year.

Thus at a rough estimate, a year elapsed between the Feeding of the Five Thousand and the Crucifixion, and we may allow a year between the Baptism and the Feeding, or between Mark 2^{23} and 6^{39}, if Mark is chronological. This will give two years as the period covered by Mark.

A ministry of one year seems too short a time for the training of the Twelve.

When we turn to our other sources, we find that two years is by no means too long a period for the duration of Christ's ministry, for we have to find time for the following in addition to the itinerary as set forth in Mark.

In Q there is mention of disappointing missions to Chorazin and Bethsaida. Mark refers to work in Bethsaida in chapter 8, but no gospel refers to Chorazin. Q also implies more than one visit to Jerusalem, as against the one in Mark, which was the final visit leading to the Crucifixion. Besides, more than one visit to Jerusalem is necessary to explain the existence of friends and disciples in and about Jerusalem, and the bitter hostility of the priestly party in the city. Again, Jesus, as a loyal Jew, would not miss the great feasts of the Jews which were observed in Jerusalem ; this is clearly brought out in John's Gospel.

L, like Mark, gives the story as if the ministry lasted one year ; L implies a year in 4^{19}, " the acceptable year of the Lord " ; also the special non-Marcan section 9^{51}–18^{14} is the story of a regular and gradual progress of Jesus from Galilee through Samaria to His death in Jerusalem (Luke 13^{22} ; 17^{11} ; 18^{31} ; 19^{11}). But we have already noticed that in it are certain incidents which are placed in different contexts in Mark, e.g. the Beelzebub controversy, and the Great Commandment; this circumstance indicates not only that in 9^{51}–18^{14} other incidents from other days are included in it but also points to the impossibility of constructing a regular and orderly account of the course of events.

As it is quite possible that some of the events in Luke's special section (9^{51}–18^{14}) include happenings of a previous visit to Samaria and that all the episodes described in the section are not to be connected with the final journey to the Holy City, the references in John to a ministry in

Samaria (4^{1-42} ; 8^{48}) will fit in with this special section in Luke ; in this case Jesus will have made one of his visits to Jerusalem by the direct route through Samaria, and the final visit by the longer route through Peræa.

In John, three Passovers are referred to : 2^{13}, after the cleansing of the Temple ; 6^4, after the Feeding of the Five Thousand · 12^1, at the time of the Crucifixion. Mention is also made of the Feast of the Tabernacles in 7^2, of the Dedication (December) in 10^{22}, and an un-named Feast in 5^1. In John, as two years must elapse between the first and third Passovers, a period of at least two years is indicated as the duration of the ministry.

On the whole, we may therefore conclude that at least two years is suggested by all our sources as the duration of the ministry.

The Value of Mark.

Mark is not a biography of Jesus ; it does not claim to be an exhaustive life of Christ, but it claims to be the good news of Jesus the Messiah, the Son of Man, set forth but not yet recognised as the Saviour. Mark is the story of the initial stages in the recognition of Jesus. The good news of Jesus is set in a framework of theology which runs concurrently with the historical framework.

1. By the Jordan.—The Baptism. Jesus is revealed to Himself as the Son of God.
2. In Galilee.—Teaching on the kingdom of heaven. Jesus recognised as a Rabbi and Prophet. The selection of the Twelve as a body to carry out the ideals of the kingdom.
3. Outside Galilee.—Peter's Confession of the Messiahship, followed by teaching of Jesus that the Messiah is the Saviour of men.
4. In Jerusalem.—Salvation through His Death, and the proof of Jesus as Divine by His Resurrection.

History, according to Mark, is an aid to faith, but is not identical with faith. It is not enough to know about Jesus ; we must know Him. To understand Mark, we must see Jesus as the disciples saw Him ; they gradually awakened to the truth of His Person that He was as truly Divine as He was truly human. The Gospel of S. Mark is the Gospel of the beginning of the progressive epiphanies of Jesus.

The Personality of Jesus is described in the right perspective, just as He seemed to the dull and ignorant and blind disciples—a truly human Jew of the first century, subject to human emotions and human desires, and one who was a great Rabbi or Teacher. So well did He train the disciples, bearing with them, encouraging them and leading them, that Peter at last had come to perceive that there was something supernatural in Him ; He was the Messiah, the supernatural Son of Man of Enoch and Daniel. When Mark wrote, Faith had begun to find out that He was more ; He was the Saviour. Mark's Gospel is the story of the beginning of that faith which ended in the Creed of the Apostles when they preached of the Risen and Glorified Jesus, now in Heaven, who would one day appear in power to judge. The sequel of Mark's Gospel is the Acts of the Apostles ; the Gospel is an introduction to the Acts. Mark gives us a true record of what the Apostles thought of Jesus as He lived and moved and died amongst them ; his record is therefore of incalculable value.

There is no trace in the Gospel that Jesus was God who had become incarnate. That came later. In Mark the Church had gone far on the way towards this belief in the Incarnation. Jesus stood in a unique relation to God, but was not yet recognised as God and Lord. He was the Son of God, *i.e.* He was a supernatural Being with supernatural powers, but He was not recognised as God. Voices from heaven had so called Him (1^{11} ; 9^7). The insane, with

their uncanny knowledge, held him supernatural when they called Him the Son of God or the Holy One of God ($1^{24,\ 34}$; 3^{11}; 5^{7}), but in Mark, Jesus was never called "Lord" in a divine sense ; only once was He thus addressed, and that by the Syro-phœnician woman, who could not have used the title in a Christian sense. In Mark, Jesus the Rabbi and Prophet recognised as the Son of Man was also the Son of God. His power was shown by His mighty acts. He gave His life a ransom for many, and He claimed He would rise again ($9^{9,\ 31}$; 10^{36}) ; He now sits at the right hand of power and will come with the clouds of heaven (14^{62}). The good news in Mark is that Jesus the Messiah, the Son of Man and the Son of God, is the Redeemer, though He was not yet so recognised at first ; the good news in the early chapters of the Acts is the recognition by the Church that Jesus is the Saviour and Redeemer through whom comes salvation ; the good news in the later chapters of Acts is that He is more than Saviour, He is Lord ; the good news in John is that Jesus the Messiah and the Saviour and Lord is God Incarnate.

Mark and the Gentiles.

John Mark was the son of Mary, a woman of wealth, whose home in Jerusalem was used as a meeting-place for Christians. Mary's house had a porch, and there was a maid who attended to the door (Acts 12^{12-17}). There was a large room in the house, where, it is said, the Lord's Supper was instituted and Christ appeared to the Apostles. We know nothing of John Mark's early life, but tradition has identified him with the man bearing the pitcher of water (Mark 14^{13}), and also with the young man who was present at the arrest of Jesus and fled away (Mark 14^{51-52}). He was cousin to Barnabas, and was con-verted by Peter, who speaks of him as his son (1 Peter 5^{13}) ; Papias, as we saw, called him a disciple not of Jesus but

of Peter (Eusebius H.E. ii. 15, iii. 39). When Peter was
released from prison, it was to the house of Mary that he
returned.

We first hear of Mark's interest in the Church when he
was taken to Antioch by Barnabas and Saul at the close of
their relief visit to Jerusalem, A.D. 46 (Acts 12²⁵). The
following year he accompanied them on their first missionary journey as their dragoman or attendant, but
parted company in Pamphylia and returned to Jerusalem.
This defection led to a quarrel between Barnabas and Saul,
with the result that Barnabas took Mark to his own home
in Cyprus, A.D. 49 (Acts 13⁵, ¹³ ; 15³⁷⁻³⁹). Eleven years
later Mark was with Paul in Rome, worked with him, and
was a comfort to the imprisoned Apostle, especially in
arguments with certain Jews (Col. 4¹⁰, ¹¹ ; Phil. 24).
Three years later Mark is found in Asia Minor, not far from
Lystra (2 Tim. 4¹¹), and in the second Epistle to Timothy,
Paul earnestly desires Timothy to bring Mark to Rome,
for he is useful for the ministry. Tradition connects the
final years of Mark with Alexandria.

According to Hippolytus, Mark was known as the
" curt-fingered," probably owing to some defect in his
hands.

The two influencing personalities of Mark's early life as
a Christian were Barnabas and Peter, the latter the great
apostle of the circumcision. When he accompanied
Barnabas and Saul on their first journey, he was bound by
ties of consanguinity to Barnabas and by his spiritual
relationship to Peter. His part in that mission was a
minor one ; he had not been set apart for it by the Holy
Spirit, and the Church had laid no hands of consecration
on him. His name is only mentioned when the historian is
describing the preaching of the missionaries in the Jewish
synagogues in Cyprus ; this is instructive, for it is a pointer
to Mark's views and his leaning towards a Jewish

Christianity. Shortly afterwards, the missionaries reached Paphos, and there, in a Roman house, Saul, the junior missionary, assumed the leadership, a fact clearly brought out by the historian, who wrote that " Paul and his company " set sail from Paphos (Acts 13[13]). It was Barnabas and Saul, not Saul and Barnabas, who had been appointed to go on a mission ; Barnabas first and then Saul speak to the Apostolic Council about their journey ; Barnabas first and Saul second are officially mentioned in James' letter (Acts 15[12, 25]), but in the narrative of the Acts in which the historian speaks for himself, the order of names is different ; it is Paul and Barnabas (Acts 13[43, 46, 50] ; 15[2, 22, 35]). Luke, by the order in which he names the two missionaries, gives us one of the causes of the desertion of Mark, namely, his loyalty to his cousin Barnabas.

There was a second cause. Mark went not with them to " the work " was Paul's opinion of him (Acts 15[37-39]). The " work " to Paul could only be one thing—the appeal to the Gentiles. Mark was satisfied as long as the mission was confined to the synagogue, but when the change in leadership meant the extension of the Gospel to the Gentiles, he showed himself to be the spiritual son of Peter by leaving the mission and returning to Jerusalem. But age and experience widened his outlook, and we find him once again with Paul and Peter in Rome. As the " interpreter " of Peter, he composed a Gospel for the Gentiles, to whom Paul was the great Apostle. In one passage in his Gospel he has exposed his new point of view, for he puts into our Lord's mouth the words, " My house shall be called a house of prayer for all the nations " (Mark 11[17]). The Temple, however, was not a house of prayer " for all the nations " (Matthew and Luke therefore omit these three words) ; but as well by the retention of the three words in the passage, which is a quotation from the Septuagint of

Isaiah 56⁷, as by the destination of the Gospel, Mark has made atonement for the desertion which in the past withdrew him from " the work."

The Style of Mark.

A literal translation of two sections of the Gospel is given below from Allen's " Gospel According to St. Mark." The translation brings out Mark's style in clear fashion. The following characteristics can be noted in them :

1. Reduplication and redundancy of expression, of which there are 39 examples in the Gospel.

   1¹⁶. Simon, and Andrew the brother of Simon.

   1²⁸. Everywhere, into all the . . . district.

   1³². And it being evening, when the sun set.

   5²³. That she may be saved and live.

   5⁴⁰⁻⁴¹. Where the child was, and he took the hand of the child.

2. The preposition is first in a compound word, and is repeated before the noun that follows, *e.g. :*

   1¹⁶. Passing-along by.

   1²¹. Enter-in into.

   1²⁵. Come-out out.

   1²⁹. Going-out out.

3. (a) The Historic present, *i.e.* the present tense used by Mark to give vividness to the narrative, is common even after a past tense. This occurs 151 times in the Gospel. Of this number Matthew retains only 21 and Luke only 1, both preferring some form of the past tense.

(b) The imperfect tense is about as common. The sections quoted abound in illustrations.

(c) A participle is used with the verb " to be."

   1¹³. Was being tempted.

   1²². Was teaching.

   1³³. Was gathered.

4. "Straightway" or "forthwith" is common, and found 41 times. "And" frequently begins a sentence. "Again" occurs over 25 times, and "much" over a dozen times. "That" after verbs of saying followed by *oratio recta* occurs about 50 times, *e.g.* in 1^{15}, 5^{23}, 5^{28}, 5^{35}. "They" is vaguely used, *e.g.* 5^{35}. The forcible word "drives" in 1^{12} is used 17 times by Mark.

5. The language is often harsh, *e.g.* Mark 4^{31-32}. "As a grain of mustard seed, which when it is sown upon the earth—being less than all seeds on the earth—and when it is sown, it comes up. . . ."

In short, Mark's style is that of one who is making his first attempt at writing a record, and who is aiming amongst other things to reproduce Peter's recollections of the Master whilst they are still fresh in his memory. The vivid and graphic touches in many a narrative show the art of story-telling—the reader or listener sees the scene unfolding itself, and can imagine himself an eye-witness of what is happening. Mark is an artist of no mean degree.

Mark 1^{9-34}

(The characteristic words and phrases and grammatical forms are in italics.)

9. And it came to pass in those days that Jesus came from Nazareth of Galilee, and was baptized by John *into* the Jordan. 10. *And forthwith* as He went up out of the water, He saw the heavens rent, and the Spirit as a dove coming down *into* Him. 11. And a voice came out of the heavens, Thou art My Son, the Beloved, in Thee I am well pleased. 12. *And forthwith* the Spirit *drives* Him out into the desert. 13. And He was in the desert forty days being tempted by the Satan. And he was with the wild beasts. And the angels *were ministering* to Him. 14. And after that John was delivered up, Jesus came into Galilee, preaching the good tidings of God, 15. and saying *that* the time

has been fulfilled, and the Kingdom of God is at hand, repent, and believe in the good tidings. 16. And passing *along by* the sea of Galilee, He saw Simon and Andrew, the brother of Simon, fishing in the sea, for they were fishermen. 17. And Jesus said to them, Come after me, and I will make you to become fishermen of men. 18. *And forthwith* they left the nets and followed Him. 19. And He went on a little, and saw James the (son) of Alphæus, and John his brother, and they (were) in the boat, mending their nets. 20. *And forthwith* He called them. And they left their father Zebedee in the boat with the hired servants, and went away after Him. 21. And they *enter-in into* Capharnaoun. *And forthwith* on the Sabbath He *was teaching into* the synagogue. 22. And they *were being astonished* at His teaching, for He *was teaching* as one having authority, and not as the Scribes. 23. *And forthwith* there was in their synagogue a man in an unclean spirit, and he cried out, 24. saying "What have we to do with Thee, Jesus of Nazareth ? Art Thou come to destroy us ? I know Thee who Thou art, the Holy One of God." 25. And Jesus censured him, saying, "Be quiet, and *come-out out* from him," 26. And the unclean spirit rent him, and gave voice with a great voice, and *came-out out* from him. 27. And all were amazed, so that they questioned together, saying, "What is this ? A new teaching ! With authority He issues orders to the unclean spirits also, and they obey Him." 28. And His fame went out *forthwith* everywhere into all the surrounding district of Galilee. 29. *And forthwith, going-out out* of the synagogue, they came into the house of Simon and Andrew with James and John. 30. And the mother-in-law of Simon kept her bed with a fever. *And forthwith* they *tell* Him about her. And He came up and raised her, taking her by the hand, 31. And the fever left her, and she *was ministering* to them. 32. And it being evening, when the sun set, they *were bringing* to Him all that were sick, and the demon-ridden. 33. And the whole city *was gathered* together to the door. 34. And he healed many who were sick with divers diseases, and cast out many demons. And He *was not suffering* the demons to speak, because they knew Him.

5^{21-43}

Jairus' Daughter and the Woman with the Issue of Blood.

21. And when Jesus had crossed over in the boat *again* to the other side there was gathered to Him a great crowd. And He

was by the sea. 22. And there *comes* one of the rulers of the synagogue, by name Jairus. And seeing Him he falls at His feet. 23. And *exhorts* Him *much*, saying *that* My little daughter is very bad. (I pray) that Thou wilt come and lay hands on her that she may be saved and live. 24. And He departed with him. And there *was following* Him a great crowd, and they *were thronging* Him. 25. And a woman with an issue of blood twelve years, 26. who had suffered much by many doctors, and had spent all her substance and had not benefited, but rather had become worse, 27. having heard the reports about Jesus, came in the crowd behind and touched His coat. 28. For she *was saying* that If I may touch even His garments I shall be saved. 29. *And forthwith* the flow of her blood was dried up, and she knew in her body that she was being healed from the plague. 30. *And forthwith* Jesus recognised in Himself the power gone *out from* Him, turned round in the crowd and *was saying*, Who touched My garments ? 31. And His disciples *were saying* to Him, Thou seest the crowd thronging Thee, and sayest, Who touched Me ? 32. And He *was looking* round to see who (fem.) had done this. 33. And the woman, fearing and trembling, knowing what had happened to her, came and fell before Him and told Him all the truth. 34. And He said to her, Daughter, thy faith hath saved thee, go in peace and be whole from thy plague. 35. While He was speaking they *come* from the ruler of the synagogue saying *that* Thy daughter is dead, why troublest thou the teacher further ? 36. And Jesus chanced to hear the word spoken, and *saith* to the ruler of the synagogue, Fear not, only believe. 37. And He permitted no one to accompany Him, save Peter and James and John the brother of James. 38. And they *come* into the house of the ruler of the synagogue, and He *beholds* a tumult, and people weeping and wailing *much*. 39. And He entered in and *saith* to them, Why do ye make a tumult and weep ? The child is not dead, but is sleeping. 40. And they *were laughing* Him to scorn. But He thrust them all out and *takes* the father of the child and the mother, and those that were with Him, and *enters* where the child was. 41. And He took the hand of the child and *saith* to her, Talitha Koum, which is being interpreted, Damsel, I say to thee, Arise. 42. *And forthwith* the damsel rose up and *was walking about*, for she was twelve years old. And they were *forthwith* astonished with a great astonishment. 43. And He *charged* them *much* that no one should know it. And He commanded that something should be given her to eat.

CHAPTER XI

THE KINGDOM OF GOD, ETC.

The Kingdom of God (or Heaven).

AFTER John was delivered up, says Mark, Jesus came into Galilee preaching and saying " The Kingdom of God is at hand." No such phrase is to be found in the Old Testament, or in the Apocrypha, or in the apocalyptic literature, that is the literature before and after the Christian era which proposes to reveal the future. Yet to understand the meaning attached by Jesus to the phrase we must go far back into Jewish history ; it cannot be understood apart from that history. It was the genius of Jesus to seize on a phrase which would not only embody the finest teaching of the prophets and apocalyptists of old, but which could be clarified and vitalised by Him and embodied in a concrete and present reality.

The word " Kingdom " involves the idea of rule and sovereignty, and the idea of the sovereignty of Yahweh over Israel prevails in prophetic literature from the eighth century onwards. But long before the eighth century, in fact, from the very earliest days of its existence as a people, there was in the belief of Israel a nexus between their God and themselves. This was a covenant relationship ; the Kingdom of God was a heritage from it.

By a covenant made between Yahweh and Israel, Yahweh became the God of Israel and Israel became His people, His son, His first-born. In this relationship, it was not the

individual but the nation that was intimately bound to Yahweh. One outstanding result of this filial relationship was that Israel never ceased to have a hope and a future ; Yahweh was bound by the covenant to bless and succour Israel, however sinful Israel might be. This idea of a covenant by its very nature was not an abstract idea ; the community of Israel was inseparably involved in it. In the same way, the idea of the sovereignty of God, which developed from the idea of a covenant relationship, was not a mere abstract idea, but one which could not be dissociated from that of a community. Had it been otherwise, Israel would have lost its soul, its sonship would have been an illusion, and its hope a phantasy. There was a grievous error, however, in their idea of the bond ; it was their unethical interpretation of it that, irrespective of their moral condition, their God would ever be on their side. It was exactly on this point that the eighth century prophets fastened when they proclaimed their great idea of sovereignty. By these prophets, their proclamation was linked up with " the Day of Yahweh "—a phrase used for the first time by Amos. In his use of it, he assumed a knowledge of it amongst his hearers as indicating their belief in a day when by an act of judgment Yahweh would inaugurate His reign over His people and over them alone, and give them material prosperity and political supremacy over other nations. Israel, the populace thought, was His son and His only son, however immoral and unrighteous it might be.

Amos (c. 750 B.C.) was the first of the great prophets. His main attack was directed against the popular view that in all circumstances and at all times Yahweh was on the side of Israel ($3^{2 \text{ ff.}}$). If Yahweh had given Israel special privileges, they would more deservedly be punished for their iniquities ; the greater their privileges the greater their responsibilities. The sovereignty of Yahweh demanded

moral righteousness. He further taught that Yahweh as a moral Being demanded righteousness as well from the surrounding nations as from Israel; he did not call Yahweh the God of Israel only, but spoke of Him as the Lord Yahweh, the Yahweh of hosts. The day of Yahweh was a day of darkness and not of light ; that day would vindicate the righteousness of Yahweh and not of Israel ; only righteous Israel and not all Israel would share in the blessedness of the future. With this interpretation Hosea and Isaiah, the contemporaries of Amos, agreed. The teaching of these prophets was not wholly without effect, but it took long to sink even partially into the national consciousness. Over a century after Amos we find in Zephaniah (*c.* 620 B.C.) a striking expression of the nature of this Kingdom. Zephaniah taught that the day of Yahweh was a day of judgment not only of Israel but of all nations, and that its effect extended to the brute creation ; he declared that the judgment would be universal and that after the judgment only the righteous remnant of Israel would be found in the Kingdom and that all nations would serve Yahweh. But the people could not rise to the heights of this prophet's vision ; in fact, the old popular view still held sway. For it was the age when the great Assyrian empire was casting its baleful shadow even on prophecy, and at this juncture came the Deuteronomic reformation under Josiah. Israel, because of Josiah's reforms (*c.* 621 B.C.), were inclined to draw the self-satisfied conclusion that Yahweh would not fail them since they were more righteous than Assyria ; in this they were encouraged by Habbakuk (*c.* 600 B.C.), who taught that because of this relative righteousness Yahweh would intervene for Israel against Assyria and that the Kingdom of Yahweh, bringing prosperity to Israel, would follow the destruction of Assyria.

A decade later came the fall of Jerusalem (586 B.C.) followed by the exile, events which transformed the whole

conception of the sovereignty of Yahweh. After the exile, great advances in the details of this conception are to be noticed ; it will suffice if some of these are given. The Kingdom becomes less political and more spiritual by a change of emphasis, for the reign of God in righteousness and peace is taught rather than the destruction of Israel's foes ; the individual and not the nation comes into prominence, for the individual and not the nation as a whole is to be judged ; the day of Yahweh as a day of judgment becomes a day of comfort and promise, for the mercy and grace of God are set forth along with His severity ; a Deliverer, a human prince of the house of David and the representative of Yahweh is by many, but not all, of the prophets, made an essential figure in the scheme of things, On one point there is a cleavage of opinion ; for whilst on the one hand Jeremiah, the second Isaiah, and Jonah teach that the Gentiles will be included in the Kingdom through their conversion, on the other hand Ezekiel, Haggai, Zechariah 9–14, and Joel do not favour their inclusion. According to the former liberal school the Kingdom is to be established on earth in the land of Israel, and to it the exiles will return ; Jerusalem will be rebuilt, and so will the Temple ; the duty of Israel is to be missionary-hearted and to convert the nations to whom the divine mercy is to be extended. This universal outlook is also found in Psalms 22 and 87, particularly in the latter, but even the grandeur of that Psalm is surpassed in Isaiah 19^{24-25} (c. 200 B.C.), where Israel is placed third and not first in a spiritual triple alliance of Egypt, Assyria and Israel.

Four particular lines of thought are to be noted in the post-exilic teaching ; they are to be met with in the Gospel story.

1. According to the second Isaiah, the conversion of the Gentiles is to be effected by the Servant of Yahweh (Isaiah

42^{1-4}; 49^{1-6}; 50^{4-9}; $52^{13}-53^{11}$). The Servant is called to suffering and rejection and his triumph will come after death. The pious remnant of Israel seems to be represented here under the symbol of an ideal hero. These four passages were not by the prophet or later by the disciples interpreted of the expected messianic Deliverer, yet after the Resurrection of Jesus the early Christian Church found in them a prophecy of Jesus as the Messiah called to suffering and death (Acts 8^{35}).

2. In Zechariah (9–14), Jerusalem is to be the centre of the universal religion, and all that is left of the nations will attend the feast of Tabernacles (14^{16}); Yahweh is holy, but His holiness is Levitical; the Law is to be supreme in the Kingdom.

3. In Isaiah 65–66 (c. 400 B.C.), Jerusalem is to be supernaturally blessed, and the people transformed to be fitted for the new life; men will live to a great age, and even the animal world will share in the peace of the future. There is to be a new heaven and a new earth—heaven is thus for the first time brought within the conception of the Kingdom.

4. In Malachi (c. 460 B.C.), Elijah will return to the earth to prepare for the terrible day of judgment which is near at hand. This nearness was proclaimed to overcome the disappointment caused by the non-fulfilment of the prophecies of Haggai and Zechariah, who had promised its advent when the Temple was rebuilt.

Between the Old and New Testaments.

The studies of Jesus were not confined to the Hebrew Scriptures; His teaching shows that He was conversant with the apocalyptic books, especially Daniel and Enoch. The apocalyptists were men who gave speculative views or revelations of that which was to come; we find such apocalypses in Daniel, in 2 Esdras (or 4 Ezra), in the

Apocrypha, and in the Revelation in the New Testament. These imaginative writers aimed at strengthening faith in times of persecution and distress.

John the Baptist used apocalyptic language, but combined it with prophetic. Jesus also occasionally spoke in apocalyptic language, and gave evidence of His knowledge of such literature ; and the more spiritual hopes and thoughts of the Jewish people came from this literature. We find instances of such language in the setting of the parable of Dives and Lazarus, in Christ's words that the names of the Seventy would be written in heaven (Luke 10^{20}), in His references to the Messianic banquet, and of His coming in the clouds of heaven, in speaking of Gentiles as the birds of the heaven in the Mustard Seed, in His answer to Caiaphas, and in the description of the last days (Mark 13, Matthew 24, Luke 21). References to apocalyptic literature, *viz.* to Enoch and the Assumption of Moses, are made in Jude. Both Jesus and the Jews were not ignorant of this literature.

The phrase " the Kingdom of God " is not found in this period. The nearest approximations are " the Kingdom of our God," " the Kingdom of the Lord," and " God's Kingdom." The idea of the sovereignty of God, however, is very prominent.

In the teaching of this period, there are divergent views about the time of the Kingdom, the inclusion of Gentiles, the place in it of a Messiah, and the locality of the Kingdom. We shall deal with the place of the Messiah in a special chapter, and therefore we shall confine ourselves at present to the other factors referred to.

According to some apocalyptists, there will be on this earth a Golden Age or a Good Time Coming of limited duration, either with or without a Messiah ; at the end of this Good Time will come the Final Judgment ; this will be followed for the righteous by a blessed Hereafter, also called

the Age to Come, which will be the Kingdom of Heaven in a special sense, but still on this earth.   In 1 Enoch (83–90), the Kingdom on earth, in which will be found Gentiles, will be before the Judgment, and be of limited duration ; when it comes to an end, the righteous dead will rise and be transformed to share with those who are alive at the time of judgment an everlasting life which shall not pass away. The same sequence of three events is to be seen in 4 Ezra 7, who writes (i) of the Good Time coming when the Messiah, God's Son, will then be revealed, and will reign for 400 years, after which the Messiah and all human beings will die ; (ii) this is to be followed by a Resurrection and a Final Judgment ; and (iii) a blessed Hereafter when evil will cease to exist.   In 2 Enoch, the Golden Age on earth will last 1000 years.   In other writers there is a revolutionary change.   For example, in the Similitudes of Enoch (1 Enoch 37–71) the Kingdom will be established not only on this earth, but also in heaven, both of which will undergo transformation (*cf.* Isaiah 65–66), and in the Kingdom a supernatural Messiah will act for God.

Thus, as regards the time and locality of the Kingdom, there are in these apocalyptic writers three views : (1) A Golden Age or Good Time Coming on this earth before the final judgment (*a*) with a Messiah, or (*b*) without a Messiah. (2) The Age to Come after resurrection and judgment, but still on this earth ; (3) A new heaven and a new earth.

Jesus and the Kingdom.

Various ideas of the Kingdom of God and of the Messiah were thus current in our Lord's days on earth.

The meaning that He attached to the phrase was one surpassing that of previous teachers, whether prophets or apocalyptists.   To Him it was still the sovereignty of God, but a sovereignty to be exercised over a righteous community

of all nations ; it was a Kingdom which was first proclaimed to be near at hand, and became present in concrete
form during His lifetime on earth when the community of
His Apostles was formed ; it was a Kingdom to be realised
in its fullness in the future when its members, after resurrection and judgment, become the glorified community of the
Age to Come, that is, in the blessed Hereafter. Eternal
life and the Kingdom, as John clearly saw, were thus inter-
changeable terms. The Kingdom was open to all, to Jew
and Gentile, to the evil and the good, to the just and the
unjust, to the observer of the Law and to the sinner.

To Jesus, the Kingdom was both near at hand and was
here, and was not only in the future. He came preaching
" The Kingdom of God is at hand " (Mark 1^{15}) ; the scribe
who asked which was the first commandment and answered
discreetly was " not far from the Kingdom of God "
(Mark 12^{34}) ; those who saw the things which the disciples
saw were more fortunate than many prophets and Kings
(Q, Luke 10^{23-24} ; and cf. Luke 7^{22}, Christ's answer to the
inquiry of John the Baptist). To the disciples He said
" Seek ye his Kingdom " (Q, Luke 12^{31}) ; to them was
given " the mystery of the Kingdom of God " (Mark 4^{11}).
Members of the Kingdom were to be like children (Mark
10^{14}), and, said Jesus, he that is least in the Kingdom of
heaven is greater than John the Baptist, for John lived in
the pre-Messianic days (Q, Luke 7^{28}) ; it belonged to the
poor (Q, Luke 6^{20}) ; the tax-gatherers and harlots were
entering in (Matthew 21^{31}) ; others, too, were entering the
Kingdom, and the lawyers were hindering them (Q, Luke
11^{52}). The Kingdom of God, said Jesus, was in the midst
of his hearers, probably meaning the community already
attached to Jesus rather than in the hearts of the people
(Q, Luke 17^{21}) ; its existence was shown by His power in
casting out devils (Q, Luke 11^{20}). It is like the grain of
mustard seed which, when it grows, will shelter " the birds

of the heaven," that is, the Gentiles. The Kingdom will be consummated in the future as He taught in the Wheat and the Tares ; some of the Twelve will not taste of death till they see the Kingdom of God come with power (Mark 9[1]) ; in the Great Supper the room was not yet full (Luke 14[15-23]).

The linking of the present and the future is brought out in the story of the rich young man who asks what he should do " to inherit eternal life," and our Lord, at the end of the interview turns to the disciples and says, " How hardly shall they that have riches enter into the Kingdom of God " (Mark 10[17-22]). The Kingdom of God, which can be entered now, is thus identified with eternal life ; a rich man will find the demands of life in the Kingdom impossible for him if he continued to be a slave to riches (cf. Luke 6[20, 24]).

In His teaching we are conscious of the immensity of His conception both as regards time and as regards place. It was not temporal and it was not of limited duration ; it was not limited to this earth, but embraced heaven or the other world ; a community on earth was to exhibit the character required of those who would share in the Kingdom in the Hereafter. The Kingdom was already present, though unrealised, on earth when He came, for He was the Messiah ; it was present when He chose His disciples as the first community of believers and adherents—but neither the multitude nor the Twelve could realise it till He was accepted as Messiah. In a real sense the Kingdom of God was in the midst of the Jews and manifested to them by signs such as the casting out of devils, signs which the Twelve were to perform on their own mission (Mark 6[7]). The Kingdom has come, but it will come again with power ; the Messiah has come, but He, too, will come again with power.

Did Jesus give a name or title to this community ?

Here we turn to the special Jerusalem sayings-document used by Matthew, namely M. This community was called by Him the Church; Jesus spoke of it as " *my* Church." It was a term used in the Greek version of the Old Testament, known as the Septuagint, for the community of God's chosen people; fuller development of the Church was to come later during the age of the Apostles. The Kingdom of God is the sovereignty and rule of God; it is not identical with the Church, but it is the Church which has to manifest the fullness of this sovereignty. Jesus did not equate the Church with the Kingdom, for the Kingdom included not only persons but also values.

The possibilities of this Kingdom were so glorious that we can understand why the Founder declared that it had been the unrealised hope of prophets and kings, and that the least in the Kingdom was greater than John the Baptist.

Our Lord utilised the finest ideas of the prophets and apocalyptists before His time. He accepted and taught the inclusion of the Gentiles in His Kingdom, emphasised the spiritual character of His Kingdom, expected a catastrophic end of this world to be followed by a Resurrection and Judgment of all. But he surpassed them in linking up the Golden Age and the Age to come by His teaching that eternal life in the Kingdom begins on this earth and is consummated in heaven. He also went beyond the conception of the righteous remnant by His practical act in forming a righteous community, the Church. He enlarged their view of the place of the Messiah in His Kingdom by His presence on earth as the Messiah and by proclaiming that He would come again with power in the clouds of heaven; and lastly, He taught that Heaven was a condition of existence which was possible on this earth. The transformation and transfiguration of human lives need not await the future.

The Messiah.

In the Old Testament the Greek word *Christos* is the equivalent of the Hebrew word " Messiah," which means " anointed." In ancient times kings and priests were anointed with oil as a religious act, but, when this custom fell into disuse, the idea of being consecrated or anointed in a figurative sense was retained. The term " anointed " or " messiah " in this figurative sense was applied to other than Israelites, *e.g.* Cyrus in " his anointed " or " his messiah " (Isaiah 45^1), because his policy favoured the Jews. So also we find that the sense of being consecrated is applied to Saul (1 Sam. 24^{10}), to the priests (Lev. 4^3), to the nation, which is " his anointed " or " his messiah " (Psalm 28^8) ; to Israel, which is " thine anointed " or " thy messiah" (Psalm 84^9) ; to the prophets, who are " my anointed " or " my messiahs " (Psalm 105^{15}). The same idea meets us in the Psalms in reference to David, *e.g.* 18^{50}; 89^{20}; 132$^{11, 17}$, all of which look back to 2 Samuel 7^{12}, but in none of these references is there a thought of a scion of the house of David who is to come in the future. Psalm 2 stands by itself ; its date is uncertain and it may be post-exilic, but a king there is called God's anointed or messiah (2^2) and on the day of his anointing is held to beome Yahweh's son (2^7), and to him is given the promise of dominion over all nations. Thus Psalm 2 speaks of a messiah in terms very much in advance of anything pre-exilic in time.

In the Prophets, the Messiah in the technical sense is not mentioned ; reference is made often but not by all the prophets to a deliverer or leader as the agent of God. Such a deliverer does not appear, for example, in the fine passages which refer to the Good Time Coming in Zephaniah. But when he is an essential part of the scheme, he is to be of the house of David (Hosea 1$^{10-11}$; 3^5. Amos 9$^{8-15}$) ; he will come from the clan of Ephrathah, to whose district

Bethlehem belongs, and rule in Yahweh's name to initiate the future (Micah 5²). He will be a great judge, ruler and warrior and will possess superhuman powers (Isaiah 9⁶⁻⁷), and be inspired by Yahweh's spirit (Isaiah 7¹⁴ ; 11¹⁻⁵). As representative of Yahweh he will enter Jerusalem riding on an ass, and victory will be granted him by Yahweh but he will not himself bring victory (Zech. 9⁹ᶠ·). In Zechariah 1–8 and by Haggai, this future deliverer is identified with Zerubbabel, who is called the Righteous Branch (Zech. 3⁸⁻⁹ ; 6¹²). Thus we may sum up the Old Testament idea of the expected deliverer as a prince of the line of David or of a new line represented by the Righteous Branch. He will not inaugurate the Kingdom, the initiation being the act of Yahweh ; he is a human leader, a man of eminent gifts but always the ambassador or viceroy of Yahweh and in no sense equal to Yahweh.

In the literature between the Old and New Testaments, the technical sense of the word " Messiah " appears. He will be according to some writers a human Messiah, according to others a superhuman Messiah. In some of the literature there is no mention of any Messiah at all. But, whether human or superhuman, he will be, as in the Old Testament, the representative of Yahweh and possess both wisdom and righteousness. (a) The human Messiah is either a warrior, or a scion of the house of David or a sacerdotal prince of the tribe of Levi ; in no instance is he identified with any personage in history, though Simon Maccabæus came very near to it. This human Messiah will secure political supremacy for righteous Israel, and, in more than one writer, this will be effected by the destruction of Rome. (b) The superhuman Messiah appears specially in the Similitudes of Enoch (1 Enoch 37–71), where he is called the Son of Man who is pre-existent and next to God ; he is higher than the angels, but not God, even though He is to judge men and angels at the Great

Assize ; his reign begins not before but after the Resurrection and the Judgment. His intervention is expected when the mighty and the kings, who deny the Lord of Spirits, possess the earth. These mighty ones, according to the late Canon Charles, are the Sadducees and native rulers of Palestine.

In 4 Ezra (or 2 Esdras) the superhuman and human elements are mixed. The duty of the Messiah is to destroy the enemies of Israel and to establish peace in Jerusalem ; after a reign of 400 years the Messiah and those with him will die.

Thus there were two ideas of the Messiah held when our Lord began His ministry—the human and the superhuman.

Jesus and the Messiah.

In our Lord's time the popular idea was that the Messiah would be human, and the Son of David, *e.g.* Bartimæus, a blind beggar, addressed Him as " Jesus, thou son of David," and on His entry into Jerusalem the people hailed the coming of the Kingdom of " our father David." After the feeding of the five thousand, Jesus refused the offer of kingship of a temporal kingdom ; to Pilate He said that His Kingdom was not of this world. The scribes said that the Christ was the son of David, but Jesus repudiated it and challenged it from scripture (Mark 12^{35-37}). Jesus would not allow any human Messiahship or encourage a nationalistic view of a political kingdom ruled by a scion of David's house.

Did Jesus then claim to be in some special sense the superhuman Messiah, the Anointed One who was to judge the earth ? When Peter confessed " Thou art the Messiah," what did he mean, and did Jesus accept his meaning ?

According to Mark, the multitudes admitted His power to heal, the authority with which He spoke, His independence

11 *

of thought surpassing that of the scribes, His ability in meeting argument. At Nazareth He claimed to be in the line of the prophets, and sadly admitted that no prophet was acceptable in his own country. It was as a prophet that He proclaimed the nearness of the Kingdom. The disciples who followed Him were as a school of the prophet Jesus ; to them He was at first no more than a Rabbi and a prophet ; He was never addressed by them as " Lord " in the divine sense ; even the miracles of the feeding of multitudes made no impression of supernatural power on them (Mark 8^{19-21}). Yet continual intercourse with Jesus had its effect ; when Peter made his confession of belief, he undoubtedly implied that Jesus was more than a prophet (Mark 8^{28-29}). How much further had he gone ? Peter admitted that others had thought Him to be John the Baptist risen from the dead, or Jeremiah, or Elijah. The prevailing idea in these identifications of the populace is the thought of another world than this, for John the Baptist, Jeremiah and Elijah had all passed away. Peter's answer must at least have involved the thought of another world, but if it was to be of value he must have surpassed them. He, too, therefore, thought of a supramundane existence, but not of Sheol. It could only have been an existence with God. Further, had Peter by his answer meant no more than that Jesus was a human Messiah, he would not have gone a step beyond the belief of blind Bartimæus or of the scribes or of the crowds of Palm Sunday ; and Jesus Himself had contradicted the view that the Messiah was the son of David. That the human Messiah was in Peter's mind or in our Lord's mind when Peter made his confession is therefore impossible. The alternative is a super-human Messiah, a Being pre-existent with God but not God, a Being called by Enoch " the Son of Man " ; in fact, Jesus began to speak of Himself as the Son of Man immediately after the Confession, as if He was continuing Peter's own belief and identification and building on it (v. p. 180).

It is therefore almost conclusive that Jesus accepted Peter's answer in the sense that the Messiah was the super-human Messiah of Enoch and Daniel. The evidence of M is conclusive, for there it is stated that it could only have been a revelation of God and not of " flesh and blood " (Matthew 16[17]) ; it is further supported by the words in Mark which follow the confession. " He charged them under a penalty that they should tell no man about Him " —the same censure as Jesus laid on the demons who pro-claimed Him the Son of God, a supernatural Being with supernatural power (Mark 3[12]). Jesus, in other words, laid the Twelve under a penalty if they made it known that He was the supernatural Messiah ; that declaration He would make Himself at the right time.

For the present it was enough for Jesus that Peter had admitted He was more than human, but Jesus would not stop there. From that moment He began to give the Twelve further enlightenment and teaching to prepare them for the great paradox that the proof of Messiahship was in suffering and death, as the proof of Divinity was in the rising from the dead. Jesus began to advance beyond the teaching of Enoch and Daniel, and in going beyond it, He went back to the teaching of the second Isaiah and identified Himself with his ideal hero, the Servant who was to suffer vicariously to redeem mankind. Peter, as representative of the Twelve, had advanced from the thought of Jesus as a prophet to that of the supernatural Son of Man. He had further to go before He believed that Jesus was the Saviour of man. The meaning of the Atonement did not become clear to him till after he had suffered the horrors of betraying his Master and had received pardon and re-storation when Jesus rose from the dead. It was only after the Resurrection and Pentecost that the Apostles learned why Jesus sought death and found it on the Cross ; only then was the Messiah identified by them with the

Saviour of mankind. Jesus as the Messiah was not enough ; Jesus as the Saviour was more wonderful still. The time was yet to come when the Messiah and the Saviour was seen to be the Incarnate Son of God, not merely the supernatural Son of God. Knowledge and revelation came by degrees.

The moment chosen by Jesus to acknowledge His Messiahship was when, standing before Caiaphas, He was questioned by him (Mark 14$^{61-62}$). " Art thou the Christ, the Son of the Blessed ? " the high priest asked Him ; the form of the question is clearly framed in apocalyptic language, being based on Enoch and 4 Ezra, where the Messiah is called by God " My son." Mark, if the text is correct, says that Jesus answered " I am " ; but some Cæsarean texts give the answer as " Thou sayest that I am," which means that Jesus in admitting the Messiahship, was careful to state that the high priest's view of Messiahship was His. In either case, Jesus added, " Ye shall see the Son of man sitting at the right hand of power (*i.e.* God), and coming with the clouds of heaven." The answer is in apocalyptic language, as the question was in apocalyptic language. Jesus claimed not that the Messiah was yet to come, but that the Messiah had come once, and would come again with the clouds of heaven. Jesus claimed at least the full attributes of the superhuman Messiah, to be higher than the angels, to be pre-existent, to be next to God ; He claimed them as He stood before the high priest as the Messiah. If the apocalyptists expected the Messiah to die, He would die too, but He would come with the clouds of heaven.

The Son of Man.

This English phrase is the translation of a Greek phrase which in its turn is a literal translation of the Hebrew and Aramaic for " man." It is not the same as Ezekiel's " son of man."

There are three important references to the phrase in the literature before the New Testament.

1. Daniel (c. 160 B.C.). After a reference to the Judgment (7^{10}), the text continues, " I saw in the night visions, and, behold, there came with the clouds of heaven one like unto a son of man. . . . And there was given him dominion, and glory, and a kingdom . . . his dominion is an everlasting dominion . . ." (7^{13-14}). This supernatural figure is in human form a being " like unto a son of man " (not " like unto the Son of man," as in the A.V.). In 7^{27} this figure is identified with " the people of the saints of the Most High," that is, the glorified people of Israel, and therefore is not the Messiah or a king of David's line but the ideal Israel.

2. The Similitudes of Enoch (c. 94–64 B.C.). In these visions, given in 1 Enoch 37–71 and stated to have been seen by Enoch, we find a description of the Judgment and the Age to Come, and also of the figure of a superhuman Messiah. Enoch is carried into heaven and sees the " Lord of Spirits," also called the " Head of Days " who is the Almighty ; he sees also the Son of Man who was created before the sun and stars and " chosen and hidden " before the Lord of Spirits. This " Elect one " stands before the Lord of Spirits. Both the Lord of Spirits and the Son of Man will suddenly appear to execute judgment. The Earth and Sheol will give back their dead ; the risen dead and men and angels will be judged by the Son of Man, to whom judgment is committed. The righteous will be blessed, the fallen angels will be cast into a fiery furnace, the wicked will be destroyed. Heaven and earth will be transformed, the righteous will be clothed with garments of life which shall not grow old, and they will become angels in heaven and dwell for ever with the Son of Man. We notice that Daniel's one " like unto a son of man " has in Enoch become a heavenly being.

The Elect One is also called the Anointed or " The Messiah." He is not God, but acts as judge for Him. He is pre-existent, though hidden from the beginning. He is a superhuman being and cannot therefore be a scion of the house of David. In one verse the text reads, " You are the Son of Man " in words addressed to Enoch, thereby implying that Enoch is the Son of Man, but this is probably a scribal error for the correct text, " This is the Son of Man."

The Messiah intervenes when the mighty and the Kings possess the earth, they who cast down the righteous, and shed their blood and also deny the Lord of Spirits. These mighty ones have been identified with the Sadducees and the native rulers who were oppressing the godly Israelites and putting them to death.

3. 4 Ezra or the Second Book of Esdras (c. A.D. 65–70), which though written after the time of Christ gives us information of views held in His days. The writer has a dream of a Son of man coming out of the sea, appearing with the clouds of heaven and graving for himself a great mountain to which he flies. Against him comes a great multitude whom he destroys with a flood of fire and flaming breath out of his mouth ; then comes a second huge multitude with peaceable intent. The dreamer awakes and God gives him the interpretation of his dream. The man ascending out of the sea is " My Son " who is to be a deliverer and a judge, *i.e.* the Messiah, and the peaceable multitude is the Ten Tribes.

In the Gospels, the phrase is always used by Christ and is never used by the disciples. Only twice is it found in Mark before Peter's Confession ; in 2^{10} where Jesus says, " But that ye may know that the Son of man hath power on earth to forgive sins," and in 2^{28} where He says, " So that the Son of man is lord even of the sabbath," and in both the sense is that of " a man," not particularly the

Son of Man (*v.* p. 172). All the other instances in Mark appear after Peter's Confession and in connexions which refer either (*a*) to the Passion or (*b*) to the Parousia, that is, the Appearance.

(*a*) 8[31].   The Son of man must suffer many things.

9[9].   Save when the Son of man should have risen again from the dead.

9[12].   How it is written of the Son of man, that he should suffer many things.

9[31].   The Son of man is delivered up into the hands of men.

10[33]. The Son of man shall be delivered unto the chief priests and the scribes.

10[45]. For verily the Son of man came not to be ministered unto, but to minister, and to give his life a ransom for many.

14[21]. For the Son of man goeth, even as it is written of him : but woe unto that man through whom the Son of man is betrayed.

14[41]. Behold, the Son of man is betrayed into the hands of sinners.

(*b*) 8[38].   For whosoever shall be ashamed of me and of my words . . . the Son of man also shall be ashamed of him, when he cometh in the glory of his Father with the holy angels.

13[26]. And then shall they see the Son of man coming in clouds with great power and glory.

14[62]. And Jesus said, I am : and ye shall see the Son of man sitting at the right hand of power, and coming with the clouds of heaven.

All but one of these eleven sayings were spoken to the Apostles, the last being spoken to the high priest.

In Q the phrase occurs eleven times ; six of these are apocalyptic, and these are all spoken to the disciples.

Luke 12⁸. Every one who shall confess me before men, him shall the Son of man also confess before the angels of God.

12⁴⁰. Be ye also ready : for in an hour that ye think not the Son of man cometh.

17²². The days will come, when ye shall desire to see one of the days of the Son of man, and ye shall not see it.

17²⁴. So shall the Son of man be in his day.

17²⁶. So shall it be also in the days of the Son of man.

17³⁰. After the same manner shall it be in the day that the Son of man is revealed.

In the other five instances, which are not apocalyptic, the meaning of the phrase may be either " a man " or " I."

Luke 12¹⁰. (= a man) And every one who shall speak a word against the Son of man, it shall be forgiven him . . . (see p. 138).

6²². (= I) Blessed are ye, when men shall hate you . . . for the Son of man's sake.

7³⁴. (= I) The Son of man is come eating and drinking ; and ye say, Behold, a gluttonous man, and a wine-bibber.

9⁵⁸. (= I) But the Son of man hath not where to lay his head.

11³⁰. (= I) For even as Jonah became a sign unto the Ninevites, so shall also the Son of man be to this generation.

There is no indication in Q where Peter's Confession may be placed ; we have no guide to the time when any of these sayings may have been spoken.

The tendency to replace Christ's " I " by " the Son of man " is to be seen in the treatment of Mark by Matthew.

Mark 8²⁷. Who do men say that I am ?

Matthew 16[13].   Who do men say that the Son of man is ?

In M, the phrase " the Son of man " appears twice in sayings which can be placed before Peter's Confession ; the first is in the mission address to the Twelve, " Ye shall not have gone through the cities of Israel before the Son of man come," where the meaning is " I " (see p. 82). The second is in the saying where Jonah is the sign of the burial of Jesus (Matthew 12[40]) ; here it is more than probable that the verse is a scribal addition. Two instances also occur in the Wheat and the Tares, an apocalyptic parable, but the occasion of its being spoken is uncertain (Matthew 13) ; here in verse 31 the meaning is " I " and in verse 41 it refers to the future. Other instances are found in Matthew 19[28] ; 24[30] ; 25[31] ; 26[2].

In L the phrase occurs in the following :

Luke 18[8].   Howbeit when the Son of man cometh, shall he find faith on the earth ?

19[10].   For the Son of man came to seek and to save that which was lost.

22[48].   But Jesus said unto him, Judas, betrayest thou the Son of man with a kiss ?

22[69].   But from henceforth shall the Son of man be seated at the right hand of the power of God.

24[6-7].   Remember how he spake unto you when he was yet in Galilee, saying that the Son of man must be delivered up. . . .

Of these, 18[8] and 22[69] are apocalyptic, 19[10] has the meaning " I " ; and the remaining two refer to the Passion. But the important point to be noticed is that in L, which, like Mark, contains narrative, the phrase is only used after Peter's Confession.

The weight of the evidence is in favour of the phrase being used by Jesus alone, of its being used by Him after Peter's Confession, and always used with reference to the Passion and the Parousia.

Though Jesus used the phrase " The Son of Man," He did not publicly identify Himself with the Son of Man until His appearance before the High Priest. He meant to keep the Messianic secret private ; to declare Himself the Son of Man before the time was ripe would have been contrary to His plan to wait for the suitable occasion for the declaration which must, He felt, be made in the Holy City. Hence, when Peter made his Confession, Jesus accepted it, but forbade publication under a penalty. The Apostles evidently understood the request, for they kept the saying secret until after the Resurrection, though they questioned, as within their rights and not against Christ's charge, not whether Christ was the Messiah in spite of His prediction of suffering and death, but what the rising again from the dead should mean (Mark 9^{9-10}). Thus, from the time of Peter's Confession, the Apostles knew He was the Son of Man in the Enochian sense, and after His Resurrection He was openly declared by them to have been so (Acts 7^{56}). It is possible, and probably certain, that in writing the Gospels, the phrase was occasionally inserted where Jesus used the personal pronoun " I " in speaking to the general public, as in the four cases mentioned in Q and one both in L and in M. This suggestion is borne out by the fact that in every instance in Mark where the phrase definitely is " the Son of Man " it was spoken to the disciples, and to them only, until He declared Himself before the High Priest (Mark 14^{62}). Mark's careful use of the phrase is in keeping with Christ's intention ; in two instances only is the Aramaic capable of meaning " a man " ($=$ I), and these were spoken in the presence of the public. In every other single instance except 14^{62} the phrase was spoken to the disciples and them alone, and in all these instances He used " the Son of Man." It is only to be expected that the disciples would not use the phrase before the Resurrection ; they were strict in carrying out the charge of Jesus to keep silent until He rose from the dead.

CHAPTER XII

OUTLINE OF THE LIFE OF CHRIST

Two thousand years ago the Jews were in great expectation that there was a Golden Age coming in the future which would restore to them on this earth the past glories of their race. For centuries past their prophets had declared its advent and had spoken of a Deliverer ; apocalyptists had given this Deliverer the title of the Messiah, who by some of them, as by the prophets, was declared to be a prince of the house of David, and by others to be a supernatural being, called " the Elect One " or " The Son of Man," and by one writer said to have been called by God " His Son."

In the fifteenth year of the reign of Tiberius Cæsar " came the word of the Lord " unto John, the son of Zacharias, a priest. It was the call of John to the work of a prophet. This revival of prophecy meant a fresh announcement of the near approach of the Golden Age or Good Time coming. The call was accepted by John, who was known as the Baptiser and also as the Fore-runner. John's preaching was a summons to preparation for the day of the Lord ; the people were called to repent or turn from their evil ways, and as a sign of this conversion to be washed in water. John proclaimed that there was coming a Mightier One than himself, and He would baptize with fire ; this coming would be to judgment, and therefore the multitudes must bring forth worthy fruit, else the tree would be hewn down and cast into the fire. Amongst those who came to hear John was Jesus, a carpenter of Nazareth.

On Jesus John made an overwhelming impression. He recognised that no one greater than John had yet been born of woman ; and probably in response to the preaching of John, He accepted baptism at his hands, not as a sign of repentance but in order to fulfil all righteousness. The baptism was a critical event to Jesus, for it was then revealed to Him that He was the Son of God, supernatural in being and in power ; this revelation was in line with the filial consciousness which had been with Him at least as early as His visit to the Temple at the age of twelve, when He spoke of God as " my Father." This revelation, according to the methods of the Rabbis, is described in Mark as the voice of God speaking to Jesus and as the Spirit or essence of God descending on Jesus in the form of a dove. The Baptism was a wondrous subjective experience ; so intense was it that He was compelled to go into retirement and face the fact and meaning of the revelation, that though He was the Son of God and therefore the Messiah, who was to represent God on earth, He was to be called to suffering (*cf.* Isaiah 42¹). How was He to act in order to win Jewish acceptance of His Messiahship ?

In the wilderness He considered what He should do, knowing Himself to be the Son of God and to possess supernatural powers. It was borne in on Him, as revealed to us by the first temptation, that His first step was to leave His family and trust His Father for the means of sustenance ; further, He decided that He must not encourage any belief in the human Messiah who was to play the part of a warrior-deliverer ; and lastly, that the Messiahship, as He meant to live it, would not be accepted by the ecclesiastical authorities. The disclosure of His being the Messiah must not be made by Him ; He would act in such ways as to enable men to draw the conclusion for themselves.

After His return from the wilderness Jesus waited for the opportunity to begin His ministry ; it was not idle waiting.

In Judæa and in Samaria, according to John and L, He spent some time manifesting His power and then He journeyed north. When He was in Galilee news reached Him of the imprisonment of John. This gave Him his opportunity, and He came forth preaching His good news or gospel. This good news was not only that the long-desired Kingdom was coming—that had been proclaimed many a time and oft by the prophets of old—but that the Kingdom was at hand. The good news was the near approach of the Kingdom of God ; it was imminent ; it was soon to be established on earth. Not Nazareth, where He had been brought up and lived, but Capernaum was His headquarters ; and from it He preached saying, " The Kingdom of God is at hand ; repent and believe in the good news." The Jewish nation was roused ; God had at last visited His people and remembered His covenant ; God was about to restore the glories of the reign of David and give them a blessed and glorious future. The Golden Age was about to dawn.

Thus began the ministry, that is the life of service, of Jesus. Of the sequence of its external history we know little, but there are clear developments in its progress ; it is not until we reach the last stages of the final journey to Jerusalem and the Passion that we get good chronological detail. These stages of development are :

1. His extreme popularity amongst the masses who, misled by their own conception of what the Kingdom implied, hailed Him as a prophet mighty in deed and word.

2. The gradual formation of a body of disciples from whom He chose Twelve who were sent forth to carry the good news to people He could not reach.

3. The unsympathetic reception given Him by the leaders of religious thought, which drove Him from the synagogue and compelled Him to preach by the sea and in the open country, until, owing to Herod's suspicion of His motives,

He had to leave Galilee, which was within Herod's jurisdiction.

4. The acceptance of Jesus as the Messiah by Peter,
followed by the Transfiguration.

None of our Gospels gives us a biography of Jesus;
the interest of the writers lay not in the journeys and travels
of Jesus but in Himself. Their Gospels and records were
not written to give a chronological history, but to reveal
Him to their readers. Their interest was centred wholly
in Him and in a secondary sense on the Apostles. They
saw that in His ministry there were certain critical events,
and they were the turning-points of the history; these
events were the Baptism of Jesus, the choice of the Twelve,
Peter's Confession, the Transfiguration, the Death and the
Resurrection of Jesus. Details of the ministry given by
the writers of the Gospels were details to illuminate these
events. Hence any sketch of our Lord's ministry can only
be the emphasising of these events.

The synagogue in Capernaum witnessed the first effects
of the power of Jesus (Mark 1^{21-28}). These were the recognition of the authority with which He spoke and of
His power to heal. The authority astonished His hearers,
for He taught without recourse to the opinions and teachings
of Rabbis, as was the method of scribes; He spoke as a Rabbi
of independent views; He spoke as One who knew what
was right. As to His power of healing there could be no
doubt; the man in the synagogue was healed and the
insanity cured instantaneously by the spoken word. The
Personality of Jesus is what Mark desires to portray in
his description of the scene. The fame of Jesus spread;
crowds flocked to hear Him; crowds came to be cured of
Him. He was one day compelled to seek retirement, and
when His first disciples found Him the next morning they
found Him at prayer (Mark 1^{35}). Jesus returned from this
retreat and once again the scenes were repeated; driven out

of the synagogue, He ceased His mission there, and only once did He enter it again, and that was in Nazareth· henceforth, from a boat and in a house (both probably Simon's) and in the open country, He taught and preached and healed until He found Himself in His own town of Nazareth. But He was received without honour ; the inhabitants resented the fact that He had made Capernaum and not Nazareth the centre of His work. Besides, rumours had reached them that He was out of His mind ; His own folk had actually tried to reach Him and to induce Him to return, but had met with failure. Hence His visit was doomed to disappointment. The inhabitants were astonished at His wisdom, but was He not known to them as a carpenter ? They had heard of the wonderful works that " his hands performed," the hands that had done a joiner's work. He did use these hands in Nazareth to heal a few sick folk, but nothing mighty was done ; the people lacked faith and they were repelled by Him (Mark 6^{1-6} ; Luke 4^{16-30}).

The ministry was continued in Galilee ; crowds kept flocking to hear Him, but they were unresponsive. Jesus saw that they sought Him for what they could get from Him, not for Himself. But whilst Jesus was a popular idol, the Jewish leaders, and the Pharisees and the scribes, had from the early stages of the ministry formed an opposition. Jealous of their law and its traditions, they found Him a transgressor of the law even to breaking the Sabbath ; thinking themselves to be the favoured of God, they found Him claiming the attributes of God, claiming to be closer to God than any human being, and even claiming powers such as the power to forgive sins, which they thought belonged to God alone. They acknowledged His power to heal and to cast out devils, but they did not scruple to assert that He was in league with the prince of the devils. They recognised in Him a Rabbi, but they observed with intolerance that He consorted with tax-gatherers and other

outcasts. Jew though He was, He did not observe the fasts and they therefore called Him a glutton and a wine-bibber. To strengthen their hands in opposition they eventually sought the help of Herod's own party-men in the hope that in a province ruled by Herod they might check His popularity and drive Him out of Galilee. They would not persecute Jesus, but they would stand apart from Him as one who was unworthy of their patronage. Jesus was disappointed at the seeming failure of His mission. He saw His own nation deaf to His appeals and foresaw the time when the Gentiles would get the blessings which His own people refused, and that these Gentiles would come from all points of the compass to enter the Kingdom.

Mark makes it clear that Jesus did not desire to declare Himself openly as the Messiah. Q, in its account of the Temptation, implies the same. Thus He could not have publicly applied to Himself any Messianic title till He had actually revealed Himself. His main teaching at first was about the Kingdom and its imminence. It was to Him much more than a mere abstraction; it was a concrete reality. Its inauguration could not take place before a community existed over whom the sovereignty of God could be exercised; it was inaugurated when, in the choice of the Twelve, the community came into being. Further, this Kingdom on earth was by Jesus linked with the Kingdom to come in the future; the link was Himself. He was the Messiah now, the Messiah of the Kingdom here, but He was also the Messiah who would one day come in the clouds of heaven. Through Him the Good Time here and the Age to Come in the hereafter were united. Jesus preached no *interim ethic* therefore, no ethic for the interval; He did not preach that because He was expecting the end of the world to come soon nothing mattered but preparation for the approaching end. His coming was not merely the coming of Himself as Messiah after He had been

received into heaven. He was no such dreamer, no such visionary, for He was the Messiah now in His days on earth, the Founder of the Church. The ethic He preached was an ethic of eternal life, but this eternal life was life in the Kingdom now, to be consummated in the Kingdom of the blessed Hereafter.

For about a year, from one spring to the next, Jesus continued His ministry. In the early part of this year He had chosen from amongst His followers twelve men ; later He gave them a charge and sent them out with His own Gospel message, " The Kingdom of heaven is at hand." His orders were that they should confine their tour to the cities of Israel, for they were untrained men and had not yet recognised Him as the Messiah. This ministry in Galilee was interrupted by a visit through Samaria to Jerusalem ; it probably took place during the mission of the Twelve who, said Jesus, would not have gone through the cities of Israel before He came.

When spring had come again, about May, Jesus met His disciples on their return from their mission and took them into retreat to a desert place near Bethsaida, that is the country just beyond the cultivated land. But a large crowd, numbering thousands, followed Him. He fed them and they in turn desired to make Him King. Jesus would not encourage this spirit of militarism ; the idea was in itself dangerous, and to add to its danger Herod was inquiring about Jesus. The Tetrarch had just put John the Baptist to death and it was clear to Jesus that his own life was in danger. It was time for Him to leave Galilee. He therefore went on a long tour through Tyre and Sidon and the Decapolis and ultimately reached Cæsarea Philippi about the time of the Feast of Tabernacles (September).

Eighteen months had passed from the beginning of the ministry in Galilee when the party reached Cæsarea Philippi. There Jesus put the Twelve to the test. What had their

experience taught them ? Did they think He was only a Rabbi and a prophet as the masses held Him to be ? " Who do you say I am ? " He asked them, and Simon answered, " Thou art the Messiah." At this point probably were uttered those great words found in Q. " I thank thee, O Father, Lord of heaven and earth, that thou didst hide these things from the wise and understanding, and didst reveal them unto babes " (Luke 10^{21-22}). To mark the occasion and the supreme importance of the Confession, Jesus gave to Simon not only a new name, Peter, but also a new position as leader of the community with power to bind and to loose ; to the community He gave a new name, the Ecclesia, the Church. The confession meant that Peter had gone beyond the popular expectation of a Messiah who was merely human, the son of David, the Deliverer. Peter had raised Jesus from a human to a supernatural plane, a Being above the angels but not God (see p. 163 f.). The first epoch in the training of the Twelve ended with this confession, and with it the whole tenour of the teaching of Jesus changed. Henceforth Jesus spoke less of the Kingdom, but more of Himself. His rejection by the leaders and people had convinced Him that His hope for the future growth of the Kingdom rested on the Twelve and that His duty was to fit them for the task. " Fear not, little flock," He said to them by way of encouragement, " it is my Father's good pleasure to give you the Kingdom " (Q, Luke 12^{32}). He therefore concentrated on the Twelve. But in His teaching He does not use the title " The Messiah " but the title " The Son of Man." The use of this new title is significant, for Peter had acknowledged Jesus as " the Messiah." It strengthens our argument that Peter, when he made his confession, had in mind a supernatural Messiah and not a human Messiah, and that Jesus accepted it in that sense and was therefore able to use the title " the Son of Man," which was a supernatural designation.

Six days later came the Transfiguration. Once again, as at the Baptism, the Divine Voice was heard. According to Luke, the Transfiguration was a subjective experience which took place when Jesus was at prayer ; according to Mark the vision was seen by three chosen Apostles. Luke also connects the Transfiguration with the Passion, for he says that Moses and Elias spake with Jesus of the approaching decease. Much in the narrative is symbolic, but the experience, whether subjective or objective, was real. Guided by the context of sayings and the events that followed, we may with some confidence infer that the voice of God meant the Divine approval of our Lord's intention to face death, and the communication of His intention to the three Apostles ; that the Transfiguration was the identification of Christ with the Suffering Servant of prophecy, an identification that was revealed to the three Apostles for the first time ; that the Transfiguration was the setting of the seal on the revelation which came to Jesus at the Baptism. The time was the Feast of Tabernacles, and on the mount Peter desired to build three booths, possibly to observe it. The Transfiguration was followed by the Apostles asking a question about the coming of Elijah—a question which recalls that put by John the Baptist when in prison. Jesus answered that John and not He was Elijah who was to come, that John had been put to death, and that it was written that the Son of Man must suffer too and be set at naught.

From the mount Jesus journeyed to Galilee, visited Capernaum, and then set forth on His last journey to Jerusalem to keep the Feast of the Passover. His route lay through trans-Jordania (Mark 10^1), and when He was once more in Herod's domain the Pharisees questioned Him to get His views on divorce and adultery, an obvious trap to enable them to lay a charge before Herod. Of the incidents of this journey Mark gives us the Blessing of

Children, the Rich Young Ruler, and the Ambition of James and John, who sought places of honour when Jesus came in His glory.

Jesus had now to advance the training of the Twelve a stage further on the lines of the revelation at the Transfiguration. He therefore continued to impress on them that the Son of Man must suffer and die ; that in fact He was more than the Messiah ; He was the Saviour who must die to win salvation. It was hard teaching. With tragedy awaiting their Master, it does not surprise us to read that the disciples were awe-stricken and afraid as they journeyed to the Holy City (Mark 10^{32}) ; they were overcome by the natural emotions of awe and reverence. The journey was slow, but the teaching was more advanced and more personal. " The Son of man came not to be ministered unto but to give his life a ransom for many." We see clearly that thoughts of the Suffering Servant were constantly in His mind, but the minds of the Twelve saw it not till after His rising from the dead ; the blending of the supernatural with the natural was to them difficult. But it was part of the teaching of Jesus to lead them on to see in Him one who was greater than the Messiah, and greater than the Saviour—one who was as fully Divine as He was fully human. Through Jericho Jesus made His way to Jerusalem. He entered the city amidst scenes of enthusiasm, visited the Temple, and with the Twelve spent the night in Bethany. According to Mark, Jesus cleansed the Temple on the Monday, according to Matthew and L, on the day of His entry into the city. The day is immaterial, but not so the effect of the cleansing. " The chief priests and the scribes heard of it and sought how they might destroy him."

On the second day after the entry Jesus was again in the Temple, teaching. The ecclesiastical authorities, much concerned over the cleansing and afraid of the multitude,

went warily on their intention to destroy Him.   Questioned as to His authority for His action in the Temple, He answered them in the Rabbinic manner by asking them a question in His turn, and then spake the parable of the Vineyard against them, as they perceived.   Questioned as to paying tribute by the Pharisees and Herod's party-men, who appear again on the scene (Mark 3^6), He replied that they should render to Cæsar the things which were Cæsar's ; this answer lost Him the support of the multitudes, who were nationalists.   Matthew interpreted the effect aright. " They marvelled, and left him, and went their way." Questioned by the Sadducees, He replied that their views were contrary to Scripture ; they would therefore not give Him any support in the Sanhedrin (*cf*. Acts $23^{6\ ff.}$).   Finally, the religious teachers were aggrieved when Jesus taught that their expectation of a human Deliverer was wrong. By the end of the day, Jesus had only His disciples left ; they stood alone with their Leader, and of that band one turned traitor.   Judas determined to sell His master.

That night Jesus and His party returned to Bethany ; the end was approaching, and the final words had to be spoken.   Two days of intimate intercourse followed ; Jesus had been asked on the way to Bethany what He had meant when He said that the huge stones of the Temple would soon be a ruin.   So when they reached Bethany, He gave four favoured disciples a detailed exposition of the end of Jerusalem.   Traces of an intimate converse may be seen in the Apocalypse of Mark 13.   Jesus still kept the thoughts of the Twelve on a supernatural plane, still using the language of Enoch and Daniel.   The Messiah will die, as the apocalyptists taught, but they will see the Son of man coming in clouds with great power and glory.   Of that day knoweth no man but the Father.   " Watch therefore," and again, " Watch."   Whilst in seclusion, a woman's act of devotion was to Him symbolic ; she came to Jesus with a valuable

cruse of ointment, broke it, and poured the contents on His head. " She hath anointed my body aforehand for the burying," said Jesus. As for this act, He continued, it would be recounted all the world over wheresoever the Gospel would be preached. On the eve of His death, Jesus knew that the Gospel would be world-wide. Then Judas went unto the chief priests and for the equivalent of £5 of our money sold His Master.

The high priests had decided to destroy Jesus, but not on the feast day. The Passover that year, says Mark, coincided with the Sabbath, and if Jesus was to die, His death, said the high priest, must take place before the Sabbath, that is, before the Passover was eaten. Thursday had come when Jesus decided to have a last meal with His Apostles. That morning He sent two of them who were to carry out arrangements already made by Jesus with a householder in the city. All the Gospels agree that the supper took place on the Thursday, but they differ whether the Passover was observed by the Jews on the Thursday or the Friday. Probably Jesus had a meal anticipatory of the Passover, for no lamb was eaten at it. He anticipated the feast on the lamb, but He fed the eleven on bread and wine, which He declared was His Body and Blood. Mark does not call the supper the Passover ; he says that the disciples made ready the Passover. Jesus did not say the supper was the Passover, but He did say that He had desired to eat it—but it was not to be. Judas the betrayer had left the room where the supper was eaten.

After supper Jesus washed the feet of the disciples and delivered His final message, meditated on and interpreted by John before it was written down in his Gospel. Thence they went to Gethsemane, and there He prayed. He did not know how He would die ; never once, according to Mark, had the word " crucified " been used by Him in His teaching. He knew He would suffer, and in the Garden

He prayed that the cup would pass from Him. He was alone as He prayed, forsaken by men and deserted. Was this desertion symbolic? Was he forsaken by God? He fought down the temptation to believe that God was forsaking Him and repressed the thought. The victory here is represented in the same language as the victory in the wilderness; temptation came to Him here as in the wilderness; in both, we are told that angels attended Him, a symbolism of victory achieved over temptation from the evil one. The mental agony of the temptation in the Garden was so great that the sweat poured down as if drops of blood.

From the Garden He was taken to trial, first before the Sanhedrin and then before Pilate. Both trials were necessary if Jesus was to be put to death. Of the exact sequence of the incidents of these two trials we are uncertain. He was taken first to Annas, the power behind the Sanhedrin, for a preliminary inquiry, but He claimed His right to legal trial with witnesses produced to substantiate any charge. Therefore, early on the Friday morning He was formally tried before Caiaphas, the High Priest. Evidence produced against the prisoner was unsatisfactory, and, as He would not commit Himself, the judge resorted to an adjuration. This was the moment for the public avowal of the Messiahship. Jesus knew it would mean conviction, but He was prepared. The question put to Him was framed in language which Jesus would understand; there was no ambiguity in it. Jesus was asked whether He claimed to be the supernatural Messiah whom God had called His Son. " Art thou the Christ, the Son of the Blessed? " The reply was direct and clear, " I am "; and to prevent any misunderstanding Jesus continued to use apocalyptic language, which recalled the visions of Enoch and Daniel: " Ye shall see the Son of man sitting at the right hand of power and coming with the clouds of heaven." This was

blasphemy; to have claimed to be the human Messiah who would restore the nation's political glories could not possibly be blasphemy. On this Confession of Jesus, Caiaphas and the members of the Hebrew court convicted Him and sent Him for trial before Pilate the Roman Governor, who alone could pass sentence of death. The initial stages of this Roman trial in L read true; they fit in with the correct Roman procedure as revealed in the life of Paul when he was accused before Gallio and Festus. "What accusation bring ye against this man?" began Pilate. At once there began a conflict between the Roman and the Jews; the voice of the Jews prevailed. Jesus was charged with treason, a correct charge against anyone claiming to be a human Messiah; Jewish national hopes if successful would follow the destruction of the Roman power. Pilate therefore interviewed Jesus privately and asked Him whether He was a King, and Jesus answered that His Kingdom was not of this world and he had no body of men under arms. Pilate at once went out to the crowd and pronounced Jesus innocent; further cries were heard and Galilee was mentioned. Jesus therefore was hurried to Herod, who, too, found no fault in Him. The crowd became restive, and Pilate offered them a choice, Jesus the King or Jesus Barabbas. The crowd chose Barabbas, and for the first time Jesus heard of the fate intended for Him, "Crucify Him." And this was followed by the charge on which the Hebrew court had convicted Him of blasphemy. Jesus, they said, claimed to be the Son of God. Once again Pilate questioned Jesus, but by now the mob had got the measure of the Governor. They would report him to Cæsar, they cried out. Pilate yielded, and about 9 a.m. that Friday morning Jesus was crucified.

On the Cross, Jesus, according to Mark, spoke one word with a great cry after a long silence. It was just before He died. The fear and doubt repressed in the temptation in

the Garden after a severe mental struggle broke forth, for Jesus was losing consciousness. Psychology here helps us to grasp the meaning of the cry of dereliction. It was not a cry of despair, but it was the welling out from the un-conscious of the thoughts which He had refused to harbour and encourage. The cry reveals not defeat but victory, victory gained at Gethsemane, victory symbolised in L by the appearance of an angel " strengthening him." God never forsakes any human soul ; to attribute such a char-acter to God would be to stultify the teaching of Jesus. Man forsakes God, but God does not forsake man.

The death of Jesus was followed by His burial. But the life of Jesus did not end there. Two days later He was seen alive and gave many " proofs " of His being alive ; of these a sound tradition is preserved in 1 Cor. 15^{3-8}, the earliest record we possess. The Resurrection is a fact of history ; the witness to it is the existence of the Church, the forgiveness of Peter and his changed life, the conversion of James the Lord's brother, the changed life of Saul of Tarsus ; the Acts of the Apostles could not have been written as the sequel to the story of a dead Christ. Mark, Q, L and M add their witness to the fact of the Resurrection.

The Gospel of Jesus Christ is to us the good news of Jesus who went about doing good, of Jesus who was more than a prophet mighty in deed and word, more than the Messiah, more than a Saviour. To Thomas and to those who believe as he did, though they have not seen Him in the days of His flesh, Jesus is their God and their Lord.

THE TEXT OF Q

The Preaching of John the Baptist

7. He said therefore to the multitudes that went out to be baptized of him, Ye offspring of vipers, who warned you to flee from the wrath to come ? 8. Bring forth therefore fruits worthy of repentance, and begin not to say within yourselves, We have Abraham to our father : for I say unto you, that God is able of these stones to raise up children unto Abraham. 9. And even now is the axe also laid unto the root of the trees : every tree therefore that bringeth not forth good fruit is hewn down, and cast into the fire.

3^{16-17} *John's Saying about the Mighty One*

16. John answered, saying unto them all, I indeed baptize you with water ; but there cometh he that is mightier than I, the latchet of whose shoes I am not worthy to unloose : he shall baptize you with the Holy Ghost and *with* fire : 17. whose fan is in his hand, throughly to cleanse his threshing-floor, and to gather the wheat into his garner ; but the chaff he will burn up with unquenchable fire.

4^{3-12} *The Temptation of Jesus*

3. And the devil said unto him, If thou art the Son of God, command this stone that it become bread. 4. And Jesus answered unto him, It is written, Man shall not live by bread alone. 5. And he led him up, and shewed him all the kingdoms of the world in a moment of time. 6. And the devil said unto him, To thee will I give all this authority, and the glory of them : for it hath been delivered unto me ; and to whomsoever I will I give it. 7. If thou therefore wilt worship before me, it shall all be thine. 8. And Jesus answered and said unto him, It is written, Thou shalt worship the Lord thy God, and him only shalt thou serve. 9.

And he led him to Jerusalem, and set him on the pinnacle of the temple, and said unto him, If thou art the Son of God, cast thyself down from hence : 10. for it is written,

> He shall give his angels charge concerning thee,
> to guard thee :

11. and,

> On their hands they shall bear thee up,
> Lest haply thou dash thy foot against a stone.

12. And Jesus answering said unto him, It is said, Thou shall not tempt the Lord thy God.

6²⁰⁻⁴⁹   *The Sermon on the Plain*

20. And he lifted up his eyes on his disciples, and said, Blessed *are* ye poor : for yours is the kingdom of God. 21. Blessed *are* ye that hunger now : for ye shall be filled. Blessed *are* ye that weep now : for ye shall laugh. 22. Blessed are ye, when men shall hate you, and when they shall separate you *from their company*, and reproach you, and cast out your name as evil, for the Son of man's sake. 23. Rejoice in that day, and leap *for joy :* for behold, your reward is great in heaven : for in the same manner did their fathers unto the prophets. 24. But woe unto you that are rich ! for ye have received your consolation. 25. Woe unto you, ye that are full now ! for ye shall hunger. Woe *unto you*, ye that laugh now ! for ye shall mourn and weep. 26. Woe *unto you*, when all men shall speak well of you ! for in the same manner did their fathers to the false prophets.

27. But I say unto you which hear, Love your enemies, do good to them that hate you, 28. bless them that curse you, pray for them that despitefully use you. 29. To him that smiteth thee on the *one* cheek offer also the other ; and from him that taketh away thy cloke withhold not thy coat also. 30. Give to every one that asketh thee ; and of him that taketh away thy goods ask them not again. 31. And as ye would that men should do to you, do ye also to them likewise. 32. And if ye love them that love you, what thank have ye ? for even sinners love those that love them. 33. And if ye do good to them that do good to you, what thank have ye ? for even sinners do the same. 34. And if ye lend to them of whom ye hope to receive, what thank have ye ? even sinners lend to sinners, to receive again as much. 35. But love your enemies, and do *them* good, and lend, never

despairing ; and your reward shall be great, and ye shall be sons of the Most High : for he is kind toward the unthankful and evil. 36. Be ye merciful, even as your Father is merciful. 37. And judge not, and ye shall not be judged : and condemn not, and ye shall not be condemned : release, and ye shall be released : 38. give, and it shall be given unto you ; good measure, pressed down, shaken together, running over, shall they give into your bosom. For with what measure ye mete it shall be measured to you again.

39. And he spake also a parable unto them, Can the blind guide the blind ? shall they not both fall into a pit ? 40. The disciple is not above his master : but every one when he is perfected shall be as his master. 41. And why beholdest thou the mote that is in thy brother's eye, but considerest not the beam that is in thine own eye ? 42. Or how canst thou say to thy brother, Brother, let me cast out the mote that is in thine eye, when thou thyself beholdest not the beam that is in thine own eye ? Thou hypocrite, cast out first the beam out of thine own eye, and then shalt thou see clearly to cast out the mote that is in thy brother's eye. 43. For there is no good tree that bringeth forth corrupt fruit ; nor again a corrupt tree that bringeth forth good fruit. 44. For each tree is known by its own fruit. For of thorns men do not gather figs, nor of a bramble bush gather they grapes. 45. The good man out of the good treasure of his heart bringeth forth that which is good ; and the evil *man* out of the evil *treasure* bringeth forth that which is evil : for out of the abundance of the heart his mouth speaketh.

46. And why call ye me, Lord, Lord, and do not the things which I say ? 47. Every one that cometh unto me, and heareth my words, and doeth them, I will shew you to whom he is like : 48. he is like a man building a house, who digged and went deep, and laid a foundation upon the rock : and when a flood arose, the stream brake against that house, and could not shake it : because it had been well builded. 49. But he that heareth, and doeth not, is like a man that built a house upon the earth without a foundation ; against which the stream brake, and straightway it fell in ; and the ruin of that house was great.

7^{6b-9} *The Centurion's Faith*

6. The centurion sent friends to him, saying unto him, Lord, trouble not thyself : for I am not worthy that thou shouldest come under my roof : 7. wherefore neither thought I myself

worthy to come unto thee : but say the word, and my servant shall be healed. 8. For I also am a man set under authority, having under myself soldiers : and I say to this one, Go, and he goeth ; and to another, Come, and he cometh ; and to my servant, Do this, and he doeth it. 9. And when Jesus heard these things, he marvelled at him, and turned and said unto the multitude that followed him, I say unto you, I have not found so great faith, no, not in Israel.

7¹⁸⁻²³   *The Message of John the Baptist and our Lord's Reply*

18. And the disciples of John told him of all these things. 19. And John calling unto him two of his disciples sent them to the Lord, saying, Art thou he that cometh, or look we for another ? 20. And when the men were come unto him, they said, John the Baptist hath sent us unto thee, saying, Art thou he that cometh, or look we for another ? 21. In that hour he cured many of diseases and plagues and evil spirits ; and on many that were blind he bestowed sight. 22. And he answered and said unto them, Go your way, and tell John what things ye have seen and heard ; the blind receive their sight, the lame walk, the lepers are cleansed, and the deaf hear, the dead are raised up, the poor have good tidings preached to them. 23. And blessed is he, whosoever shall find none occasion of stumbling in me.

7²⁴⁻²⁸   *Saying of Jesus regarding John*

24. And when the messengers of John were departed, he began to say unto the multitudes concerning John, What went ye out into the wilderness to behold ? a reed shaken with the wind ? 25. But what went ye out to see ? a man clothed in soft raiment ? Behold, they which are gorgeously apparelled, and live delicately, are in king's courts. 26. But what went ye out to see ? a prophet ? Yea, I say unto you, and much more than a prophet. 27. This is he of whom it is written,

> Behold, I send my messenger before thy face,
> Who shall prepare thy way before thee.

28. I say unto you, Among them that are born of women there is none greater than John : yet he that is but little in the Kingdom of God is greater than he.

7³¹⁻³⁵   *On Children at Play*

31. Whereunto then shall I liken the men of this generation,
and to what are they like ?   32. They are like unto children that
sit in the marketplace, and call one to another ; which say, We
piped unto you, and ye did not dance ; we wailed, and ye did not
weep.   33. For John the Baptist is come eating no bread nor
drinking wine ; and ye say, He hath a devil.   34. The Son of
man is come eating and drinking ; and ye say, Behold, a gluttonous
man, and a winebibber, a friend of publicans and sinners ! 35. And
wisdom is justified of all her children.

9⁵⁷⁻⁶²   *On Candidates for Discipleship*

57. And as they went in the way, a certain man said unto him,
I will follow thee whithersoever thou goest.   58. And Jesus said
unto him, The foxes have holes, and the birds of the heaven *have*
nests ; but the Son of man hath not where to lay his head.   59.
And he said unto another, Follow me.   But he said, Lord, suffer
me first to go and bury my father.   60. But he said unto him,
Leave the dead to bury their own dead ; but go thou and publish
abroad the kingdom of God.   61. And another also said, I will
follow thee, Lord ; but first suffer me to bid farewell to them that
are at my house.   62. But Jesus said unto him, No man, having
put his hand to the plough, and looking back, is fit for the kingdom
of God.

10²⁻¹⁶.   *The Mission Address to the Seventy*

2. And he said unto them, The harvest is plenteous, but the
labourers are few : pray ye therefore the Lord of the harvest,
that he send forth labourers into his harvest.   3. Go your ways :
behold, I send you forth as lambs in the midst of wolves.   4.
Carry no purse, no wallet, no shoes : and salute no man on the
way.   5. And into whatsoever house ye shall enter, first say,
Peace *be* to this house.   6. And if a son of peace be there, your
peace shall rest upon him : but if not, it shall turn to you again.
7. And in that same house remain, eating and drinking such things
as they give : for the labourer is worthy of his hire.   Go not from
house to house.   8. And into whatsoever city ye enter, and they
receive you, eat such things as are set before you : 9. and heal
the sick that are therein, and say unto them, The kingdom of
God is come nigh unto you.   10. But into whatsoever city ye

shall enter, and they receive you not, go out into the streets thereof and say, 11. Even the dust from your city, that cleaveth to our feet, we do wipe off against you : howbeit know this, that the kingdom of God is come nigh. 12. I say unto you, It shall be more tolerable in that day for Sodom, than for that city. 13. Woe unto thee, Chorazin ! woe unto thee, Bethsaida ! for if the mighty works had been done in Tyre and Sidon, which were done in you, they would have repented long ago, sitting in sackcloth and ashes. 14. Howbeit it shall be more tolerable for Tyre and Sidon in the judgement, than for you. 15. And thou, Capernaum, shalt thou be exalted unto heaven ? thou shalt be brought down unto Hades. 16. He that heareth you heareth me ; and he that rejecteth you rejecteth me ; and he that rejecteth me rejecteth him that sent me.

10²¹⁻²⁴   *The Thanksgiving of Jesus*

21. In that same hour he rejoiced in the Holy Spirit, and said, I thank thee, O Father, Lord of heaven and earth, that thou didst hide these things from the wise and understanding, and didst reveal them unto babes : yea, Father ; for so it was well-pleasing in thy sight. 22. All things have been delivered unto me of my Father : and no one knoweth who the Son is, save the Father ; and who the Father is, save the Son, and he to whomsoever the Son willeth to reveal *him*. 23. And turning to the disciples, he said privately, Blessed *are* the eyes which see the things that ye see : 24. for I say unto you, that many prophets and kings desired to see the things which ye see, and saw them not ; and to hear the things which ye hear, and heard them not.

11⁹⁻¹³   *Teaching on Prayer*

9. And I say unto you, Ask, and it shall be given you ; seek, and ye shall find ; knock, and it shall be opened unto you. 10. For every one that asketh receiveth ; and he that seeketh findeth ; and to him that knocketh it shall be opened. 11. And of which of you that is a father shall his son ask a loaf, and he give him a stone ? or a fish, and he for a fish give him a serpent ? 12. Or *if* he shall ask an egg, will he give him a scorpion ? 13. If ye then, being evil, know how to give good gifts unto your children, how much more shall *your* heavenly Father give the Holy Spirit to them that ask him ?

11¹⁴⁻²⁰　　　　　　*The Beelzebub Controversy*

14. And he was casting out a devil *which was* dumb. And it came to pass, when the devil was gone out, the dumb man spake; and the multitudes marvelled. 15. But some of them said, By Beelzebub the prince of the devils casteth he out devils. 16. And others, tempting *him*, sought of him a sign from heaven. 17. But he, knowing their thoughts, said unto them, Every kingdom divided against itself is brought to desolation ; and a house *divided* against a house falleth. 18. And if Satan also is divided against himself, how shall his kingdom stand ? because ye say that I cast out devils by Beelzebub. 19. And if I by Beelzebub cast out devils, by whom do your sons cast them out ? therefore shall they be your judges. 20. But if I by the finger of God cast out devils, then is the kingdom of God come upon you.

11²¹⁻²⁶　　　　　　*" The Strong Man Armed "*

21. When the strong *man* fully armed guardeth his own court, his goods are in peace : 22. but when a stronger than he shall come upon him, and overcome him, he taketh from him his whole armour wherein he trusted, and divideth his spoils. 23. He that is not with me is against me ; and he that gathereth not with me scattereth. 24. The unclean spirit when he is gone out of the man, passeth through waterless places, seeking rest ; and finding none, he saith, I will turn back unto my house whence I came out. 25. And when he is come, he findeth it swept and garnished. 26. Then goeth he, and taketh *to him* seven other spirits more evil than himself ; and they enter in and dwell there : and the last state of that man becometh worse than the first.

11²⁷⁻²⁸　　*The Woman who cried out " Blessed is the Womb "*

27. And it came to pass, as he said these things, a certain woman out of the multitude lifted up her voice, and said unto him, Blessed is the womb that bare thee, and the breasts which thou didst suck. 28. But he said, Yea rather, blessed are they that hear the word of God, and keep it.

11²⁹⁻³²　　　　　　*On the Sign of Jonah*

29. And when the multitudes were gathering together unto him, he began to say, This generation is an evil generation : it seeketh

after a sign ; and there shall no sign be given to it but the sign of Jonah. 30. For even as Jonah became a sign unto the Ninevites, so shall also the Son of man be to this generation. 31. The queen of the south shall rise up in the judgement with the men of this generation, and shall condemn them : for she came from the ends of the earth to hear the wisdom of Solomon ; and behold, a greater than Solomon is here. 32. The men of Nineveh shall stand up in the judgement with this generation, and shall condemn it : for they repented at the preaching of Jonah ; and behold, a greater than Jonah is here.

11³³⁻³⁶ *Sayings on Light*

33. No man, when he hath lighted a lamp, putteth it in a cellar, neither under the bushel, but on the stand, that they which enter in may see the light. 34. The lamp of thy body is thine eye : when thine eye is single, thy whole body also is full of light ; but when it is evil, thy body also is full of darkness. 35. Look therefore whether the light that is in thee be not darkness. 36. If therefore thy whole body be full of light, having no part dark, it shall be wholly full of light, as when the lamp with its bright shining doth give thee light.

11³⁷⁻⁵² *Woes on Pharisees and Lawyers*

37. Now as he spake, a Pharisee asketh him to dine with him : and he went in, and sat down to meat. 38. And when the Pharisee saw it, he marvelled that he had not first washed before dinner. 39. And the Lord said unto him, Now do ye Pharisees cleanse the outside of the cup and of the platter ; but your inward part is full of extortion and wickedness. 40. Ye foolish ones, did not he that made the outside make the inside also ? 41. Howbeit give for alms those things which are within ; and behold, all things are clean unto you.

42. But woe unto you Pharisees ! for ye tithe mint and rue and every herb, and pass over judgement and the love of God : but these ought ye to have done, and not to leave the other undone. 43. Woe unto you Pharisees ! for ye love the chief seats in the synagogues, and the salutations in the marketplaces. 44. Woe unto you ! for ye are as the tombs which appear not, and the men that walk over *them* know it not.

45. And one of the lawyers answering saith unto him, Master, in saying this thou reproachest us also. 46. And he said, Woe

13 *

unto you lawyers also! for ye lade men with burdens grievous to be borne, and ye yourselves touch not the burdens with one of your fingers. 47. Woe unto you! for ye build the tombs of the prophets, and your fathers killed them. 48. So ye are witnesses and consent unto the works of your fathers: for they killed them, and ye build *their tombs*. 49. Therefore also said the wisdom of God, I will send unto them prophets and apostles; and *some* of them they shall kill and persecute; 50. that the blood of all the prophets, which was shed from the foundation of the world, may be required of this generation; 51. from the blood of Abel unto the blood of Zachariah, who perished between the altar and the sanctuary: yea, I say unto you, it shall be required of this generation. 52. Woe unto you lawyers! for ye took away the key of knowledge: ye entered not in yourselves, and them that were entering in ye hindered.

12^{1b-3} *On the Leaven of the Pharisees*

1. He began to say unto his disciples first of all, Beware ye of the leaven of the Pharisees, which is hypocrisy. 2. But there is nothing covered up, that shall not be revealed: and hid, that shall not be known. 3. Wherefore whatsoever ye have said in the darkness shall be heard in the light; and what ye have spoken in the ear in the inner chambers shall be proclaimed upon the housetops.

12^{4-7} *On Providence*

4. And I say unto you my friends, Be not afraid of them which kill the body, and after that have no more that they can do. 5. But I will warn you whom ye shall fear: Fear him, which after he hath killed hath power to cast into hell; yea, I say unto you, Fear him. 6. Are not five sparrows sold for two farthings? and not one of them is forgotten in the sight of God. 7. But the very hairs of your head are all numbered. Fear not: ye are of more value than many sparrows.

12^{8-9} *On Confessing Christ*

8. And I say unto you, Every one who shall confess me before men, him shall the Son of man also confess before the angels of God: 9. but he that denieth me in the presence of men shall be denied in the presence of the angels of God.

12^{10-12} *On Blasphemy against the Holy Spirit*

10. And every one who shall speak a word against the Son of man, it shall be forgiven him : but unto him that blasphemeth against the Holy Spirit it shall not be forgiven. 11. And when they bring you before the synagogues, and the rulers, and the authorities, be not anxious how or what ye shall answer, or what ye shall say : 12. for the Holy Spirit shall teach you in that very hour what ye ought to say.

12^{22-32} *On Over-anxiety*

22. And he said unto his disciples, Therefore I say unto you, Be not anxious for *your* life, what ye shall eat ; nor yet for your body, what ye shall put on. 23. For the life is more than the food, and the body than the raiment. 24. Consider the ravens, that they sow not, neither reap ; which have no store chamber nor barn ; and God feedeth them : of how much more value are ye than the birds ! 25. And which of you by being anxious can add a cubit unto his stature ? 26. If then ye are not able to do even that which is least, why are ye anxious concerning the rest ? 27. Consider the lilies, how they grow : they toil not, neither do they spin ; yet I say unto you, Even Solomon in all his glory was not arrayed like one of these. 28. But if God doth so clothe the grass in the field, which to-day is, and to-morrow is cast into the oven ; how much more *shall he clothe* you, O ye of little faith ? 29. And seek not ye what ye shall eat, and what ye shall drink, neither be ye of doubtful mind. 30. For all these things do the nations of the world seek after : but your Father knoweth that ye have need of these things. 31. Howbeit seek ye his kingdom, and these things shall be added unto you. 32. Fear not, little flock ; for it is your Father's good pleasure to give you the kingdom.

12^{33-34} *On Alms*

33. Sell that ye have, and give alms ; make for yourselves purses which wax not old, a treasure in the heavens that faileth not, where no thief draweth near, neither moth destroyeth. 34. For where your treasure is, there will your heart be also.

12^{35-48} *On Watchfulness*

35. Let your loins be girded about, and your lamps burning ; 36. and be ye yourselves like unto men looking for their lord,

when he shall return from the marriage feast; that, when he cometh and knocketh, they may straightway open unto him. 37. Blessed are those servants, whom the lord when he cometh shall find watching: verily I say unto you, that he shall gird himself, and make them sit down to meat, and shall come and serve them. 38. And if he shall come in the second watch, and if in the third, and find *them* so, blessed are those *servants*. 39. But know this, that if the master of the house had known in what hour the thief was coming, he would have watched, and not have left his house to be broken through. 40. Be ye also ready: for in an hour that ye think not the Son of man cometh.

41. And Peter said, Lord, speakest thou this parable unto us, or even unto all? 42. And the Lord said, Who then is the faithful and wise steward, whom his lord shall set over his household, to give them their portion of food in due season? 43. Blessed is that servant, whom his lord when he cometh shall find so doing. 44. Of a truth I say unto you, that he will set him over all that he hath. 45. But if that servant shall say in his heart, My lord delayeth his coming; and shall begin to beat the menservants and the maidservants, and to eat and drink, and to be drunken; 46. the lord of that servant shall come in a day when he expecteth not, and in an hour when he knoweth not, and shall cut him asunder, and appoint his portion with the unfaithful. 47. And that servant, which knew his lord's will, and made not ready, nor did according to his will, shall be beaten with many *stripes*; 48. but he that knew not, and did things worthy of stripes, shall be beaten with few *stripes*. And to whomsoever much is given, of him shall much be required: and to whom they commit much, of him will they ask the more.

12⁴⁹⁻⁵³   *On Religious Divisions*

49. I came to cast fire upon the earth; and what will I, if it is already kindled? 50. But I have a baptism to be baptized with; and how am I straitened till it be accomplished! 51. Think ye that I am come to give peace in the earth? I tell you, Nay; but rather division: 52. for there shall be from henceforth five in one house divided, three against two, and two against three. 53. They shall be divided, father against son, and son against father; mother against daughter, and daughter against her mother; mother in law against her daughter in law, and daughter in law against her mother in law.

12 54-56   *On Signs of the Weather*

54. And he said to the multitudes also, When ye see a cloud rising in the west, straightway ye say, There cometh a shower ; and so it cometh to pass. 55. And when *ye see* a south wind blowing, ye say, There will be a scorching heat ; and it cometh to pass. 56. Ye hypocrites, ye know how to interpret the face of the earth and the heaven ; but how is it that ye know not how to interpret this time ?

12 57-59   *On Being Charged before Magistrates*

57. And why even of yourselves judge ye not what is right ? 58. For as thou art going with thine adversary before the magistrate, on the way give diligence to be quit of him ; lest haply he hale thee unto the judge, and the judge shall deliver thee to the officer, and the officer shall cast thee into prison. 59. I say unto thee, Thou shalt by no means come out thence, till thou have paid the very last mite.

13 18-21   *Parables of the Mustard Seed and the Leaven*

18. He said therefore, Unto what is the kingdom of God like ? and whereunto shall I liken it ? 19. It is like unto a grain of mustard seed, which a man took, and cast into his own garden ; and it grew, and became a tree ; and the birds of the heaven lodged in the branches thereof. 20. And again he said, Whereunto shall I liken the kingdom of God ? 21. It is like unto leaven, which a woman took and hid in three measures of meal, till it was all leavened.

13 22-30   *The Strait Gate and the Shut Door*

22. And he went on his way through cities and villages, teaching, and journeying on unto Jerusalem. 23. And one said unto him, Lord, are they few that be saved ? And he said unto them, 24. Strive to enter in by the narrow door : for many, I say unto you, shall seek to enter in, and shall not be able. 25. When once the master of the house is risen up, and hath shut to the door, and ye begin to stand without, and to knock at the door, saying, Lord, open to us ; and he shall answer and say to you, I know you not whence ye are ; 26. then shall ye begin to say, We did eat and

drink in thy presence, and thou didst teach in our streets ; 27. and
he shall say, I tell you, I know not whence ye are ; depart from me,
all ye workers of iniquity. 28. There shall be the weeping and
gnashing of teeth, when ye shall see Abraham, and Isaac, and
Jacob, and all the prophets, in the kingdom of God, and yourselves
cast forth without. 29. And they shall come from the east and
west, and from the north and south, and shall sit down in the
kingdom of God. 30. And behold, there are last which shall be
first, and there are first which shall be last.

13^{31-33} *On " That Fox "*

31. In that very hour there came certain Pharisees, saying to
him, Get thee out, and go hence : for Herod would fain kill thee.
32. And he said unto them, Go and say to that fox, Behold, I
cast out devils and perform cures to-day and to-morrow, and the
third *day* I am perfected. 33. Howbeit, I must go on my way
to-day and to-morrow and the *day* following : for it cannot be
that a prophet perish out of Jerusalem.

13^{34-35} *On Jerusalem*

34. O Jerusalem, Jerusalem, which killeth the prophets, and
stoneth them that are sent unto her ! how often would I have
gathered thy children together, even as a hen *gathereth* her own
brood under her wings, and ye would not. 35. Behold, your
house is left unto you *desolate :* and I say unto you, Ye shall not
see me, until ye shall say, Blessed *is* he that cometh in the name
of the Lord.

14^{11} *On Humility*

11. For every one that exalteth himself shall be humbled ; and
he that humbleth himself shall be exalted.

14^{26-27} *On Hating Kinsfolk*

26. If any man cometh unto me, and hateth not his own father,
and mother, and wife, and children, and brethren, and sisters, yea,
and his own life also, he cannot be my disciple. 27. Whosoever
doth not bear his own cross and come after me, cannot be my
disciple.

14^{34-35} *On Salt*

34. Salt therefore is good : but if even the salt have lost its savour, wherewith shall it be seasoned ?   35. It is fit neither for the land nor for the dunghill : *men* cast it out.   He that hath ears to hear, let him hear.

16^{13} *On Two Masters*

13. No servant can serve two masters : for either he will hate the one, and love the other ; or else he will hold to one, and despise the other.   Ye cannot serve God and mammon.

16^{16-17} *On Entering the Kingdom*

16. The law and the prophets *were* until John : from that time the gospel of the kingdom of God is preached, and every man entereth violently into it.   17. But it is easier for heaven and earth to pass away, than for one tittle of the law to fall.

16^{18} *On Adultery*

18. Every one that putteth away his wife, and marrieth another, committeth adultery : and he that marrieth one that is put away from a husband committeth adultery.

17^{1-2} *On Offences*

1. And he said unto his disciples, It is impossible but that occasions of stumbling should come : but woe unto him, through whom they come !   2. It were well for him if a millstone were hanged about his neck, and he were thrown into the sea, rather than that he should cause one of these little ones to stumble.

17^{3-4} *On Forgiveness*

3. Take heed to yourselves : if thy brother sin, rebuke him ; and if he repent, forgive him.   4. And if he sin against thee seven times in the day, and seven times turn again to thee, saying, I repent ; thou shalt forgive him.

17⁵⁻⁶   *On Faith as a Grain of Mustard Seed*

5. And the apostles said unto the Lord, Increase our faith.
6. And the Lord said, If ye have faith as a grain of mustard seed,
ye would say unto this sycamine tree, Be thou rooted up, and be
thou planted in the sea ; and it would have obeyed you.

17²⁰⁻²¹   *On the Coming of the Kingdom*

20. And being asked by the Pharisees, when the kingdom of
God cometh, he answered them and said, The kingdom of God
cometh not with observation : 21. neither shall they say, Lo, here !
or, There ! for lo, the kingdom of God is within you.

17²²⁻³⁷   *On the Coming of the Son of Man*

22. And he said unto the disciples, The days will come, when
ye shall desire to see one of the days of the Son of man, and ye
shall not see it.   23. And they shall say to you, Lo, there ! Lo,
here ! go not away, nor follow after *them :*   24. for as the lightning, when it lighteneth out of the one part under the heaven,
shineth unto the other part under heaven ; so shall the Son of
man be in his day.   25. But first must he suffer many things and
be rejected of this generation.   26. And as it came to pass in the
days of Noah, even so shall it be also in the days of the Son of
man.   27. They ate, they drank, they married, they were given
in marriage, until the day that Noah entered into the ark, and
the flood came, and destroyed them all.   28. Likewise even as it
came to pass in the days of Lot ; they ate, they drank, they bought,
they sold, they planted, they builded ;   29. but in the day that
Lot went out from Sodom it rained fire and brimstone from heaven,
and destroyed them all :   30. after the same manner shall it be in
the day that the Son of man is revealed.   31. In that day, he
which shall be on the housetop, and his goods in the house, let
him not go down to take them away : and let him that is in the
field likewise not return back.   32. Remember Lot's wife.   33.
Whosoever shall seek to gain his life shall lose it : but whosoever
shall lose *his* life shall preserve it.   34. I say unto you, In that
night there shall be two men on one bed ; the one shall be taken,
and the other shall be left.   35. There shall be two women grind-
ing together ; the one shall be taken, and the other shall be left.
37. And they answering say unto him, Where, Lord ?   And he
said unto them, Where the body *is,* thither will the eagles also be
gathered together.

3^{14-15} *At the Baptism of Jesus*

14. But John would have hindered him, saying, I have need to be baptized of thee, and comest thou to me ? 15. But Jesus answering said unto him, Suffer *it* now : for thus it becometh us to fulfil all righteousness. Then he suffereth him.

The Sermon on the Mount

$5^{1-2, \, 4-5, \, 7-10, \, 13a, \, 14, \, 16-17, \, 19-24, \, 27-28, \, 33-39a, \, 41, \, 43, \, 48}$

1. And seeing the multitudes, he went up into the mountain : and when he had sat down, his disciples came unto him : 2. and he opened his mouth and taught them, saying,

4. Blessed are they that mourn : for they shall be comforted.

5. Blessed are the meek : for they shall inherit the earth.

7. Blessed are the merciful : for they shall obtain mercy.

8. Blessed are the pure in heart : for they shall see God.

9. Blessed are the peacemakers : for they shall be called sons of God. 10. Blessed are they that have been persecuted for righteousness' sake : for theirs is the kingdom of heaven.

13. Ye are the salt of the earth :

14. Ye are the light of the world. A city set on a hill cannot be hid.

16. Even so let your light shine before men, that they may see your good works, and glorify your Father which is in heaven. 17. Think not that I came to destroy the law or the prophets : I came not to destroy, but to fulfil.

19. Whosoever therefore shall break one of these least commandments, and shall teach men so, shall be called least in the kingdom of heaven : but whosoever shall do and teach them, he shall be called great in the kingdom of heaven. 20. For I say unto you, that except your righteousness shall exceed *the righteousness* of the scribes and Pharisees, ye shall in no wise enter into the kingdom of heaven. 21. Ye have heard that it was said to them of

old time, Thou shalt not kill ; and whosoever shall kill shall be in danger of the judgement : 22. but I say unto you, that every one who is angry with his brother shall be in danger of the judgement ; and whosoever shall say to his brother, Raca, shall be in danger of the council ; and whosoever shall say, Thou fool, shall be in danger of the hell of fire. 23. If therefore thou art offering thy gift at the altar, and there rememberest that thy brother hath aught against thee, 24. leave there thy gift before the altar, and go thy way, first be reconciled to thy brother, and then come and offer thy gift.

27. Ye have heard that it was said, Thou shalt not commit adultery : 28. but I say unto you, that every one that looketh on a woman to lust after her hath committed adultery with her already in his heart.

33. Again, ye have heard that it was said to them of old time, Thou shalt not forswear thyself, but shalt perform unto the Lord thine oaths : 34. but I say unto you, Swear not at all ; neither by the heaven, for it is the throne of God ; 35. nor by the earth, for it is the footstool of his feet ; nor by Jerusalem, for it is the city of the great King. 36. Neither shalt thou swear by thy head, for thou canst not make one hair white or black. 37. But let your speech be, Yea, yea ; Nay, nay : and whatsoever is more than these is of the evil *one*.

38. Ye have heard that it was said, An eye for an eye, and a tooth for a tooth : 39. but I say unto you, Resist not him that is evil :

41. And whosoever shall compel thee to go one mile, go with him twain.

43. Ye have heard that it was said, Thou shalt love thy neighbour, and hate thine enemy :

48. Ye therefore shall be perfect, as your heavenly Father is perfect.

6$^{1-19, 34}$

1. Take heed that ye do not your righteousness before men, to be seen of them : else ye have no reward with your Father which is in heaven.

2. When therefore thou doest alms, sound not a trumpet before thee, as the hypocrites do in the synagogues and in the streets, that they may have glory of men. Verily I say unto you, They have received their reward. 3. But when thou doest alms, let not thy left hand know what thy right hand doeth : 4. that thine alms

may be in secret : and thy Father which seeth in secret shall recompense thee.

5. And when ye pray, ye shall not be as the hypocrites : for they love to stand and pray in the synagogues and in the corners of the streets, that they may be seen of men. Verily I say unto you, They have received their reward.   6. But thou, when thou prayest, enter into thine inner chamber, and having shut thy door, pray to thy Father which is in secret, and thy Father which seeth in secret shall recompense thee.   7. And in praying use not vain repetitions, as the Gentiles do : for they think that they shall be heard for their much speaking.   8. Be not therefore like unto them : for your Father knoweth what things ye have need of, before ye ask him.   9. After this manner therefore pray ye : Our Father which art in heaven, Hallowed be thy name.   10. Thy kingdom come. Thy will be done, as in heaven, so on earth.   11. Give us this day our daily bread.   12. And forgive us our debts, as we also have forgiven our debtors.   13. And bring us not into temptation, but deliver us from the evil *one*.   14. For if ye forgive men their trespasses, your heavenly Father will also forgive you.   15. But if ye forgive not men their trespasses, neither will your Father forgive your trespasses.

16. Moreover when ye fast, be not as the hypocrites, of a sad countenance : for they disfigure their faces, that they may be seen of men to fast. Verily I say unto you, They have received their reward.   17. But thou, when thou fastest, anoint thy head, and wash thy face ;   18. that thou be not seen of men to fast, but of thy Father which is in secret : and thy Father, which seeth in secret, shall recompense thee.

19. Lay not up for yourselves treasures upon the earth, where moth and rust doth consume, and where thieves break through and steal :

34. Be not therefore anxious for the morrow : for the morrow will be anxious for itself. Sufficient unto the day is the evil thereof.

7⁶, ¹²ᵇ, ¹⁵, ¹⁷, ¹⁹⁻²³

6. Give not that which is holy unto the dogs, neither cast your pearls before the swine, lest haply they trample them under their feet, and turn and rend you.

12. For this is the law and the prophets.

15. Beware of false prophets, which come to you in sheep's clothing, but inwardly are ravening wolves.

17. Even so every good tree bringeth forth good fruit ; but the corrupt tree bringeth forth evil fruit.

19. Every tree that bringeth not forth good fruit is hewn down, and cast into the fire. 20. Therefore by their fruits ye shall know them. 21. Not every one that saith unto me, Lord, Lord, shall enter into the kingdom of heaven ; but he that doeth the will of my Father which is in heaven. 22. Many will say to me in that day, Lord, Lord, did we not prophesy by thy name, and by thy name cast out devils, and by thy name do many mighty works ? 23. And then will I profess unto them, I never knew you : depart from me, ye that work iniquity.

9¹³ᵃ   *" I desire mercy "*

13. But go ye and learn what *this* meaneth, I desire mercy, and not sacrifice :

10²⁻⁴   *The List of the Twelve*

2. Now the names of the twelve apostles are these : The first, Simon, who is called Peter, and Andrew his brother ; James the *son* of Zebedee, and John his brother ; 3. Philip, and Bartholomew ; Thomas, and Matthew the publican ; James the *son* of Alphæus, and Thaddæus ; 4. Simon the Cananæan, and Judas Iscariot, who also betrayed him.

10⁵⁻⁸, ¹⁶ᵇ, ²³, ²⁵ᵇ, ³⁶, ⁴¹   *The Charge to the Twelve*

5. These twelve Jesus sent forth, and charged them, saying, Go not into *any* way of the Gentiles, and enter not into any city of the Samaritans ; 6. but go rather to the lost sheep of the house of Israel. 7. And as ye go, preach, saying, The kingdom of heaven is at hand. 8. Heal the sick, raise the dead, cleanse the lepers, cast out devils : freely ye received, freely give.

16. Be ye therefore wise as serpents, and harmless as doves.

23. But when they persecute you in this city, flee into the next : for verily I say unto you, Ye shall not have gone through the cities of Israel, till the Son of man be come.

25. If they have called the master of the house Beelzebub, how much more *shall they call* them of his household !

36. And a man's foes *shall be* they of his own household.

41. He that receiveth a prophet in the name of a prophet shall receive a prophet's reward ; and he that receiveth a righteous

man in the name of a righteous man shall receive a righteous man's reward.

11^28–30   *" Come unto Me "*

28. Come unto me, all ye that labour and are heavy laden, and I will give you rest. 29. Take my yoke upon you, and learn of me ; for I am meek and lowly in heart : and ye shall find rest unto your souls. 30. For my yoke is easy, and my burden is light.

12^5–7, 11–12a   *On the Sabbath*

5. Or have ye not read in the law, how that on the sabbath day the priests in the temple profane the sabbath, and are guiltless ? 6. But I say unto you, that one greater than the temple is here. 7. But if ye had known what this meaneth, I desire mercy, and not sacrifice, ye would not have condemned the guiltless.

11. And he said unto them, What man shall there be of you, that shall have one sheep, and if this fall into a pit on the sabbath day, will he not lay hold on it, and lift it out ? 12. How much then is a man of more value than a sheep !

12^36–37   *On the Importance of Words*

36. And I say unto you, that every idle word that men shall speak, they shall give account thereof in the day of judgement. 37. For by thy words thou shalt be justified, and by thy words thou shalt be condemned.

12^40 *On the Sign of Jonah* (*Probably a scribal interpolation*)

40. For as Jonah was three days and three nights in the belly of the whale ; so shall the Son of man be three days and three nights in the heart of the earth.

13^24–30, 36–43   *The Parable of the Tares*

24. Another parable set he before them, saying, The kingdom of heaven is likened unto a man that sowed good seed in his field : 25. but while men slept, his enemy came and sowed tares also among the wheat, and went away. 26. But when the blade sprang up, and brought forth fruit, then appeared the tares also. 27. And the servants of the householder came and said unto him,

Sir, didst thou not sow good seed in thy field ? whence then hath it tares ?   28. And he said unto them, An enemy hath done this. And the servants say unto him, Wilt thou then that we go and gather them up ?   29. But he saith, Nay ; lest haply while ye gather up the tares, ye root up the wheat with them.   30. Let both grow together until the harvest : and in the time of the harvest I will say to the reapers, Gather up first the tares, and bind them in bundles to burn them : but gather the wheat into my barn.

36. Then he left the multitudes, and went into the house : and his disciples came unto him, saying, Explain unto us the parable of the tares of the field.   37. And he answered and said, He that soweth the good seed is the Son of man ;   38. and the field is the world ; and the good seed, these are the sons of the kingdom ; and the tares are the sons of the evil *one* ;   39. and the enemy that sowed them is the devil : and the harvest is the end of the world ; and the reapers are angels.   40. As therefore the tares are gathered up and burned with fire ; so shall it be in the end of the world.   41. The Son of man shall send forth his angels, and they shall gather out of his kingdom all things that cause stumbling, and them that do iniquity,   42. and shall cast them into the furnace of fire : there shall be the weeping and gnashing of teeth.   43. Then shall the righteous shine forth as the sun in the kingdom of their Father.   He that hath ears, let him hear.

13⁴⁴   *The Parable of the Hidden Treasure*

44. The kingdom of heaven is like unto a treasure hidden in the field ; which a man found, and hid ; and in his joy he goeth and selleth all that he hath, and buyeth that field.

13⁴⁵⁻⁴⁶   *The Parable of the Pearl of Great Price*

45. Again, the kingdom of heaven is like unto a man that is a merchant seeking goodly pearls :   46. and having found one pearl of great price, he went and sold all that he had, and bought it.

13⁴⁷⁻⁵²   *The Parable of the Drag-net*

47. Again, the kingdom of heaven is like unto a net, that was cast into the sea, and gathered of every kind :   48. which, when it was filled, they drew up on the beach ; and they sat down, and

gathered the good into vessels, but the bad they cast away.
49. So shall it be in the end of the world : the angels shall come
forth, and sever the wicked from among the righteous, 50. and
shall cast them into the furnace of fire : there shall be the weeping
and gnashing of teeth.   51. Have ye understood all these things ?
They say unto him, Yea.   52. And he said unto them, Therefore
every scribe who hath been made a disciple to the kingdom of
heaven is like unto a man that is a householder, which bringeth
forth out of his treasure things new and old.

15¹²⁻¹³   *On the Pharisees being Offended*

12. Then came the disciples, and said unto him, Knowest thou
that the Pharisees were offended, when they heard this saying ?
13. But he answered and said, Every plant which my heavenly
Father planted not, shall be rooted up.

15²³⁻²⁵   *The Syro-phœnician Woman*

23. But he answered her not a word.   And his disciples came
and besought him, saying, Send her away ; for she crieth after
us.   24. But he answered and said, I was not sent but unto the
lost sheep of the house of Israel.   25. But she came and worshipped him, saying, Lord, help me.

16²ᵇ⁻³   *On Signs from the Weather*

2. When it is evening, ye say, *It will be* fair weather : for the
heaven is red.   3. And in the morning, *It will be* foul weather
to-day : for the heaven is red and lowring.   Ye know how to
discern the face of the heaven ; but ye cannot *discern* the signs of
the times.

16¹¹ᵇ⁻¹² *On the Leaven of the Pharisees and Sadducees*

11. But beware of the leaven of the Pharisees and Sadducees.
12. Then understood they how that he bade them not beware of
the leaven of bread, but of the teaching of the Pharisees and
Sadducees.

16¹⁷⁻¹⁹   *" Thou art Peter "*

17. And Jesus answered and said unto him, Blessed art thou,
Simon Bar-Jonah : for flesh and blood hath not revealed it unto

14

thee, but my Father which is in heaven. 18. And I also say unto thee, that thou art Peter, and upon this rock I will build my church ; and the gates of Hades shall not prevail against it. 19. I will give unto thee the keys of the kingdom of heaven : and whatsoever thou shalt bind on earth shall be bound in heaven : and whatsoever thou shalt loose on earth shall be loosed in heaven.

18³⁻⁴, ¹⁰, ¹⁴   *On Children*

3. Verily I say unto you, Except ye turn, and become as little children, ye shall in no wise enter into the kingdom of heaven. 4. Whosoever therefore shall humble himself as this little child, the same is the greatest in the kingdom of heaven.

10. See that ye despise not one of these little ones ; for I say unto you, that in heaven their angels do always behold the face of my Father which is in heaven.

14. Even so it is not the will of your Father which is in heaven, that one of these little ones should perish.

18¹⁵⁻¹⁸   *On Discipline in the Church*

15. And if thy brother sin against thee, go, shew him his fault between thee and him alone : if he hear thee, thou hast gained thy brother. 16. But if he hear *thee* not, take with thee one or two more, that at the mouth of two witnesses or three every word may be established. 17. And if he refuse to hear them, tell it unto the church : and if he refuse to hear the church also, let him be unto thee as the Gentile and the publican. 18. Verily I say unto you, What things soever ye shall bind on earth shall be bound in heaven : and what things soever ye shall loose on earth shall be loosed in heaven.

18¹⁹⁻²⁰   *On Common Prayer*

19. Again I say unto you, that if two of you shall agree on earth as touching anything that they shall ask, it shall be done for them of my Father which is in heaven. 20. For where two or three are gathered together in my name, there am I in the midst of them.

18²¹⁻²²   *On Forgiveness*

21. Then came Peter, and said to him, Lord, how oft shall my brother sin against me, and I forgive him ? until seven times ? 22. Jesus saith unto him, I say not unto thee, Until seven times ; but, Until seventy times seven.

18²³⁻³⁵   *The Parable of the Unmerciful Servant*

23. Therefore is the kingdom of heaven likened unto a certain king, which would make a reckoning with his servants. 24. And when he had begun to reckon, one was brought unto him, which owed him ten thousand talents. 25. But forasmuch as he had not *wherewith* to pay, his lord commanded him to be sold, and his wife, and children, and all that he had, and payment to be made. 26. The servant therefore fell down and worshipped him, saying, Lord, have patience with me, and I will pay thee all. 27. And the lord of that servant, being moved with compassion, released him, and forgave him the debt. 28. But that servant went out, and found one of his fellow-servants, which owed him a hundred pence : and he laid hold on him, and took *him* by the throat, saying, Pay what thou owest. 29. So his fellow-servant fell down and besought him, saying, Have patience with me, and I will pay thee. 30. And he would not : but went and cast him into prison, till he should pay that which was due. 31. So when his fellow-servants saw what was done, they were exceeding sorry, and came and told unto their lord all that was done. 32. Then his lord called him to him, and saith unto him, Thou wicked servant, I forgave thee all that debt, because thou besoughtest me : 33. shouldest not thou also have had mercy on thy fellow-servant, even as I had mercy on thee ? 34. And his lord was wroth, and delivered him to the tormentors, till he should pay all that was due. 35. So shall also my heavenly Father do unto you, if ye forgive not every one his brother from your hearts.

19⁹⁻¹²   *On Divorce*

9. And I say unto you, Whosoever shall put away his wife, except for fornication, and shall marry another, committeth adultery : and he that marrieth her when she is put away committeth adultery. 10. The disciples say unto him, If the case of the man is so with his wife, it is not expedient to marry. 11. But

14 *

he said unto them, All men cannot receive this saying, but they to whom it is given. 12. For there are eunuchs, which were so born from their mother's womb : and there are eunuchs, which were made eunuchs by men : and there are eunuchs, which made themselves eunuchs for the kingdom of heaven's sake. He that is able to receive it, let him receive it.

19²⁸ᵃ   " *In the Regeneration* "

28. And Jesus said unto them, Verily I say unto you, that ye which have followed me, in the regeneration when the Son of man shall sit on the throne of his glory, . . .

20¹⁻¹⁶   *The Parable of the Labourers in the Vineyard*

1. For the kingdom of heaven is like unto a man that is a householder, which went out early in the morning to hire labourers into his vineyard. 2. And when he had agreed with the labourers for a penny a day, he sent them into his vineyard. 3. And he went out about the third hour, and saw others standing in the marketplace idle ; 4. and to them he said, Go ye also into the vineyard, and whatsoever is right I will give you. And they went their way. 5. Again he went out about the sixth and the ninth hour, and did likewise. 6. And about the eleventh *hour* he went out and found others standing ; and he saith unto them, Why stand ye here all the day idle ? 7. They say unto him, Because no man hath hired us. He saith unto them, Go ye also into the vineyard. 8. And when even was come, the lord of the vineyard saith unto his steward, Call the labourers, and pay them their hire, beginning from the last unto the first. 9. And when they came that *were hired* about the eleventh hour, they received every man a penny. 10. And when the first came, they supposed that they would receive more ; and they likewise received every man a penny. 11. And when they received it, they murmured against the householder, 12. saying, These last have spent *but* one hour, and thou hast made them equal unto us, which have borne the burden of the day and the scorching heat. 13. But he answered and said to one of them, Friend, I do thee no wrong : didst thou not agree with me for a penny ? 14. Take up that which is thine, and go thy way ; it is my will to give unto this last, even as unto thee. 15. Is it not lawful for me to do what I will with mine own ? or is thine eye evil, because I am good ? 16. So the last shall be first, and the first last.

21¹⁰⁻¹¹   *During the Entry into Jerusalem*

10. And when he was come into Jerusalem, all the city was stirred, saying, Who is this ?   11. And the multitudes said, This is the prophet, Jesus, from Nazareth of Galilee.

21¹⁵ᵇ⁻¹⁶   *The Children in the Temple*

15. The children that were crying in the temple and saying, Hosanna to the son of David ; they were moved with indignation, 16. and said unto him, Hearest thou what these are saying ? And Jesus saith unto them, Yea : did ye never read, Out of the mouth of babes and sucklings thou hast perfected praise ?

21²⁸⁻³²   *The Parable of the Two Sons*

28. But what think ye ?   A man had two sons ; and he came to the first, and said, Son, go work to-day in the vineyard.   29. And he answered and said, I will not : but afterward he repented himself, and went.   30. And he came to the second, and said likewise.   And he answered and said, I *go*, sir : and went not. 31. Whether of the twain did the will of his father ?   They say, The first.   Jesus saith unto them, Verily I say unto you, that the publicans and the harlots go into the kingdom of God before you.   32. For John came unto you in the way of righteousness, and ye believed him not : but the publicans and the harlots believed him : and ye, when ye saw it, did not even repent yourselves afterward, that ye might believe him.

21⁴³   *Warning to the Pharisees*

43. Therefore say I unto you, The kingdom of God shall be taken away from you, and shall be given to a nation bringing forth the fruits thereof.

22¹⁻¹⁴ *The Parables of the Marriage Feast and the Wedding Garment*

1. And Jesus answered and spake again in parables unto them, saying, 2. The kingdom of heaven is likened unto a certain king, which made a marriage feast for his son, 3. and sent forth his servants to call them that were bidden to the marriage feast : and they would not come.   4. Again he sent forth other servants,

saying, Tell them that are bidden, Behold, I have made ready my dinner : my oxen and my fatlings are killed, and all things are ready : come to the marriage feast. 5. But they made light of it, and went their ways, one to his own farm, another to his merchandise : 6. and the rest laid hold on his servants, and entreated them shamefully, and killed them. 7. But the king was wroth ; and he sent his armies, and destroyed those murderers, and burned their city. 8. Then saith he to his servants, The wedding is ready, but they that were bidden were not worthy. 9. Go ye therefore unto the partings of the highways, and as many as ye shall find, bid to the marriage feast. 10. And those servants went out into the highways, and gathered together all as many as they found, both bad and good : and the wedding was filled with guests. 11. But when the king came in to behold the guests, he saw there a man which had not on a wedding-garment : 12. and he saith unto him, Friend, how camest thou in hither not having a wedding garment ? And he was speechless. 13. Then the king said to the servants, Bind him hand and foot, and cast him out into the outer darkness ; there shall be the weeping and gnashing of teeth. 14. For many are called, but few chosen.

22[40]   *The Two Commandments*

40. On these two commandments hangeth the whole law, and the prophets.

23[1-3, 5, 7b-11, 15-22, 24, 26-33]   *Woes on the Pharisees*

1. Then spake Jesus to the multitudes and to his disciples, saying, 2. The scribes and the Pharisees sit on Moses' seat : 3. all things therefore whatsoever they bid you, *these* do and observe : but do not ye after their works ; for they say, and do not.

5. But all their works they do for to be seen of men : for they make broad their phylacteries, and enlarge the borders *of their garments*,

7. and to be called of men, Rabbi. 8. But be not ye called Rabbi : for one is your teacher, and all ye are brethren. 9. And call no man your father on the earth : for one is your Father, which is in heaven. 10. Neither be ye called masters : for one is your master, *even* the Christ. 11. But he that is greatest among you shall be your servant.

15. Woe unto you, scribes and Pharisees, hypocrites ! for ye

compass sea and land to make one proselyte ; and when he is
become so, ye make him twofold more a son of hell than yourselves.

16. Woe unto you, ye blind guides, which say, Whosoever shall
swear by the temple, it is nothing ; but whosoever shall swear by
the gold of the temple, he is a debtor. 17. Ye fools and blind :
for whether is greater, the gold, or the temple that hath sanctified
the gold ? 18. And, Whosoever shall swear by the altar, it is
nothing ; but whosoever shall swear by the gift that is upon it,
he is a debtor. 19. Ye blind : for whether is greater, the gift, or
the altar that sanctifieth the gift ? 20. He therefore that sweareth
by the altar, sweareth by it, and by all things thereon. 21. And
he that sweareth by the temple, sweareth by it, and by him that
dwelleth therein. 22. And he that sweareth by the heaven,
sweareth by the throne of God, and by him that sitteth thereon.

24. Ye blind guides, which strain out the gnat, and swallow the
camel.

26. Thou blind Pharisee, cleanse first the inside of the cup and
of the platter, that the outside thereof may become clean also.

27. Woe unto you, scribes and Pharisees, hypocrites ! for ye
are like unto whited sepulchres, which outwardly appear beautiful, but inwardly are full of dead men's bones, and of all uncleanness. 28. Even so ye also outwardly appear righteous unto
men, but inwardly ye are full of hypocrisy and iniquity.

29. Woe unto you, scribes and Pharisees, hypocrites ! for ye
build the sepulchres of the prophets, and garnish the tombs of
the righteous, 30. and say, If we had been in the days of our
fathers, we should not have been partakers with them in the
blood of the prophets. 31. Wherefore ye witness to yourselves,
that ye are sons of them that slew the prophets. 32. Fill ye up
then the measure of your fathers. 33. Ye serpents, ye offspring
of vipers, how shall ye escape the judgment of hell ?

24$^{10-12}$ *On False Prophets*

10. And then shall many stumble, and shall deliver up one
another, and shall hate one another. 11. And many false
prophets shall arise, and shall lead many astray. 12. And because
iniquity shall be multiplied, the love of the many shall wax cold.

25$^{1-13}$ *The Parable of the Ten Virgins*

1. Then shall the kingdom of heaven be likened unto ten
virgins, which took their lamps, and went forth to meet the

bridegroom. 2. And five of them were foolish, and five were wise. 3. For the foolish, when they took their lamps, took no oil with them : 4. but the wise took oil in their vessels with their lamps. 5. Now while the bridegroom tarried, they all slumbered and slept. 6. But at midnight there is a cry, Behold, the bridegroom ! Come ye forth to meet him. 7. Then all those virgins arose, and trimmed their lamps. 8. And the foolish said unto the wise, Give us of your oil ; for our lamps are going out. 9. But the wise answered, saying, Peradventure there will not be enough for us and you : go ye rather to them that sell, and buy for yourselves. 10. And while they went away to buy, the bridegroom came ; and they that were ready went in with him to the marriage feast : and the door was shut. 11. Afterward come also the other virgins, saying, Lord, Lord, open to us. 12. But he answered and said, Verily I say unto you, I know you not. 13. Watch therefore, for ye know not the day nor the hour.

25$^{14-30}$ *The Parable of the Talents*

14. For *it is* as *when* a man, going into another country, called his own servants, and delivered unto them his goods. 15. And unto one he gave five talents, to another two, to another one ; to each according to his several ability ; and he went on his journey. 16. Straightway he that received the five talents went and traded with them, and made other five talents. 17. In like manner he also that *received* the two gained other two. 18. But he that received the one went away and digged in the earth, and hid his lord's money. 19. Now after a long time the lord of those servants cometh, and maketh a reckoning with them. 20. And he that received the five talents came and brought other five talents, saying, Lord, thou deliveredst unto me five talents : lo, I have gained other five talents. 21. His lord said unto him, Well done, good and faithful servant : thou hast been faithful over a few things, I will set thee over many things : enter thou into the joy of thy lord. 22. And he also that *received* the two talents came and said, Lord, thou deliveredst unto me two talents : lo, I have gained other two talents. 23. His lord said unto him, Well done, good and faithful servant ; thou has been faithful over a few things, I will set thee over many things : enter thou into the joy of thy lord. 24. And he also that had received the one talent came and said, Lord, I knew that thou art a hard man, reaping where thou didst not sow, and gathering where thou didst

not scatter : 25. and I was afraid, and went away and hid thy
talent in the earth : lo, thou hast thine own. 26. But his lord
answered and said unto him, Thou wicked and slothful servant,
thou knewest that I reap where I sowed not, and gather where
I did not scatter ; 27. thou oughtest therefore to have put my
money to the bankers, and at my coming I should have received
back mine own with interest. 28. Take ye away therefore the
talent from him, and give it unto him that hath the ten talents.
29. For unto every one that hath shall be given, and he shall
have abundance : but from him that hath not, even that which
he hath shall be taken away. 30. And cast ye out the unprofitable
servant into the outer darkness : there shall be the weeping and
gnashing of teeth.

25$^{31-46}$ *The Parable of the Sheep and the Goats*

31. But when the Son of man shall come in his glory, and all
the angels with him, then shall he sit on the throne of his glory :
32. and before him shall be gathered all the nations : and he shall
separate them one from another, as the shepherd separateth the
sheep from the goats : 33. and he shall set the sheep on his right
hand, but the goats on the left. 34. Then shall the King say
unto them on his right hand, Come, ye blessed of my Father,
inherit the kingdom prepared for you from the foundation of the
world : 35. for I was an hungred, and ye gave me meat : I was
thirsty, and ye gave me drink : I was a stranger, and ye took me
in ; 36. naked, and ye clothed me : I was sick, and ye visited
me : I was in prison, and ye came unto me. 37. Then shall the
righteous answer him, saying, Lord, when saw we thee an hungred,
and fed thee ? or athirst, and gave thee drink ? 38. And when
saw we thee a stranger, and took thee in ? or naked, and clothed
thee ? 39. And when saw we thee sick, or in prison, and came
unto thee ? 40. And the King shall answer and say unto them,
Verily I say unto you, Inasmuch as ye did it unto one of these
my brethren, *even* these least, ye did it unto me. 41. Then shall
he say also unto them on the left hand, Depart from me, ye cursed,
into the eternal fire which is prepared for the devil and his angels :
42. for I was an hungred, and ye gave me no meat : I was thirsty,
and ye gave me no drink : 43. I was a stranger, and ye took me
not in ; naked, and ye clothed me not ; sick, and in prison, and
ye visited me not. 44. Then shall they also answer, saying, Lord,
when saw we thee an hungred, or athirst, or a stranger, or naked,

or sick, or in prison, and did not minister unto thee ? 45. Then shall he answer them, saying, Verily I say unto you, Inasmuch as ye did it not unto one of these least, ye did it not unto me. 46. And these shall go away into eternal punishment : but the righteous into eternal life.

28¹⁸⁻²⁰ *The Final Commission*

18. And Jesus came to them and spake unto them, saying, All authority hath been given unto me in heaven and on earth. 19. Go ye therefore, and make disciples of all the nations, baptizing them into the name of the Father and of the Son and of the Holy Ghost : 20. teaching them to observe all things whatsoever I commanded you : and lo, I am with you alway, even unto the end of the world.

(Also possibly)

18¹²⁻¹³ *The Parable of the Lost Sheep*

12. How think ye ? if any man have a hundred sheep, and one of them be gone astray, doth he not leave the ninety and nine, and go unto the mountains, and seek that which goeth astray ? 13. And if so be that he find it, verily I say unto you, he rejoiceth over it more than over the ninety and nine which have not gone astray.

THE TEXT OF L

3¹⁻⁶   *The Call of John*

1. Now in the fifteenth year of the reign of Tiberus Cæsar, Pontius Pilate being governor of Judæa, and Herod being tetrarch of Galilee, and his brother Philip tetrarch of the region of Ituræa and Trachonitis, and Lysanias tetrarch of Abilene, 2. in the high-priesthood of Annas and Caiaphas, the word of God came unto John the son of Zacharias in the wilderness. 3. And he came into all the region round about Jordan, preaching the baptism of repentance unto remission of sins ; 4. as it is written in the book of the words of Isaiah the prophet,

> The voice of one crying in the wilderness,
> Make ye ready the way of the Lord,
> Make his paths straight.
> 5. Every valley shall be filled,
> And every mountain and hill shall be brought low ;
> And the crooked shall become straight,
> And the rough ways smooth ;
> 6. And all flesh shall see the salvation of God.

3¹⁰⁻¹⁴   *The Preaching of John*

10. And the multitudes asked him, saying, What then must we do ? 11. And he answered and said unto them, He that hath two coats, let him impart to him that hath none ; and he that hath food, let him do likewise. 12. And there came also publicans to be baptized, and they said unto him, Master, what must we do ? 13. And he said unto them, Extort no more than that which is appointed you. 14. And soldiers also asked him, saying, And we, what must we do ? And he said unto them, Do violence to no man, neither exact *anything* wrongfully ; and be content with your wages.

3^{18-20} *The Imprisonment of John*

18. With many other exhortations therefore preached he good tidings unto the people ; 19. but Herod the tetrarch, being reproved by him for Herodias his brother's wife, and for all the evil things which Herod had done, 20. added yet this above all, that he shut up John in prison.

3^{21-22} *The Baptism of Jesus*

21. Now it came to pass, when all the people were baptized, that, Jesus also having been baptized, and praying, the heaven was opened, 22. and the Holy Ghost descended in a bodily form, as a dove, upon him, and a voice came out of heaven, Thou art my beloved Son ; in thee I am well pleased.

3^{23-38} *The Genealogy of Jesus*

23. And Jesus himself, when he began to *teach*, was about thirty years of age, being the *son* (as was supposed) of Joseph, the *son* of Heli, 24. the *son* of Matthat, the *son* of Levi, the *son* of Melchi, the *son* of Jannai, the *son* of Joseph, 25. the *son* of Mattathias, the *son* of Amos, the *son* of Nahum, the *son* of Esli, the *son* of Naggai, 26. the *son* of Maath, the *son* of Mattathias, the *son* of Semein, the *son* of Josech, the *son* of Joda, 27. the *son* of Joanan, the *son* of Rhesa, the *son* of Zerubbabel, the *son* of Shealtiel, the *son* of Neri, 28. the *son* of Melchi, the *son* of Addi, the *son* of Cosam, the *son* of Elmadam, the *son* of Er, 29. the *son* of Jesus, the *son* of Eliezer, the *son* of Jorim, the *son* of Matthat, the *son* of Levi, 30. the *son* of Symeon, the *son* of Judas, the *son* of Joseph, the *son* of Jonam, the *son* of Eliakim, 31. the *son* of Melea, the *son* of Menna, the *son* of Mattatha, the *son* of Nathan, the *son* of David, 32. the *son* of Jesse, the *son* of Obed, the *son* of Boaz, the *son* of Salmon, the *son* of Nahshon, 33. the *son* of Amminadab, the *son* of Arni, the *son* of Hezron, the *son* of Perez, the *son* of Judah, 34. the *son* of Jacob, the *son* of Isaac, the *son* of Abraham, the *son* of Terah, the *son* of Nahor, 35. the *son* of Serug, the *son* of Reu, the *son* of Peleg, the *son* of Eber, the *son* of Shelah, 36. the *son* of Cainan, the *son* of Arphaxad, the *son* of Shem, the *son* of Noah, the *son* of Lamech, 37. the *son* of Methuselah, the *son* of Enoch, the *son* of Jared, the *son* of Mahalaleel, the *son* of Cainan, 38. the *son* of Enos, the *son* of Seth, the *son* of Adam, the *son* of God.

$4^{1-2,\ 13}$ *The Temptation of Jesus*

1. And Jesus, full of the Holy Spirit, returned from the Jordan, and was led by the Spirit in the wilderness, 2. during forty days, being tempted of the devil. And he did eat nothing in those days : and when they were completed, he hungered.

13. And when the devil had completed every temptation, he departed from him for a season.

4^{14-15} *The Departure to Galilee*

14. And Jesus returned in the power of the Spirit into Galilee : and a fame went out concerning him through all the region round about.   15. And he taught in their synagogues, being glorified of all.

4^{16-30} *The Rejection at Nazareth*

16. And he came to Nazareth, where he had been brought up : and he entered, as his custom was, into the synagogue on the sabbath day, and stood up to read.   17. And there was delivered unto him the book of the prophet Isaiah. And he opened the book, and found the place where it was written,

18. The Spirit of the Lord is upon me,
      Because he anointed me to preach good tidings to the poor :
      He hath sent me to proclaim release to the captives,
      And recovering of sight to the blind,
      To set at liberty them that are bruised,
19. To proclaim the acceptable year of the Lord.

20. And he closed the book, and gave it back to the attendant, and sat down : and the eyes of all in the synagogue were fastened on him.   21. And he began to say unto them, To-day hath this scripture been fulfilled in your ears.   22. And all bare him witness, and wondered at the words of grace which proceeded out of his mouth : and they said, Is not this Joseph's son ?   23. And he said unto them, Doubtless ye will say unto me this parable, Physician, heal thyself : whatsoever we have heard done at Capernaum, do also here in thine own country.   24. And he said, Verily I say unto you, No prophet is acceptable in his own country. 25. But of a truth I say unto you, There were many widows in Israel in the days of Elijah, when the heaven was shut up three

years and six months, when there came a great famine over all the land ; 26. and unto none of them was Elijah sent, but only to Zarephath, in the land of Sidon, unto a woman that was a widow.   27. And there were many lepers in Israel in the time of Elisha the prophet ; and none of them was cleansed, but only Naaman the Syrian.   28. And they were all filled with wrath in the synagogue, as they heard these things ; 29. and they rose up, and cast him forth out of the city, and led him unto the brow of the hill whereon their city was built, that they might throw him down headlong.   30. But he passing through the midst of them went his way.

5¹⁻¹¹   *The Call of Simon*

1. Now it came to pass, while the multitude pressed upon him and heard the word of God, that he was standing by the lake of Gennesaret ; 2. and he saw two boats standing by the lake : but the fishermen had gone out of them, and were washing their nets. 3. And he entered into one of the boats, which was Simon's, and asked him to put out a little from the land.   And he sat down and taught the multitudes out of the boat.   4. And when he had left speaking, he said unto Simon, Put out into the deep, and let down your nets for a draught.   5. And Simon answered and said, Master, we toiled all night, and took nothing : but at thy word I will let down the nets.   6. And when they had this done, they inclosed a great multitude of fishes ; and their nets were breaking ; 7. and they beckoned unto their partners in the other boat, that they should come and help them.   And they came, and filled both the boats, so that they began to sink.   8. But Simon Peter, when he saw it, fell down at Jesus' knees, saying, Depart from me ; for I am a sinful man, O Lord.   9. For he was amazed, and all that were with him, at the draught of the fishes which they had taken ; 10. and so were also James and John, sons of Zebedee, which were partners with Simon.   And Jesus said unto Simon, Fear not ; from henceforth thou shalt catch men.   11. And when they had brought their boats to land, they left all, and followed him.

6¹²⁻¹⁶   *The Choice of the Twelve*

12. And it came to pass in these days, that he went out into the mountain to pray ; and he continued all night in prayer to God.   13. And when it was day, he called his disciples : and he

chose from them twelve, whom also he named apostles ; 14.
Simon, whom he also named Peter, and Andrew his brother, and
James and John, and Philip and Bartholomew, 15. and Matthew
and Thomas, and James *the son* of Alphæus, and Simon which was
called the Zealot, 16. and Judas *the son* of James, and Judas
Iscariot, which was the traitor ;

6^{17-19} *Miracles of Healing*

17. and he came down with them, and stood on a level place,
and a great multitude of his disciples, and a great number of the
people from all Judæa and Jerusalem, and the sea coast of Tyre
and Sidon, which came to hear him, and to be healed of their
diseases ; 18. and they that were troubled with unclean spirits
were healed. 19. And all the multitude sought to touch him :
for power came forth from him, and healed *them* all.

$7^{1-6a,\ 10}$ *A Centurion sends Elders to Jesus*

1. After he had ended all his sayings in the ears of the people,
he entered into Capernaum.
2. And a certain centurion's servant, who was dear unto him,
was sick and at the point of death. 3. And when he heard concerning Jesus, he sent unto him elders of the Jews, asking him
that he would come and save his servant. 4. And they, when
they came to Jesus, besought him earnestly, saying, He is worthy
that thou shouldest do this for him : 5. for he loveth our nation,
and himself built us our synagogue. 6. And Jesus went with
them.
10. And they that were sent, returning to the house, found the
servant whole.

7^{11-17} *The Raising of the Widow's Son at Nain*

11. And it came to pass soon afterwards, that he went to a city
called Nain ; and his disciples went with him, and a great multitude. 12. Now when he drew near to the gate of the city, behold,
there was carried out one that was dead, the only son of his
mother, and she was a widow : and much people of the city was
with her. 13. And when the Lord saw her, he had compassion
on her, and said unto her, Weep not. 14. And he came nigh and
touched the bier : and the bearers stood still. And he said,

Young man, I say unto thee, Arise. 15. And he that was dead sat up, and began to speak. And he gave him to his mother. 16. And fear took hold on all : and they glorified God, saying, A great prophet is arisen among us : and, God hath visited his people. 17. And this report went forth concerning him in the whole of Judæa, and all the region round about.

7³⁶⁻⁵⁰ *The Woman who was a Sinner*

36. And one of the Pharisees desired him that he would eat with him. And he entered into the Pharisee's house, and sat down to meat. 37. And behold, a woman which was in the city, a sinner ; and when she knew that he was sitting at meat in the Pharisee's house, she brought an alabaster cruse of ointment, 38. and standing behind at his feet, weeping, she began to wet his feet with her tears, and wiped them with the hair of her head, and kissed his feet, and anointed them with the ointment. 39. Now when the Pharisee which had bidden him saw it, he spake within himself, saying, This man, if he were a prophet, would have perceived who and what manner of woman this is which toucheth him, that she is a sinner. 40. And Jesus answering said unto him, Simon, I have somewhat to say unto thee. And he saith, Master, say on. 41. A certain lender had two debtors : the one owed five hundred pence, and the other fifty. 42. When they had not *wherewith* to pay, he forgave them both. Which of them therefore will love him most ? 43. Simon answered and said, He, I suppose, to whom he forgave the most. And he said unto him, Thou hast rightly judged. 44. And turning to the woman, he said unto Simon, Seest thou this woman ? I entered into thine house, thou gavest me no water for my feet : but she hath wetted my feet with her tears, and wiped them with her hair. 45. Thou gavest me no kiss : but she, since the time I came in, hath not ceased to kiss my feet. 46. My head with oil thou didst not anoint : but she hath anointed my feet with ointment. 47. Wherefore I say unto thee, Her sins, which are many, are forgiven ; for she loved much : but to whom little is forgiven, *the same* loveth little. 48. And he said unto her, Thy sins are forgiven. 49. And they that sat at meat with him began to say within themselves, Who is this that even forgiveth sins ? 50. And he said unto the woman, Thy faith hath saved thee ; go in peace.

8¹⁻³   *The Ministering Women*

1. And it came to pass soon afterwards, that he went about through the cities and villages, preaching and bringing the good tidings of the kingdom of God, and with him the twelve, 2. and certain women which had been healed of evil spirits and infirmities, Mary that was called Magdalene, from whom seven devils had gone out, 3. and Joanna the wife of Chuza Herod's steward, and Susanna, and many others, which ministered unto them of their substance.

9⁵¹⁻⁵⁶   *The Samaritan Village*

51. And it came to pass, when the days were well-nigh come that he should be received up, he steadfastly set his face to go to Jerusalem, 52. and sent messengers before his face : and they went, and entered into a village of the Samaritans, to make ready for him.   53. And they did not receive him, because his face was *as though he were* going to Jerusalem.   54. And when his disciples James and John saw *this*, they said, Lord, wilt thou that we bid fire to come down from heaven, and consume them ? 55. But he turned, and rebuked them.   56. And they went to another village.

10¹   *The Appointment of the Seventy*

1. Now after these things the Lord appointed seventy others, and sent them two and two before his face into every city and place, whither he himself was about to come.

10¹⁷⁻²⁰   *The Return of the Seventy*

17. And the seventy returned with joy, saying, Lord, even the devils are subject unto us in thy name. 18. And he said unto them, I beheld Satan fallen as lightning from heaven. 19. Behold, I have given you authority to tread upon serpents and scorpions, and over all the power of the enemy : and nothing shall in any wise hurt you. 20. Howbeit in this rejoice not, that the spirits are subject unto you ; but rejoice that your names are written in heaven.

10²⁵⁻²⁸   *The Great Commandment*

25. And behold, a certain lawyer stood up and tempted him,
saying, Master, what shall I do to inherit eternal life ?   26. And
he said unto him, What is written in the law ? how readest thou ?
27. And he answering said, Thou shalt love the Lord thy God
with all thy heart, and with all thy soul, and with all thy strength,
and with all thy mind ; and thy neighbour as thyself.   28. And
he said unto him, Thou hast answered right : this do, and thou
shalt live.

10²⁹⁻³⁷   *Parable of the Good Samaritan*

29. But he, desiring to justify himself, said unto Jesus, And
who is my neighbour ?   30. Jesus made answer and said, A
certain man was going down from Jerusalem to Jericho ; and he
fell among robbers, which both stripped him and beat him, and
departed, leaving him half dead.   31. And by chance a certain
priest was going down that way : and when he saw him, he
passed by on the other side.   32. And in like manner a Levite
also, when he came to the place, and saw him, passed by on the
other side.   33. But a certain Samaritan, as he journeyed, came
where he was : and when he saw him, he was moved with compassion, 34. and came to him, and bound up his wounds, pouring
on *them* oil and wine ; and he set him on his own beast, and brought
him to an inn, and took care of him.   35. And on the morrow he
took out two pence, and gave them to the host, and said, Take
care of him ; and whatsoever thou spendest more, I, when I come
back again, will repay thee.   36. Which of these three, thinkest
thou, proved neighbour unto him that fell among the robbers ?
37. And he said, He that shewed mercy on him.   And Jesus said
unto him, Go, and do thou likewise.

10³⁸⁻⁴²   *Martha and Mary*

38. Now as they went on their way, he entered into a certain
village : and a certain woman named Martha received him into
her house.   39. And she had a sister called Mary, which also sat
at the Lord's feet, and heard his word.   40. But Martha was
cumbered about much serving ; and she came up to him, and
said, Lord, dost thou not care that my sister did leave me to
serve alone ? bid her therefore that she help me.   41. But the
Lord answered and said unto her, Martha, Martha, thou art

anxious and troubled about many things : 42. but one thing is needful : for Mary hath chosen the good part, which shall not be taken away from her.

11¹⁻⁴ *The Lord's Prayer*

1. And it came to pass, as he was praying in a certain place, that when he ceased, one of his disciples said unto him, Lord, teach us to pray, even as John also taught his disciples. 2. And he said unto them, When ye pray, say, Father, Hallowed be thy name. Thy kingdom come. 3. Give us day by day our daily bread. 4. And forgive us our sins ; for we ourselves also forgive every one that is indebted to us. And bring us not into temptation.

11⁵⁻⁸ *Parable of the Friend at Midnight*

5. And he said unto them, Which of you shall have a friend, and shall go unto him at midnight, and say to him, Friend, lend me three loaves ; 6. for a friend of mine is come to me from a journey, and I have nothing to set before him ; 7. and he from within shall answer and say, Trouble me not : the door is now shut, and my children are with me in bed ; I cannot rise and give thee ? 8. I say unto you, Though he will not rise and give him, because he is his friend, yet because of his importunity he will arise and give him as many as he needeth.

11⁵³⁻12¹ᵃ *The Pharisees Provoke Jesus*

53. And when he was come out from thence, the scribes and the Pharisees began to press upon *him* vehemently, and to provoke him to speak of many things ; 54. laying wait for him, to catch something out of his mouth.

12¹. In the mean time, when the many thousands of the multitude were gathered together, insomuch that they trode one upon another. . . .

12¹³⁻¹⁵ *On Dividing the Inheritance*

13. And one out of the multitude said unto him, Master, bid my brother divide the inheritance with me. 14. But he said unto him, Man, who made me a judge or a divider over you ? 15. And he said unto them, Take heed, and keep yourselves from all covetousness : for a man's life consisteth not in the abundance of the things which he possesseth.

12¹⁶⁻²¹   *The Parable of the Rich Fool*

16. And he spake a parable unto them, saying, The ground of
a certain rich man brought forth plentifully : 17. and he reasoned
within himself, saying, What shall I do, because I have not where
to bestow my fruits ? 18. And he said, This will I do : I will
pull down my barns, and build greater ; and there will I bestow
all my corn and my goods. 19. And I will say to my soul, Soul,
thou hast much goods laid up for many years ; take thine ease, eat,
drink, be merry. 20. But God said unto him, Thou foolish one,
this night is thy soul required of thee ; and the things which thou
hast prepared, whose shall they be ? 21. So is he that layeth up
treasure for himself, and is not rich toward God.

13¹⁻⁵   *The Galilæans and the Tower of Siloam*

1. Now there were some present at that very season which told
him of the Galilæans, whose blood Pilate had mingled with their
sacrifices. 2. And he answered and said unto them, Think ye
that these Galilæans were sinners above all the Galilæans, because
they have suffered these things ? 3. I tell you, Nay : but, except
ye repent, ye shall all in like manner perish. 4. Or those eighteen,
upon whom the tower in Siloam fell, and killed them, think ye
that they were offenders above all the men that dwell in Jerusalem?
5. I tell you, Nay : but, except ye repent, ye shall all likewise
perish.

13⁶⁻⁹   *The Parable of the Fig Tree*

6. And he spake this parable ; A certain man had a fig tree
planted in his vineyard ; and he came seeking fruit thereon, and
found none. 7. And he said unto the vinedresser, Behold, these
three years I come seeking fruit on this fig tree, and find none :
cut it down ; why doth it also cumber the ground ? 8. And he
answering saith unto him, Lord, let it alone this year also, till I
shall dig about it, and dung it : 9. and if it bear fruit thenceforth,
well ; but if not, thou shalt cut it down.

13¹⁰⁻¹⁷ *The Healing of the Woman with a Spirit of Infirmity*

10. And he was teaching in one of the synagogues on the
sabbath day. 11. And behold, a woman which had a spirit of
infirmity eighteen years ; and she was bowed together, and could

in no wise lift herself up. 12. And when Jesus saw her, he called her, and said to her, Woman, thou are loosed from thine infirmity. 13. And he laid his hands upon her : and immediately she was made straight, and glorified God. 14. And the ruler of the synagogue, being moved with indignation because Jesus had healed on the sabbath, answered and said to the multitude, There are six days in which men ought to work : in them therefore come and be healed, and not on the day of the sabbath. 15. But the Lord answered him, and said, Ye hypocrites, doth not each one of you on the sabbath loose his ox or his ass from the stall, and lead him away to watering ? 16. And ought not this woman, being a daughter of Abraham, whom Satan had bound, lo, *these* eighteen years, to have been loosed from this bond on the day of the sabbath ? 17. And as he said these things, all his adversaries were put to shame : and all the multitude rejoiced for all the glorious things that were done by him.

14¹⁻⁶   *The Healing of a Man with Dropsy*

1. And it came to pass, when he went into the house of one of the rulers of the Pharisees on a sabbath to eat bread, that they were watching him. 2. And behold, there was before him a certain man which had the dropsy. 3. And Jesus answering spake unto the lawyers and Pharisees, saying, Is it lawful to heal on the sabbath, or not ? But they held their peace. 4. And he took him, and healed him, and let him go. 5. And he said unto them, Which of you shall have an ass or an ox fallen into a well, and will not straightway draw him up on a sabbath day ? 6. And they could not answer again unto these things.

14⁷⁻¹⁰   *On Invitations to a Marriage Feast*

7. And he spake a parable unto those which were bidden, when he marked how they chose out the chief seats ; saying unto them, 8. When thou art bidden of any man to a marriage feast, sit not down in the chief seat ; lest haply a more honourable man than thou be bidden of him, 9. and he that bade thee and him shall come and say to thee, Give this man place ; and then thou shalt begin with shame to take the lowest place. 10. But when thou art bidden, go and sit down in the lowest place ; that when he that hath bidden thee cometh, he may say to thee, Friend, go up higher : then shalt thou have glory in the presence of all that sit at meat with thee.

14¹²⁻¹⁴   *On Hospitality*

12. And he said to him also that had bidden him, When thou makest a dinner or a supper, call not thy friends, nor thy brethren, nor thy kinsmen, nor rich neighbours ; lest haply they also bid thee again, and a recompense be made thee.   13. But when thou makest a feast, bid the poor, the maimed, the lame, the blind : 14. and thou shalt be blessed ; because they have not *wherewith* to recompense thee : for thou shalt be recompensed in the resurrection of the just.

14¹⁵⁻²⁴   *The Parable of the Great Supper*

15. And when one of them that sat at meat with him heard these things, he said unto him, Blessed is he that shall eat bread in the kingdom of God.   16. But he said unto him, A certain man made a great supper ; and he bade many : 17. and he sent forth his servant at supper time to say to them that were bidden, Come ; for *all* things are now ready.   18. And they all with one *consent* began to make excuse.   The first said unto him, I have bought a field, and I must needs go out and see it : I pray thee have me excused.   19. And another said, I have bought five yoke of oxen, and I go to prove them : I pray thee have me excused.   20. And another said, I have married a wife, and therefore I cannot come. 21. And the servant came, and told his lord these things.   Then the master of the house being angry said to his servant, Go out quickly into the streets and lanes of the city, and bring in thither the poor and maimed and blind and lame.   22. And the servant said, Lord, what thou didst command is done, and yet there is room.   23. And the lord said unto the servant, Go out into the highways and hedges, and constrain *them* to come in, that my house may be filled.   24. For I say unto you, that none of those men which were bidden shall taste of my supper.

14²⁸⁻³³   *Discipleship and its Cost*

28. For which of you, desiring to build a tower, doth not first sit down and count the cost, whether he have *wherewith* to complete it ?   29. Lest haply, when he hath laid a foundation, and is not able to finish, all that behold begin to mock him, saying, 30. This man began to build, and was not able to finish.   31. Or what king, as he goeth to encounter another king in war, will not

sit down first and take counsel whether he is able with ten thousand
to meet him that cometh against him with twenty thousand ?
32. Or else, while the other is yet a great way off, he sendeth an
ambassage, and asketh conditions of peace.   33. So therefore
whosoever he be of you that renounceth not all that he hath, he
cannot be my disciple.

15¹⁻⁷   *The Parable of the Lost Sheep*

1. Now all the publicans and sinners were drawing near unto
him for to hear him.   2. And both the Pharisees and the scribes
murmured, saying, This man receiveth sinners, and eateth with
them.

3. And he spake unto them this parable, saying, 4. What man
of you, having a hundred sheep, and having lost one of them, doth
not leave the ninety and nine in the wilderness, and go after that
which is lost, until he find it ?   5. And when he hath found it,
he layeth it on his shoulders, rejoicing.   6. And when he cometh
home, he calleth together his friends and his neighbours, saying
unto them, Rejoice with me, for I have found my sheep which
was lost.   7. I say unto you, that even so there shall be joy in
heaven over one sinner that repenteth, *more* than over ninety and
nine righteous persons, which need no repentance.

15⁸⁻¹⁰   *The Parable of the Lost Coin*

8. Or what woman having ten pieces of silver, if she lose one
piece, doth not light a lamp, and sweep the house, and seek
diligently until she find it ?   9. And when she hath found it,
she calleth together her friends and neighbours, saying, Rejoice
with me, for I have found the piece which I had lost.   10. Even
so, I say unto you, there is joy in the presence of the angels of
God over one sinner that repenteth.

15¹¹⁻³²   *The Parable of the Prodigal Son*

11. And he said, A certain man had two sons :   12. and the
younger of them said to his father, Father, give me the portion of
thy substance that falleth to me.   And he divided unto them his
living.   13. And not many days after the younger son gathered
all together, and took his journey into a far country ; and there
he wasted his substance with riotous living.   14. And when he
had spent all, there arose a mighty famine in that country ; and

he began to be in want. 15. And he went and joined himself to one of the citizens of that country ; and he sent him into his fields to feed swine. 16. And he would fain have been filled with the husks that the swine did eat : and no man gave unto him. 17. But when he came to himself he said, How many hired servants of my father's have bread enough and to spare, and I perish here with hunger ! 18. I will arise and go to my father, and will say unto him, Father, I have sinned against heaven, and in thy sight : 19. I am no more worthy to be called thy son : make me as one of thy hired servants. 20. And he arose, and came to his father. But while he was yet afar off, his father saw him, and was moved with compassion, and ran, and fell on his neck, and kissed him. 21. And the son said unto him, Father, I have sinned against heaven, and in thy sight : I am no more worthy to be called thy son. 22. But the father said to his servants, Bring forth quickly the best robe, and put it on him ; and put a ring on his hand, and shoes on his feet : 23. and bring the fatted calf, *and* kill it, and let us eat, and make merry : 24. for this my son was dead, and is alive again ; he was lost, and is found. And they began to be merry. 25. Now his elder son was in the field : and as he came and drew nigh to the house, he heard music and dancing. 26. And he called to him one of the servants, and inquired what these things might be. 27. And he said unto him, Thy brother is come ; and thy father hath killed the fatted calf, because he hath received him safe and sound. 28. But he was angry, and would not go in : and his father came out, and intreated him. 29. But he answered and said to his father, Lo, these many years do I serve thee, and I never transgressed a commandment of thine : and *yet* thou never gavest me a kid, that I might make merry with my friends : 30. but when this thy son came, which hath devoured thy living with harlots, thou killedst for him the fatted calf. 31. And he said unto him, Son, thou art ever with me, and all that is mine is thine. 32. But it was meet to make merry and be glad : for this thy brother was dead, and is alive *again ;* and *was* lost, and is found.

16¹⁻¹²   *The Parable of the Unjust Steward*

1. And he said also unto the disciples, There was a certain rich man, which had a steward ; and the same was accused unto him that he was wasting his goods. 2. And he called him, and said unto him, What is this that I hear of thee ? render the

account of thy stewardship ; for thou canst be no longer steward. 3. And the steward said within himself, What shall I do, seeing that my lord taketh away the stewardship from me ? I have not strength to dig ; to beg I am ashamed. 4. I am resolved what to do, that, when I am put out of the stewardship, they may receive me into their houses. 5. And calling to him each one of his lord's debtors, he said to the first, How much owest thou unto my lord ? 6. And he said, A hundred measures of oil. And he said unto him, Take thy bond, and sit down quickly and write fifty. 7. Then said he to another, And how much owest thou ? And he said, A hundred measures of wheat. He saith unto him, Take thy bond, and write fourscore. 8. And his lord commended the unrighteous steward because he had done wisely : for the sons of this world are for their own generation wiser than the sons of the light. 9. And I say unto you, Make to yourselves friends by means of the mammon of unrighteousness ; that, when it shall fail, they may receive you into the eternal tabernacles. 10. He that is faithful in a very little is faithful also in much : and he that is unrighteous in a very little is unrighteous also in much. 11. If therefore ye have not been faithful in the unrighteous mammon, who will commit to your trust the true *riches ?* 12. And if ye have not been faithful in that which is another's, who will give you that which is your own ?

16¹⁴⁻¹⁵ *The Pharisees who Loved Money*

14. And the Pharisees, who were lovers of money, heard all these things ; and they scoffed at him. 15. And he said unto them, Ye are they that justify yourselves in the sight of men ; but God knoweth your hearts : for that which is exalted among men is an abomination in the sight of God.

16¹⁹⁻³¹ *The Parable of the Rich Man and Lazarus*

19. Now there was a certain rich man, and he was clothed in purple and fine linen, faring sumptuously every day : 20. and a certain beggar named Lazarus was laid at his gate, full of sores, 21. and desiring to be fed with the *crumbs* that fell from the rich man's table ; yea, even the dogs came and licked his sores. 22. And it came to pass, that the beggar died, and that he was carried away by the angels into Abraham's bosom : and the rich man also died, and was buried. 23. And in Hades he lifted up

his eyes, being in torments, and seeth Abraham afar off, and Lazarus in his bosom. 24. And he cried and said, Father Abraham, have mercy on me, and send Lazarus, that he may dip the tip of his finger in water, and cool my tongue ; for I am in anguish in this flame. 25. But Abraham said, Son, remember that thou in thy lifetime receivedst thy good things, and Lazarus in like manner evil things : but now here he is comforted, and thou art in anguish. 26. And beside all this, between us and you there is a great gulf fixed, that they which would pass from hence to you may not be able, and that none may cross over from thence to us. 27. And he said, I pray thee therefore, father, that thou wouldest send him to my father's house ; 28. for I have five brethren ; that he may testify unto them, lest they also come into this place of torment. 29. But Abraham saith, They have Moses and the prophets ; let them hear them. 30. And he said, Nay, father Abraham : but if one go to them from the dead, they will repent. 31. And he said unto him, If they hear not Moses and the prophets, neither will they be persuaded, if one rise from the dead.

17⁷⁻¹⁰   *The Parable of the Master and Servant*

7. But who is there of you, having a servant plowing or keeping sheep, that will say unto him, when he is come in from the field, Come straightway and sit down to meat ; 8. and will not rather say unto him, Make ready wherewith I may sup, and gird thyself, and serve me, till I have eaten and drunken ; and afterward thou shalt eat and drink ? 9. Doth he thank the servant because he did the things that were commanded ? 10. Even so ye also, when ye shall have done all the things that are commanded you, say, We are unprofitable servants ; we have done that which it was our duty to do.

17¹¹⁻¹⁹   *The Healing of the Ten Lepers*

11. And it came to pass, as they were on the way to Jerusalem, that he was passing through the midst of Samaria and Galilee. 12. And as he entered into a certain village, there met him ten men that were lepers, which stood afar off : 13. and they lifted up their voices, saying, Jesus, Master, have mercy on us. 14. And when he saw them, he said unto them, Go and shew your-selves unto the priests. And it came to pass, as they went, they were cleansed. 15. And one of them, when he saw that he was

healed, turned back, with a loud voice glorifying God ; 16. and
he fell upon his face at his feet, giving him thanks : and he was
a Samaritan.   17. And Jesus answering said, Were not the ten
cleansed ? but where are the nine ?   18. Were there none found
that returned to give glory to God, save this stranger ?   19. And
he said unto him, Arise, and go thy way : thy faith hath made
thee whole.

18¹⁻⁸   *The Parable of the Unrighteous Judge*

1. And he spake a parable unto them to the end that they
ought always to pray, and not to faint ; 2. saying, There was in
a city a judge, which feared not God, and regarded not man :
3. and there was a widow in that city ; and she came oft unto
him, saying, Avenge me of mine adversary.   4. And he would
not for a while : but afterward he said within himself, Though I
fear not God, nor regard man ; 5. yet because this widow troubleth
me, I will avenge her, lest she wear me out by her continual
coming.   6. And the Lord said, Hear what the unrighteous judge
saith.   7. And shall not God avenge his elect, which cry to him
day and night, and he is longsuffering over them ?   8. I say
unto you, that he will avenge them speedily.   Howbeit when the
Son of man cometh, shall he find faith on the earth ?

18⁹⁻¹⁴   *The Parable of the Pharisee and the Publican*

9. And he spake also this parable unto certain which trusted in
themselves that they were righteous, and set all others at nought :
10. Two men went up into the temple to pray ; the one a Pharisee,
and the other a publican.   11. The Pharisee stood and prayed
thus with himself, God, I thank thee, that I am not as the rest
of men, extortioners, unjust, adulterers, or even as this publican.
12. I fast twice in the week ; I give tithes of all that I get.   13.
But the publican, standing afar off, would not lift up so much
as his eyes unto heaven, but smote his breast, saying, God, be
merciful to me a sinner.   14. I say unto you, This man went down
to his house justified rather than the other : for every one that
exalteth himself shall be humbled ; but he that humbleth himself
shall be exalted.

19¹⁻¹⁰   *Zacchæus*

1. And he entered and was passing through Jericho. 2. And
behold, a man called by name Zacchæus ; and he was a chief

publican, and he was rich. 3. And he sought to see Jesus who he was ; and could not for the crowd, because he was little of stature. 4. And he ran on before, and climbed up into a sycomore tree to see him : for he was to pass that way. 5. And when Jesus came to the place, he looked up, and said unto him, Zacchæus, make haste, and come down ; for to-day I must abide at thy house. 6. And he made haste, and came down, and received him joyfully. 7. And when they saw it, they all murmured, saying, He is gone in to lodge with a man that is a sinner. 8. And Zacchæus stood, and said unto the Lord, Behold, Lord, the half of my goods I give to the poor ; and if I have wrongfully exacted aught of any man, I restore fourfold. 9. And Jesus said unto him, To-day is salvation come to this house, forasmuch as he also is a son of Abraham. 10. For the Son of man came to seek and to save that which was lost.

19[11-27]   *The Parable of the Pounds*

11. And as they heard these things, he added and spake a parable, because he was nigh to Jerusalem, and *because* they supposed that the kingdom of God was immediately to appear. 12. He said therefore, A certain nobleman went into a far country, to receive for himself a kingdom, and to return. 13. And he called ten servants of his, and gave them ten pounds, and said unto them, Trade ye *herewith* till I come. 14. But his citizens hated him, and sent an ambassage after him, saying, We will not that this man reign over us. 15. And it came to pass, when he was come back again, having received the kingdom, that he commanded these servants, unto whom he had given the money, to be called to him, that he might know what they had gained by trading. 16. And the first came before him, saying, Lord, thy pound hath made ten pounds more. 17. And he said unto him, Well done, thou good servant : because thou wast found faithful in a very little, have thou authority over ten cities. 18. And the second came, saying, Thy pound, Lord, hath made five pounds. 19. And he said unto him also, Be thou also over five cities. 20. And another came, saying, Lord, behold *here is* thy pound, which I kept laid up in a napkin : 21. for I feared thee, because thou art an austere man : thou takest up that thou layedst not down, and reapest that thou didst not sow. 22. He saith unto him, Out of thine own mouth will I judge thee, thou wicked servant. Thou knewest that I am austere man, taking up

that I laid not down, and reaping that I did not sow ; 23. then wherefore gavest thou not my money into the bank, and I at my coming should have required it with interest ? 24. And he said unto them that stood by, Take away from him the pound, and give it unto him that hath the ten pounds. 25. And they said unto him, Lord, he hath ten pounds. 26. I say unto you, that unto every one that hath shall be given ; but from him that hath not, even that which he hath shall be taken away from him. 27. Howbeit these mine enemies, which would not that I should reign over them, bring hither, and slay them before me.

19[37-40]   *The Rejoicing at the Mount of Olives*

37. And as he was now drawing nigh, *even* at the descent of the mount of Olives, the whole multitude of the disciples began to rejoice and praise God with a loud voice for all the mighty works which they had seen ; 38. saying, Blessed *is* the King that cometh in the name of the Lord : peace in heaven, and glory in the highest. 39. And some of the Pharisees from the multitude said unto him, Master, rebuke thy disciples. 40. And he answered and said, I tell you that, if these shall hold their peace, the stones will cry out.

19[41-44]   *The Weeping over the City*

41. And when he drew nigh, he saw the city and wept over it, 42. saying, If thou hadst known in this day, even thou, the things which belong unto peace ! but now they are hid from thine eyes. 43. For the days shall come upon thee, when thine enemies shall cast up a bank about thee, and compass thee round, and keep thee in on every side, 44. and shall dash thee to the ground, and thy children within thee ; and they shall not leave in thee one stone upon another ; because thou knewest not the time of thy visitation.

19[47-48]   *Daily Teaching in the Temple*

47. And he was teaching daily in the temple. But the chief priests and the scribes and the principal men of the people sought to destroy him : 48. and they could not find what they might do ; for the people all hung upon him, listening.

The Last Supper

14. And when the hour was come, he sat down, and the apostles with him. 15. And he said unto them, With desire I have desired to eat this passover with you before I suffer : 16. for I say unto you, I will not eat it, until it be fulfilled in the kingdom of God. 17. And he received a cup, and when he had given thanks, he said, Take this, and divide it among yourselves :

21. But behold, the hand of him that betrayeth me is with me on the table. 23. And they began to question among themselves, which of them it was that should do this thing.

24. And there arose also a contention among them, which of them is accounted to be greatest. 25. And he said unto them, The kings of the Gentiles have lordship over them ; and they that have authority over them are called Benefactors. 26. But ye *shall* not *be* so : but he that is the greater among you, let him become as the younger ; and he that is chief, as he that doth serve. 27. For whether is greater, he that sitteth at meat, or he that serveth ? is not he that sitteth at meat ? but I am in the midst of you as he that serveth. 28. But ye are they which have continued with me in my temptations ; 29. and I appoint unto you a kingdom, even as my Father appointed unto me, 30. that ye may eat and drink at my table in my kingdom ; and ye shall sit on thrones judging the twelve tribes of Israel. 31. Simon, Simon, behold, Satan asked to have you, that he might sift you as wheat : 32. but I made supplication for thee, that thy faith fail not : and do thou, when once thou hast turned again, stablish thy brethren. 33. And he said unto him, Lord, with thee I am ready to go both to prison and to death.

35. And he said unto them, When I sent you forth without purse, and wallet, and shoes, lacked ye anything ? And they said, Nothing. 36. And he said unto them, But now, he that hath a purse, let him take it, and likewise a wallet : and he that hath none, let him sell his cloke, and buy a sword. 37. For I say unto you, that this which is written must be fulfilled in me, And he was reckoned with transgressors : for that which concerneth me hath fulfilment. 38. And they said, Lord, behold, here are two swords. And he said unto them, It is enough.

The Agony in the Garden

39. And he came out, and went, as his custom was, unto the mount of Olives ; and the disciples also followed him. 40. And

when he was at the place, he said unto them, Pray that ye enter not into temptation. 41. And he was parted from them about a stone's cast ; and he kneeled down and prayed. 43. And there appeared unto him an angel from heaven, strengthening him. 44. And being in an agony he prayed more earnestly : and his sweat became as it were great drops of blood falling down upon the ground. 45. And when he rose up from his prayer, he came unto the disciples, and found them sleeping for sorrow, 46. and said unto them, Why sleep ye ? rise and pray, that ye enter not into temptation.

22^{47-53} *The Arrest*

47. While he yet spake, behold, a multitude, and he that was called Judas, one of the twelve, went before them ; and he drew near unto Jesus to kiss him. 48. But Jesus said unto him, Judas, betrayest thou the Son of man with a kiss ? 49. And when they that were about him saw what would follow, they said, Lord, shall we smite with the sword ? 50. And a certain one of them smote the servant of the high priest. 51. But Jesus answered and said, Suffer ye thus far. And he touched his ear, and healed him. 52. And Jesus said, 53. This is your hour, and the power of darkness.

22^{63-65} *The Mocking*

63. And the men that held Jesus mocked him, and beat him. 64. And they blindfolded him, and asked him, saying, Prophesy : who is he that struck thee ? 65. And many other things spake they against him, reviling him.

22^{66-70} *The Hebrew Trial*

66. And as soon as it was day, the assembly of the elders of the people was gathered together, both chief priests and scribes ; and they led him away into their council, saying, 67. If thou art the Christ, tell us. But he said unto them, If I tell you, ye will not believe : 68. and if I ask *you*, ye will not answer. 69. But from henceforth shall the Son of man be seated at the right hand of the power of God. 70. And they all said, Art thou then the Son of God ? And he said unto them, Ye say that I am.

The Roman Trial ; before Herod

1. And the whole company of them rose up, and brought him before Pilate.   2. And they began to accuse him, saying, We found this man perverting our nation, and forbidding to give tribute to Cæsar, and saying that he himself is Christ a king. 4. And Pilate said unto the chief priests and the multitudes, I find no fault in this man.   5. But they were the more urgent, saying, He stirreth up the people, teaching throughout all Judæa, and beginning from Galilee even unto this place.   6. But when Pilate heard it, he asked whether the man were a Galilæan. 7. And when he knew that he was of Herod's jurisdiction, he sent him unto Herod, who himself also was at Jerusalem in these days.

8. Now when Herod saw Jesus, he was exceeding glad : for he was of a long time desirous to see him, because he had heard concerning him ; and he hoped to see some miracle done by him. 9. And he questioned him in many words ; but he answered him nothing.   10. And the chief priests and the scribes stood, vehemently accusing him.   11. And Herod with his soldiers set him at nought, and mocked him, and arraying him in gorgeous apparel sent him back to Pilate.   12. And Herod and Pilate became friends with each other that very day : for before they were at enmity between themselves.

13. And Pilate called together the chief priests and the rulers and the people, 14. and said unto them, Ye brought unto me this man, as one that perverteth the people : and behold, I, having examined him before you, found no fault in this man touching those things whereof ye accuse him : 15. no, nor yet Herod : for he sent him back unto us ; and behold, nothing worthy of death hath been done by him.   16. I will therefore chastise him, and release him.   18. But they cried out all together, saying, Away with this man, and release unto us Barabbas : 19. one who for a certain insurrection made in the city, and for murder, was cast into prison.   20. And Pilate spake unto them again, desiring to release Jesus ;   21. but they shouted, saying, Crucify, crucify him.   22. And he said unto them the third time, Why, what evil hath this man done ?   I have found no cause of death in him : I will therefore chastise him and release him.   23. But they were instant with loud voices, asking that he might be crucified.   And their voices prevailed.   24. And Pilate gave sentence that what they asked for should be done.

23^{27-31} *The Daughters of Jerusalem*

27. And there followed him a great multitude of the people, and of women who bewailed and lamented him. 28. But Jesus turning unto them said, Daughters of Jerusalem, weep not for me, but weep for yourselves, and for your children. 29. For behold, the days are coming, in which they shall say, Blessed are the barren, and the wombs that never bare, and the breasts that never gave suck. 30. Then shall they begin to say to the mountains, Fall on us ; and to the hills, Cover us. 31. For if they do these things in the green tree, what shall be done in the dry ?

23^{32-54} *The Crucifixion*

32. And there were also two others, malefactors, led with him to be put to death.

33. And when they came unto the place which is called The skull, there they crucified him, and the malefactors, one on the right hand and the other on the left. 34. And Jesus said, Father, forgive them ; for they know not what they do. 35. And the people stood beholding. And the rulers also scoffed at him, saying, He saved others ; let him save himself, if this is the Christ of God, his chosen. 36. And the soldiers also mocked him, coming to him, offering him vinegar, 37. and saying, If thou art the King of the Jews, save thyself.

39. And one of the malefactors which were hanged railed on him, saying, Art not thou the Christ ? save thyself and us. 40. But the other answered, and rebuking him said, Dost thou not even fear God, seeing thou art in the same condemnation ? 41. And we indeed justly ; for we receive the due reward of our deeds : but this man hath done nothing amiss. 42. And he said, Jesus, remember me when thou comest in thy kingdom. 43. And he said unto him, Verily I say unto thee, To-day shalt thou be with me in Paradise. 46. And when Jesus had cried with a loud voice, he said, Father, into thy hands I commend my spirit : and having said this, he gave up the ghost. 47. And when the centurion saw what was done, he glorified God, saying, Certainly this was a righteous man. 48. And all the multitudes that came together to this sight, when they beheld the things that were done, returned smiting their breasts.

54. And it was the day of the Preparation, and the sabbath drew on.

16

23$^{55-56}$ *The Women Prepare Spices*

55. And the women, which had come with him out of Galilee. followed after, and beheld the tomb, and how his body was laid. 56. And they returned, and prepared spices and ointments. And on the sabbath they rested according to the commandment.

24$^{1-11}$ *The Women Visit the Tomb*

1. But on the first day of the week, at early dawn, they came unto the tomb, bringing the spices which they had prepared. 2. And they found the stone rolled away from the tomb. 3. And they entered in, and found not the body of the Lord Jesus. 4. And it came to pass, while they were perplexed thereabout, behold, two men stood by them in dazzling apparel : 5. and as they were affrighted, and bowed down their faces to the earth, they said unto them, Why seek ye the living among the dead ? 6. He is not here, but he is risen : remember how he spake unto you when he was yet in Galilee, 7. saying that the Son of man must be delivered up into the hands of sinful men, and be crucified, and the third day rise again. 8. And they remembered his words, 9. and returned from the tomb, and told all these things to the eleven, and to all the rest. 10. Now they were Mary Magdalene, and Joanna, and Mary the *mother* of James : and the other women with them told these things unto the apostles. 11. And these words appeared in their sight as idle talk ; and they disbelieved them.

24$^{13-35}$ *The Appearance to the Two Disciples Going to Emmaus*

13. And behold, two of them were going that very day to a village named Emmaus, which was three score furlongs from Jerusalem. 14. And they communed with each other of all these things which had happened. 15. And it came to pass, while they communed and questioned together, that Jesus himself drew near, and went with them. 16. But their eyes were holden that they should not know him. 17. And he said unto them, What communications are these that ye have one with another, as ye walk ? And they stood still, looking sad. 18. And one of them, named Cleopas, answering said unto him, Dost thou alone sojourn in Jerusalem and not know the things which are come to pass there in these days ? 19. And he said unto them, What

things ?   And they said unto him, The things concerning Jesus of Nazareth, which was a prophet mighty in deed and word before God and all the people : 20. and how the chief priests and our rulers delivered him up to be condemned to death, and crucified him.   21. But we hoped that it was he which should redeem Israel.   Yea and beside all this, it is now the third day since these things came to pass.   22. Moreover certain women of our company amazed us, having been early at the tomb ; 23. and when they found not his body, they came, saying, that they had also seen a vision of angels, which said that he was alive.   24. And certain of them that were with us went to the tomb, and found it even so as the women had said : but him they saw not.   25. And he said unto them, O foolish men, and slow of heart to believe in all that the prophets have spoken !   26. Behoved it not the Christ to suffer these things, and to enter into his glory ?   27. And beginning from Moses and from all the prophets, he interpreted to them in all the scriptures the things concerning himself.   28. And they drew nigh unto the village, whither they were going : and he made as though he would go further.   29. And they constrained him, saying, Abide with us : for it is toward evening, and the day is now far spent.   And he went in to abide with them.   30. And it came to pass, when he had sat down with them to meat, he took the bread, and blessed it, and brake, and gave to them.   31. And their eyes were opened, and they knew him ; and he vanished out of their sight.   32. And they said one to another, Was not our heart burning within us, while he spake to us in the way, while he opened to us the scriptures ?   33. And they rose up that very hour, and returned to Jerusalem, and found the eleven gathered together, and them that were with them, 34. saying, The Lord is risen indeed, and hath appeared to Simon. 35. And they rehearsed the things *that happened* in the way, and how he was known of them in the breaking of the bread.

24[36-49]   *The Appearance to the Eleven*

36. And as they spake these things, he himself stood in the midst of them, and saith unto them, Peace *be* unto you.   37. But they were terrified and affrighted, and supposed that they beheld a spirit.   38. And he said unto them, Why are ye troubled ? and wherefore do reasonings arise in your heart ?   39. See my hands and my feet, that it is I myself : handle me, and see ; for a spirit hath not flesh and bones, as ye behold me having.   41.

16 *

And while they still disbelieved for joy, and wondered, he said unto them, Have ye here anything to eat ? 42. And they gave him a piece of a broiled fish. 43. And he took it, and did eat before them.

44. And he said unto them, These are my words which I spake unto you, while I was yet with you, how that all things must needs be fulfilled, which are written in the law of Moses, and the prophets, and the psalms, concerning me. 45. Then opened he their mind, that they might understand the scriptures ; 46. and he said unto them, Thus it is written, that the Christ should suffer, and rise again from the dead the third day ; 47. and that repentance and remission of sins should be preached in his name unto all the nations, beginning from Jerusalem. 48. Ye are witnesses of these things. 49. And behold, I send forth the promise of my Father upon you : but tarry ye in the city, until ye be clothed with power from on high.

24 $^{50-53}$ *The Ascension*

50. And he led them out until *they were* over against Bethany : and he lifted up his hands, and blessed them. 51. And it came to pass, while he blessed them, he parted from them, and was carried up into heaven. 52. And they worshipped him, and returned to Jerusalem with great joy : 53. and were continually in the temple, blessing God.

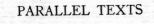
PARALLEL TEXTS

THE SICK OF THE PALSY (p. 24).

Mark 2.

1 And when he entered again into Capernaum after some days, it was noised that he was in the house. | And many were gathered together, so that there was no longer room for them, no, not even about the door : and he spake the word unto them.

2 And they come, bringing unto him a man sick of the palsy, borne of four.

4 And when they could not come nigh unto him for the crowd, they uncovered the roof where he was: and when they had broken it up, they let down the bed whereon the sick of the palsy lay.

5 And Jesus seeing their faith saith unto the sick of the palsy, Son, thy sins are forgiven.

6 But there were certain of the scribes sitting there, and reasoning in their hearts,

7 Why doth this man thus speak ? he blasphemeth : who can forgive sins but one, even God ?

8 And straightway Jesus, perceiving in his spirit that they so reasoned within themselves, saith unto them,

Matthew 9.

1 And he entered into a boat, and crossed over, and came into his own city.

2 And behold, they brought to him a man sick of the palsy, lying on a bed :

and Jesus seeing their faith said unto the sick of the palsy, Son, be of good cheer ; thy sins are forgiven.

3 And behold, certain of the scribes said within themselves,

This man blasphemeth.

4 And Jesus knowing their thoughts

said,

Luke 5.

17 And it came to pass on one of those days, that he was teaching ; and there were Pharisees and doctors of the law sitting by, which were come out of every village of Galilee and Judaea and Jerusalem : and the power of the Lord was with him to heal.

18 And behold, men bring on a bed a man that was palsied : and they sought to bring him in, and to lay him before him.

19 And not finding by what way they might bring him in because of the multitude, they went up to the house-top, and let him down through the tiles with his couch into the midst before Jesus.

20 And seeing their faith, he said, Man, thy sins are forgiven thee.

21 And the scribes and the Pharisees began to reason, saying,

Who is this that speaketh blasphemies ? Who can forgive sins, but God alone ?

22 But Jesus, perceiving their reasonings,

answered and said unto them,

Why reason ye these things in your hearts?

9 Whether is easier,
to say to the sick of the palsy,
Thy sins are forgiven;
or to say, Arise, and take up thy bed, and walk?

10 But that ye may know that the Son of man hath power on earth to forgive sins
(he saith to the sick of the palsy),

11 I say unto thee,
Arise, take up thy bed, and go unto thy house.

12 And he arose,

and straightway took up the bed, and went forth before them all;

insomuch that they were all amazed,
and glorified God,
saying, We never saw it on this fashion.

BLESSING LITTLE CHILDREN (p. 25).

Mark 10.

13 And they brought unto him little children,
that he should touch them:

and the disciples rebuked them.

14 But when Jesus saw it,

Wherefore think ye evil in your hearts?

5 For whether is easier,
to say,
Thy sins are forgiven;
or to say, Arise, and walk?

6 But that ye may know that the Son of man hath power on earth to forgive sins
(then saith he to the sick of the palsy),

Arise, and take up thy bed, and go unto thy house.

7 And he arose

and departed to his house.

8 But when the multitudes saw it, they were afraid and glorified God, which had given such power unto men.

Matthew 19.

13 Then were there brought unto him little children,
that he should lay his hands on them, and pray:
and the disciples rebuked them.

14 But Jesus

What reason ye in your hearts?

23 Whether is easier,
to say,
Thy sins are forgiven thee;
or to say, Arise and walk?

24 But that ye may know that the Son of man hath power on earth to forgive sins
(he said unto him that was palsied),
I say unto thee,
Arise, and take up thy couch, and go unto thy house.

25 And immediately he rose up before them,
and took up that whereon he lay, and departed to his house, glorifying God.

26 And amazement took hold on all, and they glorified God; and they were filled with fear, saying, We have seen strange things to-day.

Luke 18.

15 And they brought unto him also their babes,
that he should touch them:

but when the disciples saw it, they rebuked them.

16 But Jesus called them unto him,

BLESSING LITTLE CHILDREN (cont.).

Mark 10.

he was moved with indignation, and said unto them, Suffer the little children to come unto me; forbid them not: for of such is the kingdom of God.

15 Verily I say unto you, Whosoever shall not receive the kingdom of God as a little child, he shall in no wise enter therein.

16 And he took them in his arms, and blessed them, laying his hands upon them.

Matthew 19.

said, Suffer the little children, and forbid them not, to come unto me: for of such is the kingdom of heaven.

15 And he laid his hands on them, and departed thence.

Luke 18.

saying, Suffer the little children to come unto me, and forbid them not: for of such is the kingdom of God.

17 Verily I say unto you, Whosoever shall not receive the kingdom of God as a little child, he shall in no wise enter therein.

PAYING TRIBUTE TO CÆSAR (p. 26).

Mark 12.

13 And they send unto him certain of the Pharisees and of the Herodians, that they might catch him in talk.

14 And when they were come, they say unto him, Master, we know that thou art true.

and carest not for any one: for thou regardest not the person of men,

Matthew 22.

15 Then went the Pharisees, and took counsel how they might ensnare him in his talk.

16 And they send to him their disciples, with the Herodians, saying, Master, we know that thou art true, and teachest the way of God in truth,

and carest not for any one: for thou regardest not the person of men.

Luke 20.

20 And they watched him, and sent forth spies, which feigned themselves to be righteous, that they might take hold of his speech, so as to deliver him up to the rule and to the authority of the governor.

21 And they asked him, saying, Master, we know that thou sayest and teachest rightly,

and acceptest not the person of any,

but of a truth teachest the way of God :

Is it lawful to give tribute unto Caesar, or not ?

15 Shall we give, or shall we not give ?
But he, knowing their hypocrisy, said unto them,
Why tempt ye me ?
bring me a penny, that I may see it.
16 And they brought it.

And he saith unto them,
Whose is this image and superscription ?
And they said unto him, Caesar's.
17 And Jesus said unto them,
Render unto Caesar the things that are Caesar's,
and unto God the things that are God's.

And they marvelled greatly at him.

SIMON PETER'S CONFESSION (p. 26).

Mark 8.

27 And Jesus went forth, and his disciples, into the villages of Caesarea Philippi:

---

17 Tell us therefore, what thinkest thou ?
Is it lawful to give tribute unto Caesar, or not ?
18 But Jesus perceived their wickedness, and said,
Why tempt ye me, ye hypocrites ?
19 Shew me the tribute money.

And they brought unto him a penny.
20 And he saith unto them,
Whose is this image and superscription ?
21 They say unto him, Caesar's.
Then saith he unto them,
Render therefore unto Caesar the things that are Caesar's ;
and unto God the things that are God's.
22 And when they heard it,

they marvelled,
and left him, and went their way.

Matthew 16.

13 Now when Jesus came into the parts of Caesarea Philippi,

---

but of a truth teachest the way of God :

22 Is it lawful for us to give tribute unto Caesar, or not ?

23 But he perceived their craftiness, and said unto them,

24 Shew me a penny.

Whose image and superscription hath it ?
And they said, Caesar's.
25 And he said unto them,
Then render unto Caesar the things that are Caesar's,
and unto God the things that are God's.
26 And they were not able to take hold of the saying before the people :
and they marvelled at his answer, and held their peace.

Luke 9.

18 And it came to pass, as he was praying alone, the disciples were with him :

SIMON PETER'S CONFESSION (*cont.*).

Mark 8.	*Matthew 16.*	*Luke 9.*
and in the way he asked his disciples,	he asked his disciples,	and he asked them,
saying unto them, Who do men say that I am?	saying, Who do men say that the Son of man is?	saying, Who do the multitudes say that I am?
28 And they told him, saying, John the Baptist: and others Elijah; but others, One of the prophets.	14 And they said, Some say John the Baptist; some, Elijah; and others, Jeremiah, or one of the prophets.	19 And they answering said, John the Baptist; but others say, Elijah; and others, that one of the old prophets is risen again.
29 And he asked them, But who say ye that I am? Peter answereth and saith unto him, Thou art the Christ.	15 He saith unto them, But who say ye that I am? 16 And Simon Peter answered and said, Thou art the Christ, the Son of the living God. 17 And Jesus answered and said unto him, Blessed art thou, Simon Bar-Jonah: for flesh and blood hath not revealed it unto thee, but my Father which is in heaven. 18 And I also say unto thee, that thou art Peter, and upon this rock I will build my church; and the gates of Hades shall not prevail against it. │I will give unto thee the keys of the kingdom of heaven: and whatsoever thou shalt bind on earth shall be bound in heaven: and whatsoever thou shalt loose on earth shall be loosed in heaven.	20 And he said unto them, But who say ye that I am? And Peter answering said, The Christ of God.
30 And he charged them that they should tell no man of him.	20 Then charged he the disciples that they should tell no man that he was the Christ.	21 But he charged them, and commanded them to tell this to no man ;│

250

Mark 1.

²¹ And he began to teach them, that the Son of man must suffer many things, and be rejected by the elders, and the chief priests, and the scribes, and be killed, and after three days rise again.
²² And he spake the saying openly. And Peter took him, and began to rebuke him.

²³ But he turning about, and seeing his disciples, rebuked Peter, and saith, Get thee behind me, Satan.

for thou mindest not the things of God, but the things of men.

CALL AND PREACHING OF JOHN (p. 41).

Mark 1.

⁴ John came, who baptized in the wilderness and preached the baptism of repentance unto remission of sins.

Matthew.

²¹ From that time began Jesus to shew unto his disciples, how that he must go unto Jerusalem, and suffer many things of the elders and chief priests and scribes, and be killed, and the third day be raised up.
²² And Peter took him, and began to rebuke him, saying, Be it far from thee, Lord : this shall never be unto thee.
²³ But he turned

and said unto Peter, Get thee behind me, Satan : thou art a stumbling block unto me : for thou mindest not the things of God, but the things of men.

Matthew 3.

¹ And in those days

cometh John the Baptist, preaching in the wilderness of Judæa, saying,
² Repent ye; for the kingdom of heaven is at hand.

---

²² saying,
The Son of man must suffer many things,
and be rejected of the elders and chief priests
and scribes, and be killed,
and the third day be raised up.

Luke 3.

¹ Now in the fifteenth year of the reign of Tiberius Cæsar. . . . ² in the high-priesthood of Annas and Caiaphas, the word of God came unto John the son of Zacharias in the wilderness.
³ And he came into all the region round about Jordan, preaching the baptism of repentance unto remission of sins ;

The Baptism of Jesus (p. 43).

Mark 1.

9 And it came to pass in those days, that Jesus came from Nazareth of Galilee, and was baptized of John in the Jordan.

252

10 And straightway coming up out of the water,

he saw the heavens rent asunder,

and the Spirit as a dove descending upon him:

11 and a voice came out of the heavens, "Thou art my beloved Son, in thee I am well pleased."

Matthew 3.

13 Then cometh Jesus from Galilee to the Jordan unto John, to be baptized of him.

14 But John would have hindered him, saying, I have need to be baptized of thee, and comest thou to me? | But Jesus answering said unto him, Suffer it now: for thus it becometh us to fulfil all righteousness. Then he suffereth him.

16 And Jesus, when he was baptized, went up straightway from the water:

and lo, the heavens were opened unto him,

and he saw the Spirit of God descending as a dove,

and coming upon him;

17 and lo, a voice out of the heavens, saying,

"This is my beloved Son, in whom I am well pleased."

Luke 3.

21 Now it came to pass, when all the people were baptized, that Jesus also

having been baptized, and praying,

the heaven was opened,

22 and the Holy Ghost descended in a bodily form, as a dove, upon him,

and a voice came out of heaven,

"Thou art my beloved Son ; in thee I am well pleased."

The Names of the Twelve (p. 44).

Mark 3.

16 Simon he surnamed Peter;

Matthew 10.

2 The first, Simon, who is called Peter, and Andrew his brother;

Luke 6.

14 Simon, whom he also named Peter, and Andrew his brother,

Left column (Mark 12)

17 and James the son of Zebedee, and John the brother of James; and them he surnamed Boanerges, which is, Sons of thunder:
18 and Andrew, and Philip, and Bartholomew, and Matthew, and Thomas,

and James the son of Alphaeus, and Thaddaeus, and Simon the Cananaean,

19 and Judas Iscariot, which also betrayed him.

THE GREAT COMMANDMENT (p. 45).

Mark 12.

28 And one of the scribes came, and heard them questioning together, and knowing that he had answered them well, asked him, What commandment is the first of all?

29 Jesus answered, The first is, Hear, O Israel; The Lord our God, the Lord is one:

Middle column (Matthew 22)

James the son of Zebedee, and John his brother;

3 Philip, and Bartholomew; Thomas, and Matthew the publican; James the son of Alphaeus, and Thaddaeus;
4 Simon the Cananaean,

and Judas Iscariot, who also betrayed him.

Matthew 22.

34 But the Pharisees, when they heard that he had put the Sadducees to silence, gathered themselves together.
35 And one of them, a lawyer, asked him a question, tempting him,
36 Master, which is the great commandment in the law?

37 And he said unto him,

Right column (Luke 10)

and James and John,

and Philip and Bartholomew,
15 and Matthew and Thomas,

and James the son of Alphaeus,

and Simon which was called the Zealot,
16 and Judas the son of James, and Judas Iscariot, which was the traitor;

Luke 10.

25 And behold, a certain lawyer stood up and tempted him, saying,

Master,

what shall I do to inherit eternal life?
26 And he said unto him,

What is written in the Law how readest thou?

254

Mark 12.

30 and thou shalt love the Lord thy God with all thy heart, and with all thy soul, and with all thy mind, and with all thy strength.

31 The second is this, Thou shalt love thy neighbour as thyself. There is none other commandment greater than these.

32 And the scribe said unto him, Of a truth, Master, thou hast well said that he is one ; and there is none other but he : | and to love him with all the heart, and with all the understanding, and with all the strength, and to love his neighbour as himself, is much more than all whole burnt offerings and sacrifices.

34 And when Jesus saw that he answered discreetly, he said unto him, Thou art not far from the kingdom of God. And no man after that durst ask him any question.

Matthew 22.

Thou shalt love the Lord thy God with all thy heart, and with all thy soul, and with all thy mind.

38 This is the great and first commandment. And a second like unto it is this, Thou shalt love thy neighbour as thyself.

On these two commandments hangeth the whole law, and the prophets.

46 neither durst any man from that day forth ask him any more questions.

Luke 10.

27 And he answering said, Thou shalt love the Lord thy God with all thy heart, and with all thy soul, and with all thy strength, and with all thy mind ;

and thy neighbour as thyself.

28 And he said unto him,

Thou hast answered right : this do, and thou shalt live.

THE TEMPTATION (p. 46).

Mark 1.

12 And straightway the Spirit driveth him forth

into the wilderness.
13 And he was in the wilderness forty days tempted of Satan ;

and he was with the wild beasts ;

and the angels ministered unto him.

Matthew 4.

1 Then was Jesus led up of the Spirit

into the wilderness
to be tempted of the devil.

2 And when he had fasted forty days and forty nights, he afterward hungered.

11 Then the devil leaveth him ;

and behold, angels came and ministered unto him.

Luke 4.

1 And Jesus, full of the Holy Spirit, returned from the Jordan, and was led by the Spirit

in the wilderness during forty days, being tempted of the devil.

2 And he did eat nothing in those days :
and when they were completed, he hungered.

13 And when the devil had completed every temptation, he departed from him

for a season.

THE BEELZEBUB CONTROVERSY (p. 47).

Mark 3.

19 And he cometh into a house. |
20 And the multitude cometh together again, so that they could not so much as eat bread. | And
21 when his friends heard it, they went out to lay hold on him : for they said, He is beside himself.

Matthew 12.

22 Then was brought unto him one possessed with a devil, blind and dumb :

Luke 11.

14 And he was casting out a devil which was dumb.

THE BEELZEBUB CONTROVERSY (cont.).

Mark 3.

22 And the scribes which came down from Jerusalem said, He hath Beelzebub, and, By the prince of the devils casteth he out the devils.

23 And he called them unto him, and said unto them in parables, How can Satan cast out Satan?
24 And if a kingdom be divided against itself, that kingdom cannot stand.
25 And if a house be divided against itself, that house will not be able to stand.
26 And if Satan hath risen up against himself, and is divided, he cannot stand, but hath an end.

Matthew 12.

and he healed him, insomuch that the dumb man spake and saw.
23 And all the multitudes were amazed, and said, Is this the son of David?
24 But when the Pharisees heard it, they said, This man doth not cast out devils, but by Beelzebub the prince of the devils.

25 And knowing their thoughts

he said unto them,

Every kingdom divided against itself is brought to desolation; and every city or house divided against itself shall not stand:

26 and if Satan casteth out Satan, he is divided against himself; how then shall his kingdom stand?

27 And if I by Beelzebub cast out devils, by whom do your sons cast them out? Therefore shall they be your judges.

Luke 11.

And it came to pass, when the devil was gone out, the dumb man spake; and the multitudes marvelled.

15 But some of them said,

By Beelzebub the prince of the devils casteth he out devils.

16 And others, tempting him, sought of him a sign from heaven.
17 But he, knowing their thoughts,

said unto them,

Every kingdom divided against itself is brought to desolation; and a house divided against a house falleth.

18 And if Satan also is divided against himself, how shall his kingdom stand? because ye say that I cast out devils by Beelzebub.
19 But if I by Beelzebub cast out devils, by whom do your sons cast them out? Therefore shall they be your judges.

27 But no one can enter into the house of the strong man, and spoil his goods, except he first bind the strong man; and then he will spoil his house.

28 But if I by the Spirit of God cast out devils, then is the kingdom of God come upon you.
29 Or how can one enter into the house of the strong man, and spoil his goods, except he first bind the strong man? and then he will spoil his house.

20 But if I by the finger of God cast out devils, then is the kingdom of God come upon you.
21 When the strong man fully armed guardeth his own court, his goods are in peace;
22 but when a stronger than he shall come upon him, and overcome him, he taketh from him his whole armour wherein he trusted, and divideth his spoils.
23 He that is not with me is against me; and he that gathereth not with me scattereth.

30 He that is not with me is against me; and he that gathereth not with me scattereth.

Matthew 12.

31 Therefore I say unto you, Every sin and blasphemy shall be forgiven unto men;

but the blasphemy against the Spirit shall not be forgiven.

BLASPHEMY (p. 48).

Mark 3.

28 Verily I say unto you, All their sins shall be forgiven unto the sons of men, and their blasphemies wherewith soever they shall blaspheme: 29 but whosoever shall blaspheme against the Holy Spirit hath never forgiveness, but is guilty of an eternal sin:

17

257

BLASPHEMY (cont.).

Mark 3.

³⁰ because they said, He hath an unclean spirit.

THE MUSTARD TREE (p. 48).

Mark 4.

²⁰ And he said,
How shall we liken the kingdom of God? or in what parable shall we set it forth?

³¹ It is like a grain of mustard seed,

which, when it is sown upon the earth,

though it be less than all the seeds that are upon the earth,

³² yet when it is sown, groweth up, and becometh greater than all the herbs,

and putteth out great branches; so that the birds of the heaven can lodge under the shadow thereof.

Matthew 12.

³² And whosoever shall speak a word against the Son of man, it shall be forgiven him; but whosoever shall speak against the Holy Spirit, it shall not be forgiven him, neither in this world, nor in that which is to come.

Matthew 13.

³¹ Another parable set he before them, saying, The kingdom of heaven

is like unto a grain of mustard seed,

which a man took, and sowed in his field:

³² which indeed is less than all seeds;

but when it is grown, it is greater than the herbs,

and becometh a tree, so that the birds of the heaven come and lodge in the branches thereof.

Luke 12.

¹⁰ And everyone who shall speak a word against the Son of man, it shall be forgiven him: but unto him that blasphemeth against the Holy Spirit it shall not be forgiven.

Luke 13.

¹⁸ He said therefore, Unto what is the kingdom of God like? and whereunto shall I liken it?

¹⁹ It is like unto a grain of mustard seed, which a man took, and cast into his own garden;

and it grew,

and became a tree; and the birds of the heaven lodged in the branches thereof.

THE MISSION OF THE TWELVE (p. 48).

Mark 6.	Matthew 10.	Luke 9.
7 And he called unto him the twelve,	1 And he called unto him his twelve disciples,	1 And he called the twelve together,
and began to send them forth by two and two;	5 These twelve Jesus sent forth,	2 And he sent them forth
and he gave them authority over the unclean spirits ;	1 and gave them authority over unclean spirits, to cast them out, and to heal all manner of disease and all manner of sickness.	1 and gave them power and authority over all devils, and to cure diseases.
8 and he charged them	5 and charged them, saying, Go not into any way of the Gentiles, and enter not into any 6 city of the Samaritans : | but go rather to the lost sheep of the 7 house of Israel. | And as ye go, preach, saying, The kingdom of heaven is at hand. 8 Heal the sick, raise the dead, cleanse the lepers, cast out devils : freely ye received, freely give.	3 And he said unto them,
		2 to preach the kingdom of God, and to heal the sick.
that they should take nothing for their journey,	9 Get you no gold, nor silver, nor brass in your purses ; 10 no wallet for your journey,	3 Take nothing for your journey,
save a staff only ; no bread, no wallet, no money in their purse : 9 but to go shod with sandals : and, said he, put not on two coats.	nor staff : nor shoes, neither two coats, for the labourer is worthy of his food.	neither staff, nor wallet, nor bread, nor money ; neither have two coats.
10 And he said unto them,		

17 *

259

Mark 6.

Wheresoever ye enter into a house,

there abide till ye depart thence.

11 And whatsoever place shall not receive you, and they hear you not, as ye go forth thence,

shake off the dust that is under your feet for a testimony unto them.

12 And they went out, and preached that men should repent.

13 And they cast out many devils, and anointed with oil many that were sick, and healed them.

Matthew 9, 10.

260

Matthew 10.

11 And into whatsoever city or village ye shall enter, search out who in it is worthy; and there abide till ye go forth.
12 And as ye enter into the house, salute it.
13 And if the house be worthy, let your peace come upon it: but if it be not worthy, let your peace return to you.
14 And whosoever shall not receive you, nor hear your words, as ye go forth out of that house or that city, shake off the dust of your feet.
15 Verily I say unto you, It shall be more tolerable for the land of Sodom and Gomorrah in the day of judgement, than for that city.

Luke 9.

Luke 9.

4 And into whatsoever house ye enter,

there abide, and thence depart.

5 And as many as receive you not,

when ye depart from that city,

shake off the dust from your feet

for a testimony against them.

6 And they departed, and went throughout the villages, preaching the gospel,

and healing everywhere.

Luke 10.

1 Now after these things the Lord appointed seventy others, and

		sent them two and two before his face into every city and place, whether he himself was about to come.
9[37] Then saith he unto his disciples, The harvest truly is plenteous, but the labourers are few. 38 Pray ye therefore the Lord of the harvest, that he send forth labourers into his harvest.		2 And he said unto them, The harvest is plenteous, but the labourers are few : pray ye therefore the Lord of the harvest, that he send forth labourers into his harvest.
10[1] And he called unto him his twelve disciples, and gave them authority over unclean spirits, to cast them out, and to heal all manner of disease and all manner of sickness.	1 And he called the twelve together, and gave them power and authority over all devils, and to cure diseases.	
2 Now the names of the twelve apostles are these : . . .		
5 These twelve Jesus sent forth, and charged them, saying, Go not into any way of the Gentiles, and enter not into any city of the Samaritans : 6 but go rather to the lost sheep of the house of Israel.	2 And he sent them forth 3 And he said unto them,	
7 And as ye go, preach, saying, The kingdom of heaven is at hand.	2 to preach the kingdom of God,	9 and say unto them, The kingdom of God is come nigh unto you.
8 Heal the sick, raise the dead, cleanse the lepers, cast out devils : freely ye received, freely give.	and to heal the sick.	heal the sick that are therein
9 Get you no gold, nor silver, nor brass in your purses ;		4 carry no purse,

THE MISSION OF THE TWELVE (*cont.*).

262

Matthew 9, 10.

10 no wallet for your journey,

neither two coats,
nor shoes,
nor staff:
for the labourer is worthy of his food.
11 And into whatsoever city or village ye shall enter, search out who in it is worthy; and there abide till ye go forth.
12 And as ye enter into the house,

salute it.
13 And if the house be worthy, let your peace come upon it: but if it be not worthy, let your peace return to you.
14 And whosoever shall not receive you, nor hear your words, as ye go forth out of that house or that city, shake off the dust of your feet.

15 Verily I say unto you, It shall be more tolerable for the land of Sodom and Gomorrah in the day of judgement, than for that city.

Luke 9.

3 Take nothing for your journey . . . nor wallet, neither have two coats,

neither staff

4 and into whatsoever house ye enter,

there abide, and thence depart.

5 And as many as receive you not,

when ye depart from that city,

shake off the dust from your feet.

Luke 10.

no wallet,

no shoes:

7 for the labourer is worthy of his hire.
8 And into whatsoever city ye enter

5 and into whatsoever house ye shall enter, first say, Peace be to this house.
6 And if a son of peace be there, your peace shall rest upon him: but if not, it shall turn to you again.
10 But into whatsoever city ye shall enter, and they receive you not,

11 Even the dust from your city, that cleaveth to our feet, we do wipe off.
12 I say unto you, It shall be more tolerable in that day for Sodom,

than for that city.

JESUS AND JOHN (p. 53).

Luke 7.

24 And when the messengers of John
were departed,
he began to say unto the multitudes concerning John,
What went ye out into the wilderness to behold ?
a reed shaken with the wind ?
25 But what went ye out to see ?
a man clothed in soft raiment ?
Behold, they which are gorgeously
apparelled,
and live delicately,
are in kings' courts.
26 But what went ye out to see ? a
prophet ?
Yea, I say unto you, and much
more than a prophet.
27 This is he of whom it is written,
Behold, I send my messenger
before thy face,
Who shall prepare thy way before
thee.
28 I say unto you,
Among them that are born of
women
there is none greater than John :

yet he that is but little in the
kingdom of God
is greater than he.

Matthew 11.

7 And as these went their way,

Jesus began to say unto the
multitudes concerning John,
What went ye out into the wilderness to behold ?
a reed shaken with the wind ?
8 But what went ye out for to see ?
a man clothed in soft raiment ?
Behold, they that wear soft
raiment

are in kings' houses.
9 But wherefore went ye out ? to
see a prophet ?
Yea, I say unto you, and much
more than a prophet.
10 This is he, of whom it is written,
Behold, I send my messenger
before thy face,
Who shall prepare thy way before
thee.
11 Verily I say unto you,
Among them that are born of
women
there hath not arisen a greater
than John the Baptist :
yet he that is but little in the
kingdom of heaven
is greater than he.

263

I Thank Thee (p. 53).

Luke 10.

21 In that same hour he rejoiced in the Holy Spirit, and said, I thank thee, O Father, Lord of heaven and earth, that thou didst hide these things from the wise and understanding, and didst reveal them unto babes: yea, Father; for so it was well-pleasing in thy sight.

22 All things have been delivered unto me of my Father: and no one knoweth who the Son is, save the Father; and who the Father is, save the Son, and he to whomsoever the Son willeth to reveal him.

Matthew 11.

25 At that season Jesus answered and said, I thank thee, O Father, Lord of heaven and earth, that thou didst hide these things from the wise and understanding, and didst reveal them unto babes: 26 yea, Father, for so it was well-pleasing in thy sight.

27 All things have been delivered unto me of my Father: and no one knoweth the Son, save the Father; neither doth any know the Father, save the Son, and he to whomsoever the Son willeth to reveal him.

Consider the Lilies (p. 53).

Luke 12.

27 Consider the lilies, how they grow: they toil not, neither do they spin; yet I say unto you, Even Solomon in all his glory was not arrayed like one of these.

28 But if God doth so clothe the grass in the field, which to-day is, and to-morrow is cast into the oven;

Matthew 6.

28 Consider the lilies of the field, how they grow; they toil not, neither do they spin:

29 yet I say unto you, that even Solomon in all his glory was not arrayed like one of these.

30 But if God doth so clothe the grass of the field, which to-day is, and to-morrow is cast into the oven,

shall he not much more clothe
you,
O ye of like faith?

O JERUSALEM, JERUSALEM (p. 53).

Luke 13.

34 O Jerusalem, Jerusalem, which
killeth the prophets,
and stoneth them that are sent
unto her!
how often would I have gathered
thy children together,
even as a hen gathereth her own
brood under her wings,
and ye would not!
35 Behold, your house is left unto
you desolate:
and I say unto you,
Ye shall not see me, until ye shall
say,
Blessed is he that cometh in the
name of the Lord.

TWO MASTERS (p. 53).

Luke 16.

13 No servant can serve two masters:
for either he will hate the one, and
love the other;
or else he will hold to one, and
despise the other.
Ye cannot serve God and mammon.

---

how much more shall he clothe
you,
O ye of little faith?

Matthew 23.

37 O Jerusalem, Jerusalem, which
killeth the prophets,
and stoneth them that are sent
unto her!
how often would I have gathered
thy children together,
even as a hen gathereth her
chickens under her wings,
and ye would not!
38 Behold, your house is left unto
you desolate.
39 For I say unto you,
Ye shall not see me henceforth,
till ye shall say,
Blessed is he that cometh in the
name of the Lord.

Matthew 6.

24 No man can serve two masters:
for either he will hate the one, and
love the other;
or else he will hold to one, and
despise the other.
Ye cannot serve God and mammon.

Luke 6.

17 . . . and he came down with them, and stood on a level place, . . .

20 And he lifted up his eyes on his disciples, and said,
Blessed are ye poor:
for yours is the kingdom of God.
21 Blessed are ye that hunger now:

for ye shall be filled.
Blessed are ye that weep now:
for ye shall laugh.

22 Blessed are ye, when men shall hate you, and when they shall separate you from their company,

Matthew 5.

1 And seeing the multitudes, he went up into the mountain: and when he had sat down, his disciples came unto him:
2 and he opened his mouth and taught them, saying,

3 Blessed are the poor in spirit: for theirs is the kingdom of heaven.
6 Blessed are they that hunger and thirst after righteousness: for they shall be filled.
4 Blessed are they that mourn: for they shall be comforted.
5 Blessed are the meek: for they shall inherit the earth.
7 Blessed are the merciful: for they shall obtain mercy.
8 Blessed are the pure in heart: for they shall see God.
9 Blessed are the peacemakers: for they shall be called sons of God.
10 Blessed are they that have been persecuted for righteousness' sake: for theirs is the kingdom of heaven.
11 Blessed are ye when men shall

and reproach you,
and cast out your name as evil,

for the Son of man's sake.
23 Rejoice in that day, and leap for joy:
for behold, your reward is great in heaven:
for in the same manner did their fathers unto the prophets.

24 But woe unto you that are rich!

25 Woe unto you, ye that are full now! . . .
Woe unto you, ye that laugh now!

26 Woe unto you, when all men shall speak well of you! . . .

THE LORD'S PRAYER (p. 56).
Luke 11.
2 When ye pray, say,

Father,
Hallowed be thy name.
Thy kingdom come.

3 Give us day by day our daily bread.
4 And forgive us our sins;
for we ourselves also forgive every one that is indebted to us.
And bring us not into temptation.

reproach you, and persecute you, and say all manner of evil against you falsely,
for my sake.
12 Rejoice, and be exceeding glad:

for great is your reward in heaven:

for so
persecuted they the prophets which were before you.

Matthew 6.
9 After this manner therefore pray ye:
Our Father which art in heaven,
Hallowed be thy name.
10 Thy kingdom come.
Thy will be done, as in heaven, so on earth.
11 Give us this day our daily bread.

12 And forgive us our debts,
as we also have forgiven our debtors.
13 And bring us not into temptation, but deliver us from the evil one.

THE CENTURION'S SERVANT (p. 56).

Luke 7.

¹ After he had ended all his sayings in the ears of the people, he entered into Capernaum.

² And a certain centurion's servant, who was dear unto him, was sick and at the point of death. | And ³ when he heard concerning Jesus, he sent unto him elders of the Jews, asking him that he would come and save his servant. | ⁴ And they, when they came to Jesus, besought him earnestly, saying, He is worthy that thou ⁵ shouldest do this for him: | for he loveth our nation, and himself built us our synagogue.

⁶ And Jesus went with them. And when he was now not far from the house, the centurion sent friends to him, saying unto him, Lord, trouble not thyself: for I am not worthy that thou should'st come under my roof: ⁷ wherefore neither thought I myself worthy to come unto thee:

Matthew 8.

⁵ And when he was entered into Capernaum, there came unto him a centurion, beseeching him, | and ⁶ saying, Lord, my servant lieth in the house sick of the palsy, grievously tormented.

.

⁷ And he saith unto him, I will come and heal him.

⁸ And the centurion answered and said, Lord, I am not worthy

that thou shouldest come under my roof:

but say the word, and my servant shall be healed.
8 For I also am a man set under authority,
having under myself soldiers:
and I say to this one, Go, and he goeth;
and to another, Come, and he cometh;
and to my servant, Do this, and he doeth it.
9 And when Jesus heard these things, he marvelled at him,
and turned and said unto the multitude that followed him,
I say unto you,
I have not found so great faith, no, not in Israel.
10 And they that were sent, returning to the house, found the servant whole.

THE LOST SHEEP (p. 57).

Luke 15.

3 And he spake unto them this parable, saying,
4 What man of you, having a hundred sheep,

but only say the word, and my servant shall be healed.
9 For I also am a man under authority,
having under myself soldiers:
and I say to this one, Go, and he goeth;
and to another, Come, and he cometh;
and to my servant, Do this, and he doeth it.
10 And when Jesus heard it, he marvelled,
and said to them that followed,

Verily I say unto you,
I have not found so great faith, no not in Israel.

11 And I say unto you, that many shall come from the east and the west, ...
13 And Jesus said unto the centurion, Go thy way; as thou hast believed, so be it done unto thee. And the servant was healed in that hour.

Matthew 18.

12 How think ye?

if any man have a hundred sheep

The Lost Sheep (*cont.*).

Luke 15.

and having lost one of them,
doth not leave the ninety and
nine
in the wilderness,
and go after that which is lost,
until he find it?

[5] And when he hath found it,

he layeth it on his shoulders,
rejoicing.

[6] And when he cometh home, he
calleth together his friends and
his neighbours, saying unto them,
Rejoice with me, for I have found
my sheep which was lost. | I say
[7] unto you, that even so there shall
be joy in heaven over one sinner
that repenteth,
more than over ninety and nine
righteous persons,
which need no repentance.

Matthew 18.

and one of them be gone astray,
doth he not leave the ninety and
nine,
and go unto the mountains,
and seek that which goeth astray?

[13] And if so be that he find it,
verily I say unto you,
he rejoiceth over it

more than over the ninety and
nine

which have not gone astray.

The Strait Gate (p. 58).

Luke 13.

[24] Strive to enter in by the narrow
door: for many, I say unto you,
shall seek to enter in, and shall
not be able.

[25] When once the master of the
house is risen up, and hath shut
to the door, and ye begin to stand

Matthew 7.

[13] Enter ye in by the narrow gate:
for wide is the gate, and broad is
the way, that leadeth to destruction, and many be they that enter
in thereby.

without, and to knock at the door, saying, Lord, open to us; and he shall answer and say to you, I know not whence ye are; 26 then shall ye begin to say, we did eat and drink in thy presence, and thou did'st teach in our streets;

27 and he shall say, I tell you, I know not whence ye are; depart from me, all ye workers of iniquity.

22 Many will say to me in that day, Lord, Lord, did we not prophesy by thy name, and by thy name cast out devils, and by thy name do many mighty works? 23 And then will I profess unto them, I never knew you: depart from me, ye that work iniquity.

INDEX

PRINTED IN GREAT BRITAIN BY
THE UNIVERSITY PRESS, ABERDEEN